W9-CFC-691

Weatherproofing Your Landscape

UNIVERSITY PRESS OF FLORIDA

Florida A&M University, Tallahassee
Florida Atlantic University, Boca Raton
Florida Gulf Coast University, Ft. Myers
Florida International University, Miami
Florida State University, Tallahassee
New College of Florida, Sarasota
University of Central Florida, Orlando
University of Florida, Gainesville
University of North Florida, Jacksonville
University of South Florida, Tampa
University of West Florida, Pensacola

Weatherproofing

University Press of Florida | Gainesville | Tallahassee | Tampa | Boca Raton | Pensacola | Orlando | Miami | Jacksonville | Ft. Myers | Sarasota

Your Landscape

A Homeowner's Guide to Protecting and Rescuing Your Plants

Sandra Dark and Dean Hill

Copyright 2011 by Sandra Dark and Dean Hill
Printed in the United States of America. This book is printed on Glatfelter Natures Book,
a paper certified under the standards of the Forestry Stewardship Council (FSC). It is a
recycled stock that contains 30 percent post-consumer waste and is acid-free.

16 15 14 13 12 11   6 5 4 3 2 1

Library of Congress Cataloging-in-Publication Data
Dark, Sandra.
Weatherproofing your landscape : a homeowner's guide to protecting and rescuing
your plants / Sandra Dark and Dean Hill.
p. cm.
Includes index.
ISBN 978-0-8130-3682-3 (alk. paper)
1. Landscape gardening. 2. Plants, Protection of. I. Hill, Dean. II. Title. III. Title:
Homeowner's guide to protecting and rescuing your plants.
SB473.D363 2011
712'.6—dc22   2011011214

The University Press of Florida is the scholarly publishing agency for the State University
System of Florida, comprising Florida A&M University, Florida Atlantic University,
Florida Gulf Coast University, Florida International University, Florida State University,
New College of Florida, University of Central Florida, University of Florida, University
of North Florida, University of South Florida, and University of West Florida.

University Press of Florida
15 Northwest 15th Street
Gainesville, FL 32611-2079
http://www.upf.com

Contents

Introduction   vii

1. The Big Four   1
2. The Nature of Your Landscape   20
3. An Ounce of Prevention   40
4. During the Disaster   68
5. Assessing the Damage   83
6. Experts to the Rescue   100
7. Rehabilitate or Remove?   115
8. Intensive Care   132
9. Preserving "Heirloom" Plants   154
10. Replacing the Loss   170
11. Landscape Insurance and Tax Breaks   189
12. Healing the Heart   197

Acknowledgments   211
Appendix I: Trees and Shrubs for Extreme Weather   213
Appendix II: Species Ratings   219
Appendix III: Resources   223
Index   227

Introduction

Natural disasters are just that: *natural*. Like it or not, storms, droughts, floods, wildfires, and all their rowdy, destructive kinfolk are a normal part of the great, often spectacular, and always-evolving panorama of our planet's environment.

The bad news is that the weather picture is not getting any prettier. Scientists warn that ongoing climate change will bring us more intense and more frequent droughts, heat waves, floods, and other extreme-weather events as this century continues to unfold. And because nature is a notorious equal-opportunity basher, virtually every landscape in the country is potentially vulnerable to damage, no matter where it is located.

The good news is that there are many things that you can do to help mitigate the effects of extreme-weather events on your landscape's big-ticket plants, and there are plenty of reasons why you should want to make the effort.

Extreme weather and its undesirable side effects damage and destroy hundreds of thousands of forest trees and shrubs annually; in many years, those casualties range into the millions. A significant number of the unfortunate plants are elements of urban forests that include plants in public parks and empty lots, along streets, and in myriad private landscapes just like yours—perhaps even including yours.

And the value of those landscape plants? You might be very surprised. A nicely designed and maintained landscape can make a substantial contribution to the overall worth of your real estate, with individual trees of mature size and desirable species not uncommonly valued in the thousands—in special cases even tens of thousands—of dollars. Besides adding curb appeal to property that is or might go on the market, well-placed specimens can serve important utilitarian functions, offering privacy and shade while considerably reducing cooling bills.

So for both financial and aesthetic reasons, your trees and shrubs are deserving of all the consideration that you can give them. And when it comes to maintaining their health and value, the age-old maxim has never been truer: Prevention is the best medicine.

But how far can you go to prevent damage not just *to* your trees and shrubs, but *by* them? After all, ice-laden tree limbs have been known to crash through dining room windows, and entire trees can blow over onto houses and vehicles. Such is life in the urban forest.

For the sake of prevention, you can remove every tree that is within close proximity of your house to create a defensible safe zone—indeed, you should do so if you live in a wildfire-prone area. But grand old trees can add to the architecture and ambience of your property. And need we mention again their contribution to the overall value and marketability of your real estate? So the best way to protect your landscape and your property values is to maintain healthy, robust trees and shrubs with strong structures that enhance their ability to withstand onslaughts of extreme weather.

But even the best preventive measures can go only so far in the face of a severe-weather event that leaves your landscape in ruins. If that happens—and odds are good that it eventually will at least once—you will need to take a slow, deep breath and then kick into recovery mode.

Because the disaster event itself is only the beginning.

For the sake of both your landscape specimens and your real estate values, it is important to have a strategic plan in place with which to help prevent or reduce damage whenever possible, to manage the aftermath of a weather mugging when it does occur, and to restore your landscape in such a way that it will be more resilient in the face of future onslaughts.

A landscape is an extremely complex man-made ecosystem that can be healthy or unhealthy, strong or weak, as can its anchor trees and shrubs. But large, woody plants are so much a part of our everyday scenery that their presence can be easy to take for granted. So perhaps it should come as no surprise that many property owners and even landscape-maintenance crews lack a basic knowledge of arboriculture. For example, few homeowners know the difference between a tree's cambium and phloem layers, or even where they are located.

And many lawn-maintenance workers do not realize that the tender bark of a young tree or shrub can be girdled by repeated exposure to a weed whip or string trimmer—or that palms, having no cambium layer, have an inability to heal themselves when stem damage occurs.

A big mistake that too many people make is to believe that their landscape specimens can flourish, and even survive serious injuries, pretty much on their own. But once you learn the basics of *Weatherproofing Your Landscape*, you will be more aware of the condition of many trees and shrubs in the urban forest as you stroll through public parks and along neighborhood streets.

The simple fact is that landscape trees and shrubs do not necessarily thrive on benign neglect, or for that matter on inept or misguided attention. But just as you need to know when you should be seen by a doctor rather than depend on home remedies, you also need to know when the wise course of action is to consult an arborist, landscape architect, or some other trained specialist for assistance in protecting, restoring, or replacing your landscape's valuable anchor plants.

Toward that end, *Weatherproofing Your Landscape* provides you with the tools you need, either in consultation with experts or as an informed do-it-yourselfer, to help your trees and shrubs avoid as much severe damage as possible when nature throws her worst at them; to restore your battered landscape if an extreme-weather event proves to be overpowering; and even to recover your family's much-distressed peace of mind.

Weatherproofing Your Landscape

The Big Four

In our naivety, we like to think of our landscapes as self-contained territories, bounded by clearly defined curbs and fence lines. Within these boundaries, we go about manipulating our individual plots of land to reflect our personal tastes. Like interior decorators working outdoors, we carefully "arrange the furniture" to meet our needs, placing our most significant specimen trees and shrubs in attractive locations and accessorizing with perennials and annuals.

Unfortunately, we too often fail to appreciate that weather neither knows nor respects boundaries or human designs—and nature can have a violent temper. Ignorance of those simple truths, and a lack of preparedness to deal with them, can cost us dearly.

On your road to becoming a savvy steward of your trees and shrubs, consider this: an attractive landscape greatly enhances your property's appeal to a potential buyer, even in a down market. What's more, according to the Gallup Organization, a well-maintained landscape can increase the value of your real estate by 7 to 15 percent (some sources place the figure as high as 20 percent). And while giant petunias and hybrid daylilies can be charming accessories, the big-ticket trees and shrubs are what anchor your living landscape and carry the greatest value weight.

But like most homeowners, you probably have not taken into account just how much damage a single extreme-weather event can do, often literally overnight, to your property's aesthetic and market values. With mature, healthy trees of desirable species and location commonly worth from $1,000 to $10,000, according to the Council of Tree and Landscape Appraisers, a natural disaster can instantly batter your property values, way before you get into the pricy cleanup costs.

A Case in Point

As Rose Payne can attest, the cost of repairing major damage to your landscape plants can be just the beginning. Over the years, Rose had safely weathered many storms in Cherry Hill, New Jersey, without incurring serious injuries to her land- scape. But none of those previous bouts with nature measured up to the whole- sale destruction inflicted in mid-December 2007. Violent winds generated by an unseasonable weekend thunderstorm toppled a 50-foot white pine onto the roof of the 150-year-old two-story house that contains her business. Total damage to house and landscape from that one tree: an unexpected $50,000.

Can this type of disaster be averted? Not always. Truly savage winds above 75 mph can damage even healthy trees. But a certified or registered consulting ar- borist often can detect evidence of structural or root-system instability that could leave a seemingly healthy specimen vulnerable to tipping over in high winds. So a "wellness checkup" before extreme weather strikes can at least forewarn you of potential dangers.

Worst-Case Scenarios

Sometimes even a moderate storm can cause a shocking amount of devastation. Uprooted trees can damage buried utility lines. Limbs or entire trees can fall onto your house, your vehicle, you, or your neighbor. Even unsuspecting pets are at risk when wandering beneath trees destabilized by inclement weather.

But wait—those are things you only hear about on the evening news, com- plete with dramatic videos of ice-coated cities, flooded neighborhoods, and hurricane-shattered trees and houses. And perhaps you do not live in Tornado Alley, the hurricane-prone Gulf Coast, the wildfire-scorched West, or some other area known for its spectacular extreme-weather events. So what are the chances that the lovely maple tree or holly shrub in *your* landscape will actually fall victim to nature's wrath, and possibly victimize both you and your vital real estate values in the process?

The chances are good . . . and growing.

Why? Because ongoing climate changes are making record-setting extreme weather the norm in most regions. During just one season in 2008, horrific drought raged in the West; Florida and the upper Mississippi basin battled catastrophic floodwaters; and a tornado clawed through a town in New Hampshire. Reports of serious-to-severe weather mayhem appear on the news virtually every week of the year, often on a daily basis. The question is not so much *if* your landscape will take a hit, but rather *when*. So let's look at what nature might throw at you.

By far the most common weather-damage to big-ticket landscape plants comes from nature's four biggest guns: wind, frozen stuff (ice and snow, and occasionally even hail), drought, and flood. Almost no part of the country is invulnerable to at least one of these forms of extreme weather. And in many cases, the components of severe-weather events do not occur in isolation, so theoretically your landscape could be subjected to one of more than a dozen different combinations of wind, frozen stuff, drought, or flood in a single event. Knowing what kinds of damage to expect can help you prepare for the day when your landscape comes under assault.

Wind

In the Pacific Northwest, the infamous Hanukkah Eve Windstorm of December 14 to 15, 2006, delivered peak wind gusts ranging from 50 to more than 100 mph, toppling thousands of large trees. In 2008, a tornado ripped through Georgia, damaging as much as 40 percent of the urban tree canopy in Bibb County. In 2003, Hurricane Isabel damaged or destroyed 10,000 trees in Richmond, Virginia.

Destructive winds can come in many forms: hurricanes, tornadoes, straight-line winds, or powerful downbursts generated by collapsing thunderstorms. How much—or how little—damage your big-ticket trees and shrubs might incur depends upon a variety of factors that can work alone or in combination:

1. Wind Velocity. Wind speeds of 39 to 46 mph (*gale force* on the Beaufort scale) can snap twigs off woody plants. In winds from 47 to 54 mph (*severe gale*), old or structurally weakened plants can lose large limbs. *Storm winds* of 55 to 63 mph can uproot entire trees and large shrubs that have compromised root systems.
2. Property Topography. Winds compress as they pass over ridges or are funneled between natural or man-made barriers (hillsides, houses, etc.). This wind-tunnel effect can result in damage to plants located in the vulnerable "trough," while leaving nearby trees and shrubs unscathed.
3. Plant Exposure. A tall or densely foliaged tree or shrub growing in isolation in the middle of a large expanse of lawn is more vulnerable than one situated among other large plants, or on the lee side of a structure.

4. Sail Area. A plant's *sail* is the area of branches and foliage that presents itself to the wind. Sails with dense branches and foliage that do not allow air currents to flow through the crown are more vulnerable to wind damage. For example, some dense "lollipop" trees such as Bradford pears create such strong resistance that, in the face of powerful winds, the entire crown can snap off at the trunk.

5. Root Anchoring. A tree or shrub's root system is crucial to its ability to literally stand up under wind stress. Large perennial roots (not to be confused with shallow and fragile feeder roots) can reach from three to seven feet deep, anchoring the plant's aboveground growth to the soil. Inadequate or damaged anchor roots—or insufficient space in which those roots can grow—leave a plant out of balance and easily tipped over.

A Case in Point

In some areas of Keith Newcomb's front yard in Nashville, Tennessee, the soil is as shallow as a foot deep atop an impenetrable limestone shelf, providing inadequate room for anchor roots to get a grip. More than once, the restricted soil depth has proven fatal. "The bigger trees that were in areas closer to the rock sometimes just fell over," Keith says. "A little wind would come along, and then it was all over for them."

Can this type of loss be averted? Little can be done to safeguard large, established trees and shrubs growing in shallow or otherwise unstable soil, other than pruning to open up the sail area somewhat so that air currents can flow through. (See chapter 3, An Ounce of Prevention.) Your best bet where limited space or thin soil presents a potential tipping problem is to plant small-stature species that develop balanced top-growth-to-root system ratios as they mature.

Species

While judicious pruning can help to increase the wind tolerance of woody plants, species such as ginkgo (*Ginkgo biloba*) and yaupon holly (*Ilex vomitoria*) are naturally more wind resistant. Others such as silver maple (*Acer saccharinum*) and common hackberry (*Celtis occidentalis*) are notoriously susceptible to wind damage. (See appendix I for a list of wind-resistant species.)

Age and Health

Old, diseased, neglected, or infested specimens are more likely to have structural weaknesses that compromise their ability to withstand wind.

A Case in Point

In 2008, artist Pablo Solomon of Lampasas, Texas, lost a grand old live oak tree that had a trunk diameter of five feet. The tree had grown and thrived for 300 years in what is known as the Texas Hill Country. But age, heavy rains, and damage to its root anchorage finally caused it to simply tump over in a windstorm.

Can this type of loss be averted? Sometimes. But you have to look at *all* the factors involved. For instance, even at its venerable age, Pablo's oak tree might have survived still longer despite high winds and saturated soil if a family of foxes had not built a den that further destabilized the root system.

Severe weather felled Pablo Solomon's 300-year-old live oak. Courtesy of Pablo Solomon.

Other Contributing Weather Conditions

Both prolonged drought and waterlogged soil can cause damage to root systems and alter the integrity of the soil, loosening the grip of anchor roots. Waterlogged soil from torrential rains was a major contributor to the toppling of thousands of large trees during the Hanukkah Eve Windstorm, which struck the Pacific Northwest in December 2006.

A weighty buildup of frozen stuff in a tree or shrub's branches can make the plant top-heavy and more easily shattered or felled by wind.

At-Risk Regions

Santa Ana winds in California; hurricanes on the Atlantic and Gulf coasts; nor'easters in New England; high winds that strike the Pacific Northwest in 15-year cycles; twisters in Tornado Alley and elsewhere; incessant winds on the Great Plains—the list goes on and on. Virtually every landscape in the country has the potential for eventually incurring wind damage in one form or another.

Frozen Stuff

In early December 2007, a storm spread a crystal nightmare of ice from Kansas and Oklahoma to Illinois. As the horrifyingly beautiful storm rolled slowly eastward, millions of trees and shrubs stood—or lay—damaged and dying in its wake. In many towns and cities, shattered limbs and toppled trees covered yards, blocked streets, and crushed roofs, leaving entire neighborhoods resembling war zones.

Heavy snowfall also can devastate your big-ticket landscape plants. Though snow damage is seldom as widespread and spectacular as that of ice, Currier & Ives scenes of flocked trees and whipped-creamed hedges can conceal a disheartening amount of death and destruction.

And let's not forget hail. Violent storms such as the one that deposited a foot of hail on parts of New Jersey in June 2009 can batter trees and shrubs mercilessly, causing bark wounds that can leave plants open to infections.

A number of factors determine how well, or how badly, your trees and shrubs will stand up to frozen stuff. A heavy coating of ice can easily turn a 50-pound limb into a leviathan weighing three-quarters of a ton, sometimes more. Limbs with weak forks are particularly vulnerable and can succumb to ice buildup of as little as a quarter of an inch. Large limbs are at risk when ice buildup exceeds half an inch.

Snow, being less dense than ice, usually requires far higher accumulations before reaching maximum stress levels.

A heavy snow load can endanger limbs and entire specimens. Courtesy of Joseph O'Brien, USDA Forest Service, Bugwood.org.

A Case in Point

In 2009, two successive winter storms dumped a total of 20 inches of snow on Libertyville, Illinois, north of Chicago. The heavy snow load surpassed the structural limits of a 50-year-old cedar next to Bill Burnett's house, causing two-thirds of the branches on one side of the tree to fail.

Can this type of damage be averted? Snow and ice removal is a delicate operation, and impractical with very tall specimens. But in some cases, the effort can save threatened trees and shrubs from limb damage, distortion, or outright uprooting. (See chapter 4, During the Disaster.)

Species

Some tree species such as silver maple and common hackberry are highly susceptible to ice or snow damage, and this is often attributed to their brittle branches. But a study of a destructive February 1990 ice storm in Urbana, Illinois, revealed that what made a plant more vulnerable to damage was not so much the strength of its wood as the ability of its branches to accumulate ice until they surpassed their maximum load-bearing capacity. For example, hackberry trees develop many small, dense branches that can hold on to large quantities of ice or snow. Broadleaf evergreens, as well as deciduous trees that retain their foliage through winter, also can accumulate unbearable quantities of frozen stuff. (See appendix I for a list of species that are tolerant of ice and snow.)

Shape

That same Urbana study concluded that species having vertical branching habits, such as honey locusts, are less able to tolerate ice accumulations than those with horizontal branching, such as oaks. Conifers, with their short branches and central leader, are generally more able to shed or tolerate the weight of frozen stuff. Also, wide crotches in trees are stronger than narrow crotches and so fail less readily under ice or snow.

Even if actual breakage does not occur, heavy loads of frozen stuff can warp upright evergreens such as arborvitae out of shape and severely bend the leaders of flexible young trees. In some cases the deformity will correct itself once the ice or snow melts, but not always.

Maturity and Size

Large trees can be more susceptible to damage than younger or smaller specimens for the simple reason that their hefty branches are able to accumulate a greater burden of ice or snow.

Melt-off

Thawing of heavy accumulations of snow can waterlog your landscape, particularly in low-lying areas and foundation beds beneath unguttered eaves. When tall trees and shrubs are top-heavy with frozen stuff, their anchor roots can lose their grip on the soggy soil, especially when an encore snow or ice storm closely follows a thaw, adding more weight to a plant's crown.

Burial

Snow actually has insulating qualities, protecting plants from bitterly cold temperatures. But giant snowdrifts piled up by wind or man-made means can be overpowering, crushing what lies beneath.

A Case in Point

During a particularly bad winter in the Chicago area, Jennifer Raaths lost three spirea bushes near the street in front of her house when they were buried by city snow-removal crews clearing the road.

Can this type of loss be prevented? Buried shrubs that have not already been crushed by the weight can be rescued by prompt removal of snow. But the best way to avoid damage or loss from man-made snowdrifts is to plant shrubs well away from streets and driveways in regions where snowplows and snowblowers commonly are used.

Other Contributing Weather Conditions

Wind can be the most lethal combination with frozen stuff. Even light breezes can snap ice-laden twigs. Brisker winds can bring down weak or overburdened limbs, increase structural damage that can result in major limb failure, or topple the entire tree.

Previous recent drought or flood conditions that persisted long enough to damage a tree or shrub's root system and weaken its vitality can leave the plant less able to stand up under stress from frozen stuff.

At-Risk Regions

The highest-risk regions for severe ice storms are east of the Rocky Mountains— in the northeast, southern, and central states—plus there is a relatively isolated pocket of frequent activity in western Idaho and eastern Washington and Oregon. The majority of heavy-snowfall events generally occur in the northeast, southeast, and central states, with areas near the Great Lakes commonly receiving depths measured in feet rather than inches thanks to "lake effect" weather conditions.

Drought

Ongoing climate change is spreading and intensifying drought conditions in many regions of the country. With populations in drought-prone areas growing exponentially, water has become a precious commodity from coast to coast, already resulting in water wars. In recent years, parched Georgia threatened to shut off the spigot to downstream Florida. California is scrambling to overcome dire water shortages that are expected to worsen dramatically. Texas wants a share of equally drought-prone Oklahoma's water resources. The list goes on.

Serious root loss from drought means sure death, as this browned evergreen shows. Courtesy of Sandra Dark.

Short- or long-term drought conditions can do a number on your landscape-related real estate values because water shortage is potentially the most serious enemy of your big-ticket trees and shrubs. But as if that isn't bad enough, drought lays the groundwork for wildfire, which can destroy every plant and surface structure on a property in a single sweep of flames.

Water is absolutely essential for transporting nutrients back and forth between a plant's roots and top growth, thus affecting all of the life-sustaining processes of a tree or shrub. (You might be surprised to learn that water constitutes as much as half of a tree's weight.) A mature tree might take up anywhere from a dozen or so to hundreds of gallons of water per day—and transpire hundreds of gallons—depending on the species, season, and a variety of other factors. Any serious interruption of that moisture supply can result in permanent damage or death.

Unlike wind and frozen stuff, drought is a relatively slow-motion version of extreme weather. Therefore, your big-ticket trees and shrubs can take weeks, months, and even years to reveal how severely they have been injured—or even that they have been injured at all. But as dry conditions intensify, woody plants do not just stand by and suffer: they take increasingly desperate damage-control measures, employing an escalating succession of survival tactics.

Sensing a potentially dangerous shortage of soil moisture, the plant first responds by closing tiny openings called *stomates* on the undersides of leaves. To put it simply, under normal circumstances, moisture and oxygen are "exhaled" through the stomates, and carbon dioxide is "inhaled." By closing down these portals, the plant prevents some water loss. But in the process, it deprives itself of carbon dioxide, one of the essential elements needed for photosynthesis, the plant's food-manufacturing process.

As water deficits intensify, the plant attempts to increase absorption of scarce soil moisture by producing more feeder roots. Unfortunately, these delicate, hairlike roots generally live within 6 to 18 inches of the surface, so as the dry zone extends deeper into the ground, feeder roots are the first to die.

When photosynthesis slows or halts altogether, the plant is forced to fall back upon food reserves stored in its root system. The longer the water deficit continues, the more these food reserves are depleted. With each passing day, the risk grows greater that the thirsty, now-starving plant's life processes will suffer a catastrophic collapse.

Deep into the drought, the struggling plant resorts in desperation to shutting down root functions. (Beyond a certain point, this shutdown is like pulling the plug on a critically ill patient in intensive care.) Plant foliage, branches, and roots begin to die back.

Finally, unrelieved water deficit brings severe stunting or death to a specimen's vital organs, including the phloem layer (the tissue beneath the bark through which food is transported from the leaves to the rest of the plant) and the cambium layer (the tissue beneath the phloem that forms a new trunk ring each year). At best, severe water deficit results in a thinner trunk ring for that year; at worst, the plant is a goner.

At some point during your tree or shrub's journey into the depths of drought, it will exhibit leaf wilt. Just how soon this occurs can depend upon the species. The leaves of some species such as magnolia and holly possess a thick waxy coating that keeps them turgid; rather than wilting, foliage will curl and turn brown. Likewise, waxy conifer needles will simply turn brown and drop off.

By the time a woody plant wilts or begins dieback, it is in dire straits. But in some cases, serious visible symptoms might not show up until long after the dry spell has ended. Then the drought-weakened tree or shrub might suffer what appears to be an inexplicable sudden death that is actually the culmination of a process that began a year or even several years earlier.

Unfortunately, severe drought damage is pretty much irreparable and can happen behind your back as well as right before your eyes.

A Case in Point

Like many property owners, Keith Newcomb has experienced a variety of weather extremes over the years. His Nashville landscape took a serious hit from drought during a season when he was unable to monitor his plants as carefully as he likes. By the time he realized the severity of the dry spell, many shrubs were already suffering dieback. Taking emergency measures, he was able to bring his Chinese holly back from the brink, but was unable to save three inkberry holly shrubs.

You would not think of trekking across Death Valley without an adequate water supply, so do not expect plants to journey through dry spells without adequate moisture. As Keith can attest, a matter of weeks without supplemental watering during dry periods can spell doom for valued landscape plants.

Besides a simple lack of water, other factors can exacerbate drought stress on trees and shrubs:

1. Duration. The longer a drought persists, the deeper the soil dries out. Once the dry zone reaches 6 inches deep, the shallowest feeder roots begin to die. If the dry zone reaches 12 to 18 inches deep, all feeder roots will die, and then the tree or shrub is doomed.

2. Location. Trees and shrubs exposed to full sun during the heat of the day or that grow near the reflective heat of pavement or walls, require more water to sustain their life processes. Even then, they might lose more moisture through their foliage than they can take up through their roots during a 24-hour cycle, causing greater water stress than that experienced by plants in less challenging locations.

3. Soil Conditions. Soils rich in humus trap and hold more water. Sandy or heavily compacted soils, or shallow soils over rocky shelves, are least able to hold sufficient moisture to sustain plants through even short periods of drought.

4. Root Problems. Trees and shrubs need all the roots they can get during dry spells. Root systems confined by concrete surfaces, foundations, or other barriers have fewer of the feeder roots necessary for healthy plant growth. And damage to roots by construction equipment is a common tree killer. Severing a large, woody root kills all the feeder roots from that point to the root's end, reducing the plant's capacity to take up moisture and nutrients.

5. New Plantings. A newly transplanted shrub or tree has lost most of its feeder roots and requires from one to several years, depending on its size, to recover from the shock of root amputation and build a new

feeder system. Throughout its recovery period, the plant is extremely vulnerable to drought.

6. Temperature. High temperatures trigger higher water consumption. Some woody plants such as hemlocks suffer mightily when temperatures reach 95 degrees. But even relatively heat-tolerant species can have a hard time of it when high temperatures are combined with desiccating wind.

7. Competition. Turf grasses and neighboring trees and shrubs all compete for scarce water resources.

8. Watering Technique. Supplemental water is wasted if it fails to penetrate the soil down to feeder roots 6 to 18 inches deep or does not reach out to or beyond the plant's drip line. Plants replenish water deficits at night, so soaking the ground during the day is less efficient than night watering. But watering at night can cause fungal problems, so care should be taken to soak only the soil, and not foliage.

Species

Some trees and shrubs are naturally more sensitive to dry conditions. Shallow-rooted species such as silver maple, dogwood, and arborvitae are often among the first to show drought stress. By contrast, plants native to a region tend to be better equipped to handle its seasonal droughts. (See appendix I for a list of drought-tolerant species.)

Plant Health

Trees and shrubs that are diseased or infested, or that have suffered damage or stress from extreme-weather events in the past, are less able to tolerate drought conditions.

Other Contributing Weather Conditions

A woody plant that has experienced recent flooding might have lost some of its deeper feeder roots to drowning, leaving the drought-vulnerable topmost feeder roots to carry the entire water and nutrient uptake load during dry spells.

Wind increases a plant's loss of moisture through its foliage, especially when humidity is low.

Plants entering winter conditions with inadequate soil moisture are more susceptible to extreme cold.

At-Risk Regions

In most years, at least 10 percent of the country suffers from drought; as recently as 1988, more than a third of the nation was parched. During the past century, the most long-running severe droughts have focused on regions west of the Mississippi River. Ongoing climate change appears to be intensifying dry conditions out West, but the bull's eye is by no means limited to that area. Recently, Georgia and Florida were locked in a severe drought, and similar conditions have been known to creep as far northeast as New England. Occasionally, even the Desert Southwest has seen normally drought-hardy cacti dying of thirst.

Flood

When we think of flooded landscapes, Hurricane Katrina just naturally comes to mind, and with good reason. Along with the terrible human tragedy and property destruction of that 2005 disaster, New Orleans lost around 75 percent of its urban forest to a combination of flooding and wind. But as urban populations continue to spread into low-lying areas along coastlines and rivers around the country, loss of valuable trees and shrubs to high water and saturated soil becomes increasingly commonplace.

Located at the headwaters of three rivers, Roanoke, Virginia, averages a major flood every seven years. Numerous communities along the rampaging Mississippi River and its tributaries were inundated during the Great Flood of 1993

Flooding can severely stress landscape specimens. Courtesy of FEMA/Adam Dubrowa.

and again in 2008. And thanks to an aging system of levees, Sacramento, California, has the dubious distinction of being among the most flood-threatened cities in the country.

But flood damage to your big-ticket landscape plants does not always come in biblical extremes. Even without actual inundation, trees and shrubs can succumb to wet feet as a result of conditions ranging from poorly drained soil to something as simple as a leaky outdoor faucet, a dripping air conditioner, or an overwatered lawn.

A Case in Point

In 2006, so much rain fell on southern New Jersey that an entire row of a dozen eight-year-old Bradford pear trees toppled overnight at Michelle Wendt's business in Hammonton. "The ground became so saturated that it could not hold the roots. We had to stake [the trees] on all four sides to hold them in place so they would not die."

Top-heavy specimens are particularly vulnerable to tipping when soil becomes saturated, especially when roots are confined by paving or other barriers. Selecting proper species for problem locations as well as improving drainage can help prevent losses from waterlogged soil.

Flooding squeezes oxygen out of the soil, depriving roots of this vital element. In extreme cases, this can eventually result in a buildup of toxic natural compounds such as hydrogen sulfide and ethylene followed by root rot. Loss of root function, which is akin to losing your heart and lungs, shuts down a plant's life-sustaining processes, including all-important photosynthesis.

Odd though it might seem at first blush, flood damage to woody plants bears at least one striking similarity to drought damage: in both cases, root systems can suffer life-threatening injury or death, thereby resulting in many of the same symptoms.

Common symptoms of flood stress in woody plants include:

yellowing of foliage, or premature fall coloring
leaf drop
stunted leaves, or failure to leaf out
profuse water sprouts
profuse seed production the year following a flood
dieback of branches

Because most of the initial damage takes place out of sight beneath the soil surface, a tree or shrub often is already in desperate condition by the time visible symptoms appear. And, as with drought, the real damage might not reveal itself until a year or more after the event.

Drowning seems like such a straightforward way for a plant to die. But a surprising number of factors come into play in determining whether your big-ticket landscape plants will survive a flood:

1. Depth and Duration. Most tree and shrub species can tolerate saturated soil or even standing knee-deep in water for periods of anywhere from a few weeks to three or four months; they won't like it, but they will recover. Some can cope with complete submersion of the crown for up to a month. But some plants cannot survive complete submersion of the crown for more than a few days at most. And except for some species, such as bald cypress, which grow well in standing water, even relatively flood-tolerant species have their limits: repeated short-term flooding can be damaging or even deadly if the plant does not have time to recover between the events.

2. Season. Flooding and its resulting root damage are more dangerous to plants during the growing season, especially in hot weather when the demand for oxygen and water are greatest in the top growth.

3. Flowing or Stagnant. Both flowing and stagnant water have pluses and minuses. Stagnant water lacks oxygen, but exerts no force against plants. Flowing water carries oxygen—though it might not be available to the plant—but can uproot trees and shrubs or severely damage them with floating debris.

4. Soil Conditions. Plants in deep, well-drained, loamy soils are more likely to survive flooding than those in shallow soils or poorly drained clay. In flowing floodwaters, sandy soils can wash away, causing tree and shrub roots to lose their grip, or generate silting (three inches or more can suffocate root systems). And flooding can change the pH of soil, raising its acidity beyond a plant's tolerance level. In coastal areas, flooding can also pollute soil with salt water.

Species

Some species such as deciduous holly (*Ilex decidua*) and green ash (*Fraxinus pennsylvanica*) are extremely tolerant of wet feet. Others such as redbud (*Cercis canadensis*) and eastern arborvitae (*Thuja occidentalis*) give up the ghost during even short-term flooding during the growing season. Legions of tree and shrub species fall between those two extremes. (See appendix I for flood-tolerant species.)

Age and Size

Mature specimens tend to tolerate flooding better than old trees that are well past their prime or very young trees. And in deep floods, tall species can do better than short ones because they are better able to keep all or part of their heads above water.

Other Contributing Weather Conditions

Wind can be a lethal combination with flooding. As root systems lose their grip in soggy soil, straight or gusty winds can topple plants, especially fully foliaged trees and shrubs having large sail areas.

Frozen stuff adds weight to top growth, increasing the risk of tipping in wet soil.

Plants that have not recovered from recent drought stress are more vulnerable to flood damage or death.

At-Risk Regions

The greatest risk of major flood damage is near the great Mississippi, Missouri, and Ohio rivers and their tributaries, plus in California, Texas, and the mid-Atlantic states. Then in the Southeast and Pacific Northwest. But a heavy rainstorm—especially a series of deluges—has the potential to flood or waterlog almost any low-lying, poorly drained landscape no matter where you are located.

A Bolt from the Blue

In the list of threats to your valuable landscape plants, let's not overlook that rare but superdramatic weather phenomenon: lightning.

Into the Trenches

During a nocturnal thunderstorm, a bolt of lightning struck a tall post oak tree in my front yard in Norman, Oklahoma, peeling a broad strip of bark from near the top of its crown all the way down to ground level. The electrical charge dug a three-foot-long trench in the sandy soil at the base of the tree before traveling along the roots to fry a buried telephone line more than 40 feet away. Because the crowns of surrounding trees could spread to fill in the space within a few years, I chose to remove the stricken oak rather than wait to see if it would survive such wholesale high-voltage trauma.

Sandra Dark

Lightning damage isn't always fatal. Courtesy of William Jacobi, Colorado State University, Bugwood.org.

But how likely is lightning to strike *your* tree? That depends.

- Lightning is attracted to the tallest object in the area. So if your tree is taller than surrounding plants and structures or stands alone in a broad expanse of lawn, it is a natural lightning rod.
- Lightning is attracted to water, so tree species having high water content, such as oaks and maples, are frequent targets, as are trees standing in wet soil.

The amount of damage inflicted on your tree depends on where its greatest concentration of water lies at the time lightning strikes. If the bark is saturated, lightning might surge along the exterior of the tree, doing little or no damage. If a high concentration of water is present in the phloem layer just beneath the bark, the electrical charge will follow that route, blowing off strips of bark in the process. But when lightning finds a high concentration of water in the inner wood, the entire tree can explode like a bomb.

The Other Shoe

Regardless of what extreme-weather assault your big-ticket trees and shrubs endure, there are three major problems that might cause difficulties either during the event or, in some cases, much later. When these other shoes fall, they can prove deadly to an already stressed plant if not watched for and dealt with promptly.

Hidden Structural Damage

This can show up weeks, months, or even years after the obvious initial weather damage has been dealt with. Tree limbs that appeared sturdy can begin to sag as wrinkles or tears in the bark materialize. Large woody plants with hidden root damage can suddenly begin to lean or simply topple over. Badly out-of-balance trees that have lost many large limbs on one side also are inherently unstable.

Plants that have already suffered serious structural injury—even damage that has been repaired—might not be out of the woods (pardon the pun) for as many as five years after the damage was inflicted. Some victims might never stabilize.

Pests

Like pneumonia following the flu, dangerous pests just naturally turn up around weakened, vulnerable plants. One theory is that stress might cause trees or shrubs to produce larger quantities of glucose and other nutrients, resulting in larger populations of borers and other harmful insects that feed upon leaves and sap. Some species such as oaks and pines commonly suffer serious infestations while under stress and can remain vulnerable for several years.

Disease

Trees and shrubs that are already weakened by extreme-weather events are vulnerable to some really nasty diseases. Root rot comes in forms such as *Armillaria* fungi and species of *Phytophthora* (so-called water molds). And a number of fungi such as *Botryodiplodia* and *Cystospora* can invade bark and cause cankers. (See chapter 8 for more detail.)

In summary, extreme-weather events can have devastating short-term *and* long-term effects on your landscape's big-ticket trees and shrubs and on your real estate values. So let's look at how those risks pertain to your specific landscape.

The Nature of Your Landscape

Weather has been called the most complex of all the sciences, which explains why your local-television weather guru has such a tough time forecasting the next day's conditions. Throw ongoing climate change into the mix, and complexity stands on its head.

Just as each weather pattern is subject to and influenced by an incredibly complex array of variables both great and small, so is an intricate montage of elements involved in making your specific landscape unique in both its potential vulnerability to extreme weather and its durability under assault. How well you understand and deal with those elements before, during, or after a destructive weather event can be a matter of life or death for your big-ticket plants.

To begin with, just how valuable are your specimen plants?

For any number of reasons (insurance, marketing, taxes, estate planning, etc.), you have a need to know the value of your house. But putting a price tag on your beech or black gum tree probably has never entered your mind, much less evaluating its worth to your overall property values. In fact, if you are like many homeowners, you might not even know the species of every tree or shrub on your property.

But ignoring the content, health, and value of your landscape is about as wise as taking for granted the condition of your roof. Someday your ignorance of this important component of your real estate could come back to bite you in the wallet.

Fortunately, for the purpose of safeguarding your important specimen plants *and* your real estate values, what you need to know about the nature of your landscape is fairly fundamental.

The best possible time to scope out the true nature and worth of your landscape plants is before weather-related damage occurs. The reason for that is obvious: determining the value of your red maple tree is much easier if wind, ice, lightning, or some other tantrum of nature has not already left it lying in pieces on the ground. And who (besides you) knows how well your Japanese holly looked and thrived before heat and drought seared it to a crisp?

To begin the process of evaluating your landscape, it helps to ask yourself a series of questions.

Which of My Tree and Shrub Species Are Most Vulnerable to Extreme-Weather Events, and What Makes Them So?

How well your big-ticket trees and shrubs can stand up to weather assaults hinges largely on the types of extreme weather experienced by your immediate location (meaning your very own yard), and how well adapted your individual specimens are to those conditions.

But as ongoing climate change progresses, woody plants that once were considered "safe" in your area might find themselves exposed to more frequent or intense heat, droughts, floods, ice storms, or other weather events than ever before. So when it comes to vulnerability, the past is not always a reliable marker of the future.

In appendix I you will find lists of tree and shrub species that are relatively tolerant of specific extreme-weather events. But be aware that the ability of even the most tolerant species to withstand serious weather assaults can be profoundly influenced by a variety of factors, many of which are within your power to control or at least mitigate (see also chapter 3).

Soil Conditions

The quality, depth, and drainage of the soil that supports the health and stability of your specimen's root system are absolutely crucial to the plant's strength and vitality.

Sun and Shade

All plants have species-specific light requirements, ranging from full or partial sun to full shade, in order to develop sturdy growth habits.

Plant Health

Plants that are already weakened by mechanical or weather damage, infestation, or disease are far more vulnerable to additional assaults.

Pruning

Improper pruning—or none at all—can result in weak wood that contributes to major limb failure during windstorms or under the weight of frozen stuff.

Age and Size

The limited root systems of young or newly transplanted trees and shrubs make them more vulnerable to flood and drought damage, but their smaller crowns make them less prone to wind damage.

On the other hand, large, mature specimens are more threatened by frozen stuff because their branches can accumulate heavier burdens of ice or snow, but their more extensive root systems can make them less vulnerable to flood and drought.

Adaptation

In a natural environment, you will find particular species of plants in certain locations; they have adapted to these sites over hundreds of years because this is where they find their optimum growing requirements. Likewise, trees and shrubs in your landscape have specific location requirements to ensure their growing success. For instance, some plants prefer a dry location, while others require wet feet. In addition, each species has its own *required* range of soil pH, from acid to alkaline, with most preferring something in the middle.

Suitability

Plants that are native to your region have adapted to your local climate and growing conditions. Conversely, any plant that is grown outside its region or recommended hardiness zone is a possible extreme-weather disaster waiting to happen.

Habit

Trees and shrubs grow in specific shapes or forms, otherwise known as the plant's *habit*. For example, besides the familiar spreading shape of a hawthorn or fringe tree, a tree species might have a columnar (Lombardy poplar), oval (Kentucky coffee tree), pyramidal (bald cypress), round (red oak), or vase-shaped (common hackberry) growing habit. Trees also tend to have predominately horizontal or vertical branching habits.

Clockwise from top left: vase-like, columnar, oval, round, and pyramidal tree shapes. Drawing by Peggy Lovret Chaffin.

Sometimes a plant's habit can make it more or less vulnerable to extreme weather. As mentioned earlier, strong lateral branches such as those found in white oaks are better able to bear the weight of frozen stuff, while trees with vertical branches and narrow forks such as Bradford pears can be highly vulnerable to the same conditions.

Foliage

Evergreens such as magnolias and species that retain foliage in winter such as pin oaks are more vulnerable to frozen stuff, especially when combined with wind.

Why Was My Shrub Destroyed in an Ice Storm While My Neighbor's Shrub of the Same Species Did Not Lose a Twig?

A wide variety of natural and man-made elements such as air currents, shaded or sunlit areas, heat-retaining surfaces such as brick walls and paving, and water runoff from roofs can combine in your landscape to create pocket conditions known as *microclimates*. So your front yard might not have the same exact weather conditions as your backyard or side yard, or your near-neighbors' properties.

Shade from a tree or heat reflection off an air conditioner unit can cause plants growing just a few feet apart to exist in dramatically different microclimates. You might not notice those variations, but your trees and shrubs definitely will.

A microclimate can be either beneficial or harmful depending on the specific needs of plants growing there. In winter, a south-facing brick wall absorbs heat from the sun during the day and releases it slowly at night, keeping the temperature in its immediate proximity several degrees warmer than the surrounding terrain; this slight variation can mean the difference between ice forming or not forming on the branches of a tree or shrub. But the very same south wall can turn into a blast furnace during summer, drying the soil and baking drought-sensitive plants.

A Case in Point

When a big hackberry tree in Keith Newcomb's side yard lost two large limbs, the microclimate of a nearby foundation bed was instantly transformed from protected to full-sun exposure. This forced Keith to quickly rethink the newly planted bed, replacing shade-loving plants with sun-tolerant vegetation.

As Keith found out, microclimates sometimes can change with startling abruptness. But the change also can come so gradually that we hardly notice, such as when a tree canopy expands to shade out a sunny garden, or a maturing hedge blocks air circulation that once helped dry out a wet area of the landscape. So remaining attuned to your property's unique, often subtle microclimates will enable you to make timely, cost-saving choices when it comes to replacing plants or adapting your landscape specimens to an altered environment.

Becoming aware of your property's microclimates (of which there can be several in even a small yard) can help you select suitable species for each location's unique conditions. In addition, you will be better able to anticipate potential extreme-weather threats to already established specimens.

Which of My Trees and Shrubs Are Most Valuable?

Four basic elements are important in determining a plant's intrinsic worth, as well as its importance to your real estate values.

Species

All things being equal, some species simply have greater monetary value than others, but that can vary from region to region. For instance, in such diverse areas as Oregon and Oklahoma, a Japanese laceleaf maple (*Acer palmatum dissectum*) is perhaps as valuable as any landscape tree available today, while in Utah the replacement value of the same species might be rated at from 5 to 25 percent less. And a ginkgo tree (*Ginkgo biloba*) might receive a rating as much as 20 percent higher in Georgia than it does in South Dakota. Check appendix II for more information on how and why species are rated.

At the bottom end of the value scale, some tree and shrub species are worse than worthless. For instance, salt cedar (*Tamarix ramosissima*) and eastern red cedar (*Juniperus virginiana*) have become incredibly invasive pests in areas of the Southwest. In at least one under-siege state, eastern red cedars are taking over some 760 acres per day—more than 9 million acres thus far—and this environmental disaster is spreading exponentially. The problem has gotten so out of hand that in a growing number of cities it is now illegal to buy, sell, transport, plant, or possibly even discuss these infamous species in polite company. (Many big box stores sell invasives anyway, so if you see this, complain to the management.)

Age and Size

Assuming that it is in good health, a tree or shrub in the prime of maturity is of greater value than a young or newly transplanted specimen.

Plant Health

Nothing says "high value" quite like a robust, properly pruned, disease- and pest-free tree or shrub. On the other hand, neglect can turn even a Japanese laceleaf maple, the gold standard for big-ticket landscape plants in many areas, into a worthless derelict.

Proper care can easily double or triple the average lifespan of a specimen, which can range from 30 years for a Japanese flowering cherry (*Prunus serrulata*) to 500 or more years for a white oak (*Quercus alba*). While you might not care if your white oak tree outlives you by hundreds of years, treating it as if you do can benefit both the tree and your real estate values.

Location

Like any precious gem, a specimen tree or shrub has a setting, one that can enhance or detract from its value. Specimens that are arranged with a sense of balance and eye appeal improve both the appearance and value of your property.

In addition, trees and shrubs can serve a number of important utilitarian purposes whether or not they rank high on the desirable-species scale. Well-located plants can cut the energy consumption of your house by as much as 50 percent, a definite selling point in this age of budget-bleeding energy costs. Or a hedge or tree barrier might create privacy, block an ugly view of an alley or business, or create a sound buffer between your house and the busy street traffic out front. And let's not forget fruit and nut trees, which yield nutritious value-added crops.

Do Some Trees or Shrubs Have the Potential to Damage My Real Estate Values or Marketability?

Definitely. Nothing says "devalue" like a sick shrub or a ramshackle tree in the landscape.

Into the Trenches

After I purchased my current property, an arborist took one look at the huge, poorly maintained mulberry tree in the side yard and declared, "That tree is not your friend." Two weeks later, his words proved to be prophetic when the tree collapsed in a severe ice storm. Besides creating cleanup costs that included a broken fence, the downed tree put a crimp in the potential marketability of my real estate by depriving me of a substantial source of shade in a region of withering hot summers. Having learned that hard lesson, now when I shop for property the condition of the trees is a top priority on my checklist.

Sandra Dark

But a tree or shrub can reduce the marketability or value of your real estate in a number of ways even without dying.

Ramshackle Nonspecimens

Besides being unsightly, badly maintained plants reflect negatively upon your entire property. Trees and shrubs that are diseased or infested, contain

A ramshackle tree can reduce the marketability of property. Courtesy of Sandra Dark.

deadwood, or show major unrepaired damage from failed limbs can reduce the visual appeal and selling price of your property, or even frighten off potential buyers altogether.

The substantial cost of restoring or removing large ramshackle trees and shrubs that offer less than desirable ornamental or utilitarian value is an expense that few discerning real estate shoppers care to inherit, especially in a buyer's market.

Topped Trees

Topping a tree (an abomination also known as dehorning) forever weakens its crown, reduces its life span, increases its vulnerability to disease, and causes irreversible disfigurement. Whether done to downsize the tree's crown or to repair storm damage, this procedure automatically devalues even the most desirable specimen. In the case of a high-value landscape, topping a prized specimen can even devalue the landscape as a whole.

Topping a tree causes permanent disfigurement and a drastically shortened life span. Courtesy of Sandra Dark.

Jungle Fever

Rather than landscapes that are designed to create privacy, overgrown trees or shrubs that block views or walkways, or leave your house hunkered behind a green barricade, definitely make your property appear less appealing.

Damage Threat

Any tree or shrub that represents an obvious risk for causing expensive damage—including limbs scraping the roof, or aboveground roots threatening to jack up concrete walkways—might encourage a potential buyer to look askance at your property.

Older Varieties

Plant propagation has come a long way in a short period of time. Breeders have improved varieties of plants to make them more resistant to diseases and pests. For example, flowering crabapple varieties have been so improved over the last 15 years that multiple sprayings to deter apple scab and apple rust are very rarely required. So outdated specimens can, in some cases, make your landscape less desirable.

Can I Improve the Value of a Tree or Shrub That Is Not Living Up to Its Full Potential?

A specimen that is at or beyond its maximum normal life span can only decrease in intrinsic value no matter what you do. But an anchor plant that simply is not living up to its potential often can be improved.

Watering Technique

Water is as essential to a plant's life as blood is to yours. Making sure that your trees and shrubs receive the proper amount of this vital resource—neither so little that feeder roots will dry out nor so much that they will drown—is crucial to their long-term health and well-being. (See also the Preventive Watering section in chapter 3 and the Drought section in chapter 4.)

Nutrients

To maintain good health and vigor, your specimen plants also require proper amounts of nitrogen, potassium, phosphorus, and an array of micronutrients. While a mature tree rarely, if ever, needs supplemental fertilizer, a low-performing specimen might be a sign of soil deficiency, a condition that can be confirmed or discounted by a simple soil test.

When a valuable tree or shrub is suffering from a serious nutritional deficiency, a certified or registered consulting arborist can assess the specimen and prescribe a fertilization plan that might consist of deep root feedings and micronutrient amendments.

Reducing Lawn

Applications of chemical fertilizers, herbicides, and pesticides effectively sterilize the soil beneath the turf, where tree and shrub roots grow. Also, the watering regimen required for maintaining turf grass differs markedly from the needs of large woody plants, so one or the other is bound to suffer. Replacing turf with ground cover or mulch all the way out to a tree's drip line or beyond provides a healthier, more natural environment.

Pruning

Overgrown trees and shrubs, or those having weak forks, can benefit from judicious, *appropriate* pruning. If a plant has been badly neglected, several prunings over a period of two or three years might be required to gradually strengthen its framework and bring it into a desirable shape.

Annual and rehabilitative pruning can not only improve a plant's appearance and health—as well as its ability to withstand extreme-weather events—it can also increase the tree or shrub's sex appeal to potential buyers of your property. (See chapters 3 and 7 for information on preventive and rehabilitative pruning.)

Transplanting

The value of a badly located plant sometimes can be improved or preserved by simply moving it, especially if storm damage to surrounding trees and shrubs has changed its heretofore favorable location into a horticultural death trap. This is especially the case when disaster has left a shade garden exposed to full sun.

Of course, transplanting is not an option for an established tree or large shrub unless you are willing to shell out big bucks to have it scooped out with heavy machinery. But any number of shrubs such as roses and crape myrtles, especially dwarf varieties, can be transplanted successfully with proper care. (See Chapter 7 for information on transplanting poorly situated specimens.)

Into the Trenches

The previous owner of my property planted a variety of attractive shrubs, but arranged them like ranks of West Point cadets along the distant fence line. In early spring, I successfully transplanted two large heavenly bamboo specimens and three mature crape myrtles to sites where their berries and flowers show off to better advantage.

Sandra Dark

Such labor-intensive rearranging of a landscape's living furniture can be avoided by devising a long-term landscape master plan before you ever stick a spade in the ground. You can do this with the help of a landscape architect or designer, or by studying do-it-yourself landscape books.

Why Is It Important That I Know the Value of My Specimen Plants?

For better or worse, the plants that anchor your landscape are an integral part of your property's overall worth. By knowing whether those important trees and shrubs are of significant worth or if they are actually dragging down the value of your real estate, you are better able to make informed decisions before or after an extreme-weather event strikes.

Into the Trenches

The ice storm of December 2007 severely damaged all nine trees on my property. Five clearly were goners, but the remaining four—an American elm, a large Japanese laceleaf maple, a sizeable Scotch pine, and a young pin oak—potentially could be saved.

Crowding by a taller tree nearby had caused the elm to grow at a sharp angle, and it was vulnerable to eventual infestation by elm bark beetles, so I chose to have it removed.

The valuable double-trunk Japanese laceleaf maple had split in half near the base of the trunk, but the remaining half appeared to be sturdy, with an appealing canopy shape that served as an architectural accent to the front of the house. The pin oak, also quite valuable before it was damaged, might, with time and a lot of tender loving care, eventually recover at least some utilitarian function, if not its former glory. The Scotch pine had lost several large lower limbs, but still looked impressive. So I chose to have all three of these repaired.

Prior to the ice storm, all nine trees had been examined by a professional arborist. Therefore, I already knew which were and were not valuable. This enabled me to make snap decisions regarding which trees were valuable enough to warrant the cost and effort of trying to salvage.

Sandra Dark

In addition, valuating your anchor plants while they are still healthy *might* help you recover at least some of your financial losses should they be severely damaged or destroyed. (See chapter 11, Landscape Insurance and Tax Breaks.)

How Can I Assess the Value of My Woody Plants?

Unless you live in a brand new development, your landscape is most likely populated by an eclectic variety of trees and shrubs. Calculating their individual or collective replacement value is a complicated process with a set of variables that is sometimes confusing to the nonprofessional. So a tree worth $1,000 in less-than-ideal circumstances might be valued at $5,000, or much more, in the best of all worlds.

Therefore, unless you possess extensive knowledge of arboriculture and are prepared to shop around to determine the current going price in your area for each of your anchor plants, a definitive appraisal of your landscape should be left to a pro. Also, even if you do have the skills to appraise your own anchor plants, you might still require documentation from a certified professional for insurance, tax, or legal purposes.

But even without the help of a pro, you can make a useful seat-of-the-pants inventory of the important anchor plants in your landscape. While your amateur appraisal of your trees and shrubs is likely to result in only a general estimation of their desirability rather than an accurate assessment of their true monetary value, you will gain some idea as to which of your major plants measure up to big-ticket status. And you might be surprised: even a modest-sized landscape can have a surprising number of potentially valuable trees and shrubs.

For the do-it-yourself evaluation of your landscape specimens, you will need to address the following issues.

Species

If you cannot identify the species of each tree or shrub, take photos and/or stem cuttings, including foliage, to your local nursery or Cooperative Extension office for assistance.

Age and Size

Do you know, or can you learn from longtime residents of your neighborhood, when a specific tree or shrub was planted? Old photos of your property also can be helpful. If such information is not available, at least attempt to estimate the stage of maturity: sapling, still maturing, or fully grown.

For valuation purposes, the size of a tree is usually established by measuring its trunk diameter. Take this measurement 4.5 feet above ground for a large tree. For trunks less than 8 inches in diameter, move the tape to a foot above ground. For trees under 4 inches in diameter, measure 6 inches from ground level. (An easy method for the math-challenged among us: Wrap a cord around the tree at the proper point. Then lay the cord on the ground in a circle and measure across its widest point to get the diameter.)

The diameter of a trunk is stated as its *caliper*. The caliper of a tree in relation to its species is usually more important than its years except when a well-maintained specimen is of venerable age. After all, a 100-year-old red oak can make a big impression!

Judging a tree or shrub's age simply by its size can be difficult. Growth rates are influenced by a number of factors such as location, soil structure and nutrients, water availability, and stress.

Into the Trenches

Based on the size of a 25-year-old mulberry tree on my previous property, I had assumed that the huge mulberry tree in my current side yard was at least 50 years old. But when the giant—more than twice the size of its kin across town—was brought down by the ice storm of 2007, a ring count revealed that both trees were the exact same age!

Sandra Dark

Plant Health

Has the tree or shrub been well maintained and properly pruned? Does it appear to be free of disease, pests, and damage? "No" answers to any of these can downgrade the value of a specimen.

Location

Ask yourself if the plant is in a location that complements the general landscape. Does the tree or shrub have utilitarian value, such as providing energy-saving shade or a sound barrier? Are its mature dimensions in scale with its site?

On the negative side, are the roots constricted by paving, foundations, or other obstacles? Or is your pecan tree growing too close to the house or other important structures, beneath a power line, or in a too-small backyard?

Into the Trenches

When it reached maturity, my late mulberry tree was located too close to the house. By the time of the 2007 ice storm, it had many weak forks and overlapping limbs, and a large scar indicated a major limb failure in the not-distant past. As the storm began breaking the tree apart, large limbs came crashing down on the roof, only narrowly missing an outside air-conditioner unit.

Sandra Dark

Large trees located close to structures always pose a potential threat, especially if they are poorly maintained, of advanced age, or of a weather-vulnerable species. With mature trees, this can be at least partially mitigated with timely pruning. But if you are making new planting choices, make sure that you understand

Severe restriction of roots leaves trees easy prey to drought or toppling. Courtesy of Sandra Dark.

the *mature* sizes of the plants you are locating in close proximity to structures, sidewalks, or driveways, septic systems, etc. (See chapter 3, An Ounce of Prevention.)

Desirability

Once you have identified and evaluated each of your anchor plants, try to find out the "desirability quotient" of your specimens by checking with nurseries in your area to determine the market price of a plant of the same species of comparable size (or, more likely, of the closest possible replacement size). Professional landscape appraisers use regional and local *species ratings lists* as one component of their involved valuation process. To learn more about how these lists work and where you might locate one for your area, see appendix II.

With your completed landscape survey in hand, place each of your trees and shrubs in one of three categories: choice, moderate, or poor. Choice specimens will have all or most of the following:

a rank of 80 or above on a species ratings list for your area, or in the top range of prices for locally recommended tree species offered in area nurseries

mature size

excellent health

a well-maintained structure through regular pruning

great utilitarian importance

a desirable location

Note: Not all valuable or highly desirable species will be available at your local nursery.

Moderate specimens will have all or most of the following:

a rank from 50 to 80 on a species ratings list for your area, or in the middle range of prices for locally recommended tree species offered in area nurseries

yet-to-mature size

good but not excellent health

a structure that is not well maintained, but that can be upgraded with proper care

some utilitarian purpose

a desirable location

Note: Sometimes a plant that falls into the moderate category can be upgraded to choice with proper care, time for maturing, or by transplanting to a better location.

Poor specimens include any plant that:

ranks below 50 on a species ratings list for your area, or in the low range of prices for locally recommended tree species offered in area nurseries

is near the end of its normal life span

is seriously diseased and/or infested

has a weak structure that cannot be significantly improved

is in an undesirable location and cannot be transplanted

poses a potential hazard

Note: If health and potential-hazard considerations are positive, a low ranking on a species ratings list does not necessarily make a specimen undesirable for purposes such as a privacy barrier. But a low ranking will influence its appraised value.

Do I Need a Professional Appraiser to Valuate My Landscape?

You do if you wish to obtain an accurate monetary assessment of your big-ticket plants—and there are good reasons why such a valuation can be beneficial.

For Insurance or Tax Purposes

If you intend to insure your landscape or file for a tax break if your landscape is damaged by an extreme-weather event, you must have an appraisal in hand. Since a predamage appraisal is likely to be more accurate, it is better to have your big-ticket specimen trees and shrubs valuated while they are in prime condition rather than after the fact.

For information on what your homeowner's insurance policy covers—or more to the point, what it probably does not cover—in the event of extreme-weather damage, as well as what tax breaks you might be entitled to, see chapter 11, Landscape Insurance and Tax Breaks.

As a Marketing Tool

An attractive landscape populated with choice specimens might be worth as much as 15 to 20 percent of your property's market value, and can be a powerful lure to potential buyers. On the other hand, an unkempt landscape is worth less than nothing, and can actually drag down the marketability and value of your real estate.

Just as having a name-brand central air conditioner or state-of-the-art kitchen appliances can enhance your property's desirability on the marketplace, so can being able to say that your big-ticket landscape plants have been appraised at, say, $20,000, $50,000, or much more. A professional appraisal provides actual documentation for how much worth your landscape might contribute to your real estate value in your local market.

If You Need to Go to Court

If an extreme-weather event causes your tree to fall on and damage a neighbor's property (and we hope not the neighbor himself), you might need to prove that the specimen was healthy and well maintained before it collapsed. Again, check chapter 11 for information on personal liability and your landscape.

This brings up another important plus to having your big-ticket anchor plants appraised by an expert: if a plant is found to be in less than prime condition or perhaps poses a threat, a certified or registered consulting arborist can advise you on the proper remedy for preventing future costly damage to either the plant or to surrounding property. This early warning has the potential to save you big bucks down the road.

What about Intangible Value?

Sometimes a tree or shrub can be of only modest intrinsic value, and yet be priceless to its owner.

Into the Trenches

I have personally moved a lilac shrub twice, most recently all the way across town, simply because I originally planted it 30 years ago and have developed a deep sentimental attachment to the thing. Go figure.

Sandra Dark

But while a homeowner's sentimental attachment to a tree or shrub can sometimes trump its intrinsic value, so can its historical significance.

The Survivor Tree in Oklahoma City, damaged by the 1995 bombing of the Alfred P. Murrah Federal Building, is an example of sentiment *and* history overriding all. The symbolism of the battered, charred, and misshapen American elm far transcends any monetary value that might be placed upon it.

But what about heritage trees such as those grown from scions of a poplar that George Washington planted at Mount Vernon more than 200 years ago? Or for that matter, what of those grown from seeds and scions of Oklahoma City's iconic Survivor Tree?

When establishing a tree or shrub's intrinsic value, landscape appraisers are ethically required to set aside considerations of sentiment and history. However, if substantial costs are involved in the maintenance of a historically significant specimen, or if the historical significance of a tree makes the property it stands on more valuable, that sometimes can influence the worth of the tree itself. But those are issues that can be hashed out only by professional appraisers, often an arborist and a real estate appraiser working together.

What Will It Cost to Have My Landscape Appraised?

The cost of appraising a full landscape depends on the purpose of the appraisal. For example, do you intend to insure your trees and shrubs? Do you want to know the replacement cost of your big-ticket plants? Or, do you want to know the *contributory value* of your trees and shrubs (such as hedges that provide visual screening, shade trees that reduce energy usage, etc.)?

Also, the appraisal fee can vary depending on the size and complexity of your landscape. If you live in a new, conventional housing development, a verbal estimate of the approximate monetary value of your landscape can be simple, and the "appraisal" might require only a phone conversation with an appraiser. The cost could be anywhere from free on up to around $200. And if you require the appraiser's valuation in the form of a letter, the cost might range from $200 to $600.

But appraising a large, established, complex landscape can require two to three days to complete. And if the appraisal is for insurance or legal purposes, you will want detailed documentation. The cost for this could be anywhere from several hundred to several thousand dollars.

Your landscape might well fall somewhere between the above two levels—in that case, so will the cost of appraisal. But before hiring any expert to valuate your trees and shrubs, always settle on the appraiser's fee up front and in writing.

Can I Have Just One Special Tree Appraised?

Yes. Requests for valuations of single, mature specimens are fairly common-place, especially when a plant might be threatened by nearby construction. And keep in mind that even nonfatal construction damage to trees or shrubs can reduce their ability to withstand future extreme-weather events.

For example, if you have a healthy 100-year-old tree on your property, you might want to have it appraised if nearby construction is planned. Then if the tree declines because of compacted or severed roots or other construction damage, you will have documentation of the condition and replacement costs for that important specimen if you decide to seek recompense from the construction company.

If you want to know the replacement cost of, say, your stately pin oak, you often can find out over the phone simply by providing the appraiser with the dimensions and species of the specimen. But estimating the specimen's value to your overall landscape (which can include the plant's health, location, utility, and other factors) requires on-site appraisal. The cost of an on-site appraisal of a single specimen by a certified arborist or landscape appraiser can range anywhere from around $50 to $900. Appraisers often charge for a minimum number of hours no matter how small the job; again, do establish the fee up front.

Anticipating Problems

Appraisals can be used as defensive weapons. Developers who value mature trees have been known to have a tree appraised and then place a price tag on the tree to remind contractors and subcontractors that they might be responsible for the replacement cost! And adjacent property owners have even leveraged the appraised value of large trees to influence the approval of zoning variances. In one case, in order to get a project approved, a developer agreed to pay for the annual maintenance of a 300-year-old oak.

Dean Hill

What Will I Get for My Money?

Whether you are having a single specimen or your entire landscape valuated, the appraiser's final written report should contain:

identification of the property appraised (either the entire property or selected specimens)

the purpose and use of the appraisal (e.g., for insurance, pre-construction, etc.)

a description of the work to be done and not done

a list of the quantity and quality of landscape elements

a reconciliation of the utilized approach to the opinion of value. *Note: That mouthful simply means that if the replacement cost of your landscape is, say, $50,000, does that estimate seem reasonable when placed in the context of your overall real estate value? For example, a landscape valued at $50,000 on property worth $350,000 would not be reasonably valued that highly if the same landscape graced property worth $150,000. Landscape appraising is all about "demonstrating reasonableness," and valuations above 20 percent of overall property value are fairly meaningless.*

a final estimate of value

Where Can I Find a Reputable Landscape Appraiser?

To find a reliable, trustworthy appraiser, check out the professional organizations listed in appendix III. And before hiring any expert, see chapter 6, Experts to the Rescue.

An Ounce of Prevention

The best, most cost-effective way to rescue your valuable landscape plants from an extreme-weather event is to try to keep them from being damaged in the first place. An ounce of prevention might be the difference between survival and failure.

Big-ticket specimens that are subjected to extreme-weather events have at least one thing in common with what we humans face during the flu season; the very young, the very old, and those with underlying health issues are most vulnerable. Taking that comparison out into your landscape, the most vigorous, best-maintained trees and shrubs tend to suffer the least damage and have the best chance of recovery when nature throws a hissy fit.

Growing robust, weather-resistant trees and shrubs requires both nature and nurture. While some preventive measures are specific to the type of condition being experienced, many apply to pretty much any extreme-weather event.

The Right Species for the Right Place

Trees and shrubs that are unsuited to your growing area will be among the first to succumb to extreme-weather assaults.

Subjected to weather extremes over millennia, a plant gradually develops natural defenses that help protect it from the extreme-weather conditions common *to the locale in which it has evolved.* Flood-tolerant bald cypress (*Taxodium distichum*) has adapted to swampy environs by producing shallow roots, root extensions called knees, and a broad-based trunk that helps to anchor the tree to soggy soil. On the other end of the scale, drought-tolerant blue palo verde (*Cercidium floridum*) both sheds water and creates water-repellant soil beneath its crown, effectively eliminating most other plants that would compete for precious water resources.

Some non-native (exotic) trees and shrubs have adapted to wind, flooding, drought, or heavy loads of frozen stuff in their own native lands. If chosen carefully, these specimens can make useful additions to your landscape. But if you are selecting a species that can handle stiff winds, for example, a wind-resistant exotic might not have developed a native plant's co-tolerance for other extreme conditions such as drought, flooding, or frozen stuff that are common to your locale.

For more on selecting weather-resistant plants, see chapter 10, Replacing the Loss, and appendix I, Trees and Shrubs for Extreme Weather.

Why Some Specimens Are Impossible to Safeguard

Some trees and shrubs are almost destined to be severely damaged or killed by severe-weather events. There are a number of reasons why this happens.

Wrong Zone

Trees and shrubs that are being grown outside their recommended climate zones (dry, wet, windy, etc.) will be among the first to succumb to adversity. A mail-ordered exotic plant runs the added risk of being installed outside its natural hardiness zone. This makes the specimen highly vulnerable not only to forms of extreme weather to which it has not become adapted but also to your landscape's normal seasonal temperature cycles.

What to do: For long-term protection of your real estate values, remove unsuitable specimens and replace them with desirable species native to your location.

Wrong Root Space

A specimen with root space that is severely constricted by concrete walkways, rock ledges, or other barriers develops weak, weather-vulnerable top growth.

What to do: If top growth cannot be reduced to bring it into balance with the root dimensions—a job best left to a professional arborist—remove the inappropriate specimen and replace it with a smaller species.

Wrong Habit

Perhaps a tree has developed a major weak fork, or a shrub has grown severely lopsided for reasons such as crowding from neighboring plants, old injuries, or strong prevailing winds. Or a specimen might have suffered serious crown damage in the past that left it misshapen.

What to do: If major structural or aesthetic flaws in a plant's habit cannot be remedied with a long-term pruning program, or a cabling/bracing system is not practical or affordable, the tree or shrub does not merit valuable specimen status. So it is best to remove the plant and start over with new stock.

Preventive Health

Landscape specimens do not grow in isolation: a plant's health is rooted in and exposed to both its immediate *and* surrounding environment. By taking an integrated approach to the well-being of your trees and shrubs and how they fit into your landscape, you can help them maintain the soil-to-sky strength and vitality necessary to endure nature's worst.

Begin with Soil

No tree or shrub is native to a putting-green lawn. In nature, soil is a dynamic, complex ecosystem teeming with earthworms and untold millions of beneficial microorganisms. This thriving subterranean population is fed by layer upon layer of fallen leaves, animal droppings, decaying logs, and other natural debris, which are broken down over time into rich soil nutrients.

These waterborne nutrients are then taken up by intricate networks of plant roots, where they are either stored or transported upward through the stems and branches. The branches produce an abundance of leaves that comprise the plant's great photosynthesis engine, using carbon dioxide, water, and energy from the sun to produce sugar and oxygen, thus completing the endless natural cycle of birth, death, and renewal.

Unfortunately, soil beneath a flawless, chemically treated expanse of turf grass can be a sterile place that is functionally devoid of earthworms and other beneficial microorganisms—alien territory to any plant other than the turf grass. And as if being an environmental wasteland were not bad enough, putting-green lawns have many other downsides:

- Because grass roots and the topmost feeder roots of trees intermingle just below the soil surface, herbicides targeted at turf grasses can cause severe damage to trees.

- Dense turf-grass roots compete for precious soil nutrients and water and can hinder surface moisture from making its way down to the feeder roots of specimen plants.
- The water needs of turf grass differ substantially from those of woody plants. Meeting the moisture needs of heavy-drinking turf grasses can end up drowning trees.
- Some very competitive turf-grass species such as Bermuda grass and Kentucky bluegrass release chemicals that can actually stunt trees.

Constructing lawn-free beds that extend *at least* out to the drip line will give your big-ticket trees and shrubs the competition-free root space necessary for their overall health. Specimen beds also enable you to maintain watering and feeding regimens that are best suited for important landscape plants separate from the lawn.

With large planting beds, you can begin to replicate a woody plant's natural environment by covering the bare ground with several inches of mulch such as bark chips, shredded leaves, or other organic materials. Gradually decaying hardwood and leaf mulches will feed a growing population of the beneficial surface and soil organisms that are an integral part of a healthy tree or shrub's natural community.

Root Zones

A tree's *drip line* (the outer edge of its canopy) is considered to be the outside boundary of its *critical root zone*, the area of feeder roots that is most crucial to the specimen's survival. Major damage within this zone can often prove fatal to the plant. But the diameter of the total feeder-root network can extend out more than twice the equivalent height of the tree—as much as two to three times the reach of the drip line. This entire area needs to be protected from compaction, trenching, and other soil- and root-disrupting activities ranging from construction to human or mechanical traffic.

Elbow Room

Turf grass is not the only competition of which you need to be mindful. Trees and shrubs that are grown too closely together are in constant competition for nutrients, water, and sunlight. In addition, overcrowding restricts the development of a plant's normal shape and encourages spindly, vertical growth habits.

A Case in Point

More than half of Adrienne Travis's two acres of property near St. Louis, Missouri, consists of dense cedar and deciduous woods. A severe ice storm in 2006 brought down around twenty trees, including five 30- to 50-foot cedar trees that crashed into her backyard. The cleanup "has been taking forever."

While crowding results in weak growth habits, ample elbow room can beget strength. The constant swaying that well-spaced specimens experience when exposed to normal wind currents strengthens them structurally, making them more resistant to extreme-weather events. So properly thinning overcrowded trees and shrubs can enable each to grow to its full potential.

Caution: Dense groupings should be thinned gradually over several seasons, allowing spindly specimens time to develop sturdier frameworks. Otherwise, newly thinned specimens will be highly vulnerable to wind and frozen stuff.

Drainage

Without corrective measures, too little or too much drainage can result in serious damage to delicate feeder-root systems, weakening plants and lowering their tolerance of extreme-weather conditions.

Wet areas that remain saturated for extended periods, such as low-lying terrain or locations where roof runoff keeps foundation beds waterlogged, can drown tree and shrub roots. Specimens weakened by persistent soil saturation are destined to play host to fungal diseases and are sitting ducks for pest infestations and extreme-weather events.

Installing rain guttering on eaves to direct water away from a structure or into collection receptacles might be all that is needed to remedy wet foundation beds.

Welcoming Change

In many cases, the easiest and least expensive cure for a chronically waterlogged spot is to **embrace the low areas.** A natural low area in your landscape can act as a sink to collect and store surface water so that it percolates back into the groundwater table rather than flowing into storm sewers. These are perfect locations for rain gardens and water-tolerant specimens such as bald cypress trees.

Dean Hill

Misguided interventions such as arbitrarily trenching French drains through root systems or spreading additional soil over wet areas to raise the grade can be deadly to trees and shrubs. For a proper assessment of your options for protecting your existing big-ticket trees and shrubs from damage in boggy, low-lying terrain, you might want to consult a landscape architect. Do not be surprised if an expert recommends that the drowning specimen be replaced with a more suitable species.

Dry zones such as elevated areas of your property might be too well drained, especially in sandy soil. Or rain guttering might create desert conditions in foundation beds during even moderately dry spells. As with wet areas, the resulting root damage can encourage pests and diseases and leave weakened specimens vulnerable to extreme-weather events.

In dry zones, established specimens need more frequent watering regimens in the absence of regular precipitation. But when chronic drought conditions prevail, planting drought-tolerant species of native trees and shrubs is the best strategy for maintaining a healthy landscape *and* conserving precious water resources.

Preventing Disease and Infestation

Trees and shrubs that are pest- and disease-free are less susceptible to damage during extreme-weather events. Toward that end, a plant's best line of defense against a host of life-threatening pathogens is a low-stress environment. Assuming that you are growing the appropriate species for your location, the game plan for creating a low-stress milieu for your big-ticket plants should include meeting their specific water and soil-nutrient needs, pruning properly, and reducing overcrowding.

But if symptoms of infestation or disease do appear, the problem should be dealt with *immediately*.

If you are unable to identify the pathogen, collect a sample or close-up photo of the pest or diseased tissue (roots, wood, leaves, or other affected plant material). Seal the sample in a plastic bag and take it to your local nurseryman or Cooperative Extension office for diagnostic assistance. Or contact a certified or registered consulting arborist for expert diagnosis and treatment. For more on diseases, pests, and Integrated Pest Management, see chapter 8.

Why You Should Get a "Preventive Health" Evaluation

A certified or registered consulting arborist can spot weaknesses and problems in trees and shrubs that you might overlook but that extreme weather will find every time. Detecting and correcting problems beforehand can save you money in the long run by preventing costly damage.

You should check with an arborist if:

- You have mature trees and shrubs that were poorly maintained in the past. If the plants are candidates for rehabilitation, a certified arborist can develop an appropriate pruning and maintenance program aimed at increasing their health and value.
- You have specimens that are showing signs of infestation, disease, or stress. A certified arborist can accurately identify pests and diagnose health problems then institute finely targeted treatment. An arborist also can tell whether the disease or infestation has become pervasive, in which case the best solution might be to remove the specimen altogether.
- You are considering purchasing property that has established trees and shrubs. The condition of large, mature trees, in particular, should be evaluated by a professional, especially if they do not appear to have been well maintained. Otherwise, you might unknowingly buy into landscape problems that could prove costly down the road or even reduce the future value and marketability of your real estate.

These are things an arborist might find that you might have missed:

early signs of disease or infestation that might be easily treated before they seriously weaken or kill a specimen
soil deficiencies that can affect a specimen's growth and vitality
badly positioned young branches that will create problems as they mature
indications of stress, such as overabundant leaf production, branch suckers, and leaves changing colors
old wounds that have not callused over properly, and through which diseases or pests can invade the tree

Soil Testing

Mature trees and shrubs seldom if ever require fertilizing. But some soils, especially in newer developments where native topsoil has been disturbed or scraped away, have deficiencies that can make new plantings difficult to establish.

Having your soil tested is the only way you can be sure that your newly planted American holly has a proper balance of the nitrogen, potassium, phosphorous, and trace elements that it requires to maintain good health. And a test can tell you whether the pH of your soil is too acid for your yew tree, or not acid enough for your hydrangea.

A standard soil test analyzes those basic nitrogen, phosphorous, potassium, and pH levels. More extensive tests can cover trace elements such as iron and magnesium. For soil-testing guidelines, contact your local Cooperative Extension office.

Preventive Pruning

For many homeowners, proper pruning of valuable specimen plants is one of the most overlooked and misunderstood aspects of landscape maintenance. Improperly pruned trees and shrubs—or those that go through life completely unpruned—can develop weak growth habits that leave them prone to limb failure or split trunks during extreme-weather events.

Even after repairs are made, damaged trees never truly heal. Though bark eventually grows over the injury, the wound remains forever "beneath the skin," leaving that area weaker and more vulnerable to future storm damage. So employing proper pruning practices which help keep a tree from developing such built-in weaknesses can not only reduce the chance of the initial damage occurring but also can prevent additional damage on down the road.

There are a number of ways that you can use pruning to help protect your big-ticket plants from major damage.

Codominant branch failure in a large hackberry tree. Courtesy of Joseph O'Brien, USDA Forest Service, Bugwood.org.

Prune Young

Small wounds heal relatively quickly: if possible, remove unwanted branches when they are still less than an inch in diameter. Pruning early also helps ensure that a tree or shrub will develop a form that is both appealing and durable.

Prevent Double Trunks

Unless a tree variety has been grown as a "clump" form, it should have only one main stem. Some nurseries grow varieties of serviceberry, hawthorn, river birch, and even some crabapples specifically to have multiple stems or trunks; these should be advertised and sold as clump forms.

For standard nonclump trees: if two stems, also called codominant branches, sprout opposite each other forming a V, one should be removed to prevent a weak double trunk from developing.

Into the Trenches

When I purchased my current property, I was captivated by a 25-year-old double-trunked Japanese laceleaf maple—one of the largest specimens in town—that stood sentry near the front door. Within weeks, the weight of ice from a major winter storm had split the valuable tree in half near the ground at the juncture of the two trunks. The remainder of the tree was undamaged.

If the codominant branch of my Japanese maple had been removed at an early age, when it first developed, the mature tree probably would have weathered the ice storm unscathed.

Sandra Dark

Reduce Buildup of Frozen Stuff

In heavy-snow areas, flat-topped shrubs serve as table tops for collecting crushing amounts of snow and ice. Pruning evergreen shrubs into mound or pyramid shapes helps them shed frozen stuff.

Build a Strong Structure

Removing weak or crowded interior branches of a tree or deciduous shrub can result in sturdier, more wind- and weight-tolerant branches, as well as less sun-deprived interior foliage. But do not overdo it!

As a tree matures, branches should be spaced about 18 to 36 inches apart laterally. The branches should form a rising, evenly arranged scaffold around the tree's leader so that, viewed from above, limbs have the symmetry of a starfish.

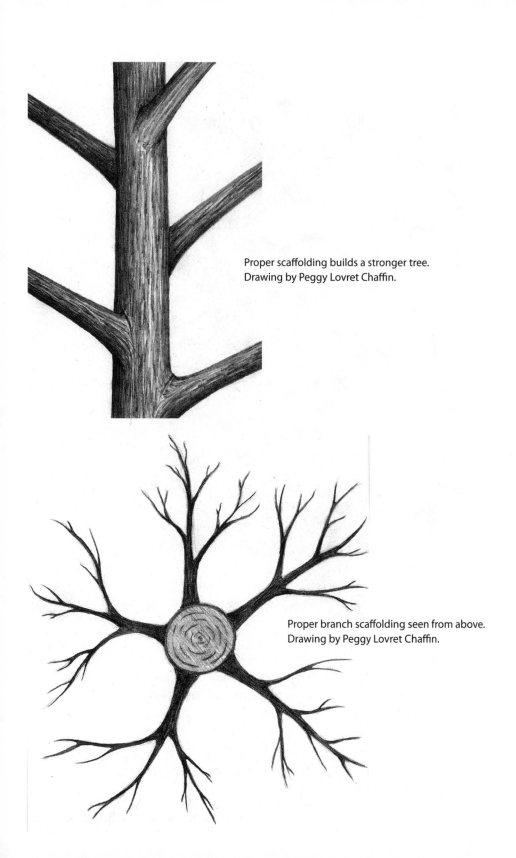

Proper scaffolding builds a stronger tree.
Drawing by Peggy Lovret Chaffin.

Proper branch scaffolding seen from above.
Drawing by Peggy Lovret Chaffin.

"Included" bark also causes weak branch union. Courtesy of Joseph O'Brien, USDA Forest Service, Bugwood.org.

To avoid weakening a tree's structure, gradually prune or thin dense branches over several seasons. Remove crowded growth from the interior of limbs but never enough to create "lion's tale" clumps of foliage near the ends. Eliminate weak forks.

Hold up a hand with your fingers splayed: proper tree branching should resemble the angle between your thumb and forefinger and not the angle between your fingers. Sharp angles of under 45 degrees form weak junctures and should be remedied as early as possible during a tree's development.

Sharp forks that are not eradicated early also tend to develop "included" bark, bark that is trapped between two close-growing branches near the base of the fork. Common to some species such as Bradford pears, this condition further weakens the canopy structure.

Besides weak forks and double trunks, plants can have serious structural flaws that reduce their potential value and leave them prone to weather damage:

- Young branches that sprout too close together can grow into major limbs that overlap and sometimes even grow together, forming an inherently weak, weather-vulnerable structure. Again, branches should be spaced at least 18 inches apart along the central leader at maturity and be evenly arranged around the tree.

- Trees and shrubs should have symmetrical shapes, but they can become seriously out of balance because of crowding from neighboring plants or structures, the loss of major branches, or improper pruning practices. This can leave a specimen in mortal danger of tipping over in high winds or under a burden of frozen stuff, especially if its root anchorage is compromised by constricted space or soggy soil. In some cases, an arborist can gradually bring a plant back into balance with staged restoration pruning extended over several seasons.

Reduce Hazards

Major limbs that overhang structures and driveways can pose a threat to property during extreme-weather events. Even small branches that come into contact with the roof can cause shingle damage in windy conditions. Major overhanging limbs should be inspected for structural soundness; small branches should be removed or pruned back to a sturdy lateral if they become a problem.

Also, most people are aware of the potential dangers associated with trees that grow in close proximity to power lines. Power companies dedicate enormous financial and human resources to dealing with this problem; most companies go so far as to provide lists on their Web sites of appropriate plant selections for growing under or near power lines. Contact your local power company to discuss or assess any potential dangers that you detect on your property.

Should I Leave Curbside Pruning to Utility Companies?

For starters, a homeowner should never—ever—attempt to prune a tree or tall shrub that encroaches upon power lines. Period. Besides that, you are not allowed to trim trees growing in municipal rights-of-way without permission.

Unfortunately, each year thousands of curbside trees across the country are butchered beyond repair by crews hired by utility companies and municipalities to lop off limbs and treetops that interfere with overhead lines. All too often, these crews are grievously untrained in proper pruning methods and are all too likely to leave behind disfigured trees.

Worse than just ruining appearances, such damage weakens trees and leaves

Utility-company pruning crews often leave mutilated trees in their wake. Courtesy of Sandra Dark.

them vulnerable to pests, diseases, and extreme-weather events. Their long-term prognosis is, to say the least, bleak. By planning ahead rather than waiting until cutting crews appear on your street, you have the power to choose alternatives:

- Contact your utility company or city forester to find out if cutting crews have—or can be—trained in proper pruning methods.
- If you can afford the expense, you might ask if you can hire an arborist to properly maintain the trees in front of your property, keeping them downsized so they will not interfere with utility lines. Maintenance of public trees is not your responsibility, but it can be a better option than having your curbside lined with permanently mutilated victims.
- If the trees are too large to be downsized without causing serious disfigurement, or if they already have been butchered, ask your city forester or other officials if the street trees can be removed and replaced with a smaller species.

What If I Do It Myself?

Pruning shrubs and small trees can be handled by the do-it-yourselfer if you are willing to educate yourself on proper pruning practices. Comprehensive books are available (see appendix III), and your Cooperative Extension office can provide basic pruning instructions. But unless you have experience, any pruning that requires a ladder or chainsaw is best left to a trained arborist. Falling limbs are heavier than they might look and can be lethal, whether brought down by a storm or by power tools.

Six rules of do-it-yourself pruning:

1. Always prune to a lateral branch that is no less than half the diameter of the branch segment being removed.
2. When removing limbs large enough to require a saw, use a three-cut method.

   a. First make a partial cut from below about a foot from the final cut point; this will prevent the bark from tearing.

   b. Next, cut completely through the branch from above just outside the first cut.

   c. Make your final cut close to, but not flush with, the trunk, making sure to preserve the branch collar and tree ridge.

Three cuts should be used to remove large limbs, taking care to protect the branch collar next to the trunk. Drawing by Peggy Lovret Chaffin.

Bark tearing due to improper pruning cuts. Courtesy of Joseph O'Brien, USDA Forest Service, Bugwood.org.

3. Do not use wound paint or other sealants, except on oak trees in areas where oak wilt is common.

4. Prune most specimens in early spring, just as leaf buds are beginning to swell. This speeds the callusing over of wounds. But for spring-blossoming trees and shrubs, wait until after the bloom period to prune.

5. Never climb into trees to use power tools. Leave that to professionals.

6. Remember, do not ever top trees! This cannot be overemphasized. Topping, also called dehorning, causes permanent disfigurement and shortens a plant's life span. You might as well remove the specimen and start over with fresh stock. If your contractor suggests topping as a pruning technique, find another contractor.

The *branch collar* is a bulge of stem wood that develops where a limb grows from the trunk, and is more visible in some tree species than in others. When a limb is removed or dies back naturally, this collar helps a wound to callus over. So when removing a limb, preserve the branch collar by never pruning flush with the trunk.

A *tree ridge* is a clearly discernible crease that forms at the juncture of a tree branch (see figure on page 53). When removing a limb, never cut behind the tree ridge—always make your cut on the limb side of the ridge.

Poor callusing of a flush cut. Courtesy of Peter Bedker, Bugwood.org.

Properly callusing cut. Courtesy of Sandra Dark.

For more on pruning, see chapter 4, During the Disaster; chapter 5, Assessing the Damage; and chapter 7, Rehabilitate or Remove?

Preventive Watering

All trees and shrubs need a steady supply of water through the entire year, even during the winter dormant season. If that flow is interrupted for long, specimens can suffer severe damage to their tissues as well as to their ability to withstand extreme weather, pests, and diseases. So practicing smart watering techniques when natural precipitation is inadequate is a key factor in weatherproofing your big-ticket landscape plants.

Lawn versus Trees and Shrubs

The relatively shallow root systems of turf grasses require more frequent watering than do trees and shrubs, which have feeder roots that reach down as far as 18 inches. Also, woody specimens prefer to dry out somewhat between deep soakings. So frequent lawn sprinkling will either fail to get water down to the deeper feeder roots of trees and shrubs, or more rarely, in some soils, result in overwatering of those roots. Either way, specimen plants will suffer.

For that and other reasons discussed earlier, turf grass should not be grown inside the critical root zones of trees and shrubs, thus allowing the desired water regimens of the two types of plants to be kept separate. This is an important consideration: planting beds and turf areas should be separated into zones in your irrigation system.

The Right Time of Day

During the growing season, woody plants replenish their daytime water deficits at night. So the best time to provide supplemental water to trees and shrubs is between sunset and sunup. This also reduces water waste from heat-of-the-day evaporation.

Get Water to the Right Place

Water the feeder-root zone at least out to the drip line, and extend the soak area several more feet for evergreens. Avoid using water-wasting sprinklers, and do not wet the trunk and foliage. Soaking anything but the soil at night can encourage fungal problems.

How Much and How Often

The objective is to thoroughly soak a specimen's feeder-root system. In the absence of regular rainfall, there are several rules of thumb that you can follow when watering to make sure your big-ticket plants receive sufficient water:

- Use a drip hose to apply an inch of water out to the drip line or beyond. Place the hose near the trunk for new transplants. For established plants, begin at least three feet from the trunk.
- Supply about 10 gallons of water per inch of trunk caliper.
- If a slow-running hose is used instead of a drip hose, move it to a new location within the root zone every 15 minutes.

The ability of your landscape's soil to absorb and retain water can vary widely depending on its composition. Sandy soil allows water to drain away rapidly, while fine clay absorbs moisture relatively slowly but holds on to it longer. In many regions, in the absence of at least an inch of precipitation weekly, plants grown in sandy soils will need supplemental watering more often, while those in clay or high-humus soils might get by with less frequent soakings. Established drought-tolerant native species also require less frequent watering.

Though soil variation, climate, the types of plants being grown, and other conditions ensure that there is no one-size-fits-all watering schedule for every landscape, there are certain rules of the road:

- Newly transplanted trees and shrubs need deep soaking twice weekly (daily during warm dry spells) until established. Studies show that a tree with a one-inch-caliper trunk needs a full year to regenerate the roots lost during transplantation; a tree with a four-inch-caliper trunk can take up to five years.
- During extended dry spells, established specimens need deep soaking at least two to three times a month during the growing season, and monthly throughout winter if the ground is not frozen. (For more on this, see the Drought section in chapter 4.)
- If in doubt as to whether supplemental water is needed, dig down a few inches inside the drip zone. If the soil is moist enough to form a ball in your fist, watering can wait.

Winterize

A good soaking before the first hard freeze of winter will help insulate specimens against the cold.

Adjust to Microconditions

Specimens exposed to winds or heat-reflective surfaces such as bricks and paving require more water to sustain their vigor; those grown in shielded, shady areas might need less. Being aware of the microclimates and soil conditions on your property will allow you to apply the proper amount of supplemental water to each area.

Preventive Support

Staking or Guying

Newly planted trees and shrubs should not be staked as a matter of routine. Staking or guying is necessary only if the plants are grown in windy locations, sandy or shallow soil, or on precipitous slopes. Even then, supports should remain in place no longer than necessary—usually six to nine months, and no more than a year.

Old, conventional methods of staking trees called for holding plants rigidly between taut tethers. This is still true for palms, which must be held securely while they grow all-new root systems. But for other trees, taut lines prevent the plant from swaying naturally in breezes, movement that helps to create stronger root, stem, and crown growth. So how you stake a young tree makes an important difference in its development of wind tolerance:

- For trees with a trunk caliper of less than four inches, drive two stakes firmly into solid ground on either side of the root ball, outside the planting hole and placed upwind or downwind from prevailing winds. The stakes should be no taller than half the height of the tree. Tether the tree to the stakes at a location *below* a point halfway up the tree's height.
- For trees with a trunk caliper larger than four inches, use a guy system. Drive three 18-inch stakes firmly into the ground, evenly spaced around the trunk. Place these far enough away from the trunk so the tether lines create 45-degree angles when you connect them to the tree at the lowest ladder of branches.
- Spindly shrubs more than three feet tall that are transplanted into windy exposures might require staking or guying—but only if conditions warrant it.
- When installing the tethers, use a wide strip of grommeted rubber or cloth where the restraint contacts the tree. Do not use the outdated method of running wire through a section of rubber hose. The strip will help protect the bark from damage, a common problem with staking or guying. Attach the tether line to the grommets and to the stake. *Note: Numerous tree-friendly flexible tethering materials are now on the market. Check with your local garden center or search "tree-staking systems" online.*
- Leave some slack in the lines so the trunk and crown can sway slightly with the wind. The objective of staking or guying is to keep the tree from tipping over, not to keep it rigid.

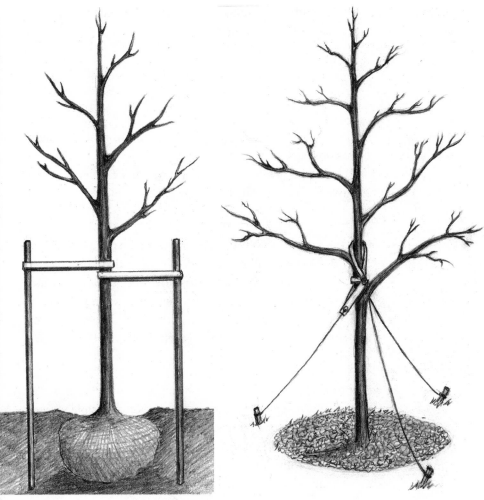

When staking a tree, use either loose or (as shown) elastic tethers. Drawing by Peggy Lovret Chaffin.

Guying a large transplant. Drawing by Peggy Lovret Chaffin.

- Check tethers frequently to make sure that bark is not being damaged at the contact points. This is important! Staking or guying can subject a plant to strain and abrasion in windy conditions. In addition, restraints left in place for too long can cause permanent scarring or even girdling.

Cabling or Bracing

Weak forks, double trunks, and unstable limbs that cannot be corrected with pruning can sometimes benefit from support cabling or bracing. In some cases, installation of mechanical support is the only way to prevent eventual splitting.

But cabling of large trees and major limbs should be left to a certified or registered consulting arborist. For more information on mechanical supports, see chapter 8.

Preventing Construction Damage

Landscape specimens can take as long as a decade to recover from serious damage incurred during construction projects, if they recover at all. During that stressful time, they remain vulnerable to pests, diseases, and extreme-weather events. With preventive action, you can avoid major losses.

Talking with Contractors

Communication is the key to preventing mechanical damage to landscape plants! Emphatically discuss with all contractors the value that you place on the health of your landscape specimens, and insist that this be communicated to their crews. If your trees have been appraised, you might even go so far as the developers in chapter 2 went, adorning them with actual replacement-cost price tags as a constant reminder to workmen of their dollar value.

Soil Compaction

To avoid the crushing of feeder roots during construction, mark off critical root zones for specimen plants, using snow fencing, tape, or other visible barriers to designate these areas as traffic-free zones. The zone should reach out at least to the drip line: the larger the traffic-free area, the better. Make sure vehicles, equipment, and people are routed away. Besides safeguarding roots, this also can help prevent mechanical damage to trunks and branches.

Grade Changes

Most of a tree's feeder roots are located within 6 to 18 inches of the soil's surface, spread out like a giant fibrous wafer. So lowering the ground level within the root zone by even several inches can expose or scrape away these vital lifelines, and raising the ground level can suffocate them. Before making any grade changes around valuable trees and shrubs, consult a landscape architect.

Trenching

Digging trenches for utility lines, French drains, or other purposes can do extensive damage to root systems. Try to route such trenching away from specimens, or limit it to areas that have already been trenched.

If trenches or other digging must intrude, avoid severing any more major roots than necessary. Destroying a major segment of feeder roots cuts off a

Severe root damage all but dooms this tree. Courtesy of Peter Bedker, Bugwood.org.

substantial part of a plant's water and nutrient supply, and can be fatal. Such root loss also can result in a tree's tipping over in high winds.

A Case in Point

Alexandra Owens's property in Boonton, New Jersey, sported a number of maple trees that were planted at the time her house was built in 1870. In 1998, a developer installed a retaining wall at the edge of her front yard, just 8 to 10 yards from one of the old maples, causing major disruption to its root system on that side. "A couple of years later," Alexandra says, "that entire side of the tree was dead. The side facing our house was still relatively healthy, but the trunk was so compromised that we felt it to be a threat."

The 130-year-old tree had to be taken down.

Without question, prior to any major construction project near valuable specimens, a landscape architect should be consulted.

Preventive Removal

Derelict trees and shrubs reduce the marketability of your real estate and are particularly vulnerable to costly damage during extreme-weather events. You should remove plants that fall prey to the following conditions.

Severe Disease

First, you might want to check with a certified or registered consulting arborist to make sure the disease cannot be successfully and affordably treated.

Structural Weakness

Again, a trained arborist can tell you if the tree or shrub can be restored to health. Just as important: the arborist can advise you as to whether the particular plant is worth the effort and expense.

Extremely Poor Shape

A young tree that develops a seriously faulty structure that goes uncorrected until the plant has grown into maturity can seldom be retrained into a desirable asset to your landscape.

Utility-Line Interference

A tree that comes into contact with overhead utility lines presents a hazard in wind, ice, or snow conditions. If professional pruning to downsize the crown cannot keep it within bounds, removal of the tree is preferable to having it severely disfigured by topping. *Note: Curbside trees usually belong to the city and cannot be pruned or removed without permission.*

Decline with Age

With care, some tree and shrub species can live for hundreds of years; others live barely a generation before reaching their dotage. Removing and replacing plants that are in serious natural decline because of advanced age will help avoid future damage from extreme-weather events while maintaining the visual appeal of your real estate. (For tips on tree removal, see chapter 7.)

Preventive Property-Line Maintenance

In some cases, a neighbor's well-maintained tree or shrub that overhangs your property can provide welcome shade, an attractive backdrop, or serve as a beneficial windbreak or privacy screen. In those instances, a neighbor's plants can enhance the visual and market appeal of your real estate.

But an unkempt tree or shrub that rudely elbows its way into your property's airspace can devalue your landscape scheme and even pose a danger to structures and vehicles during extreme-weather events. You can and should remedy the situation, sooner rather than later.

First, take stock. Are we talking minor branch overhang from a tree or shrub? Or is there major encroachment that either mars the appearance of your landscape or poses a clear-and-present hazard to your property values, structures, or vehicles? In many cases, neighbors are oblivious to what the back sides of their trees and shrubs are up to. Approached politely, they might readily agree to prune back problem plants.

Can I Do the Pruning Myself?

Definitely, especially if the problem is relatively minor. But unless you have permission from your neighbor, you cannot prune back branches farther than your own property line. When the best pruning cut happens to be across the fence, try to obtain the neighbor's permission; it's to his advantage as well as yours.

And yes, you should be worried about butchering your neighbor's overhanging plants. Your neighbor's landscape plants are part of your view, which makes them part of the market appeal of your property.

If an Arborist Is Needed, Who Pays?

If the neighbor is not inclined to have problem plants pruned on his own, you might try for a cost-sharing arrangement. But the bottom line is that, in most cases, you "own" the airspace over your property. So expect to bear any costs incurred in the removal of problem overhangs or intrusions.

However, if a neighbor's unhealthy or ramshackle tree poses a clear-and-present danger to life and property—and he refuses to take action—you might want to point out to him that he is liable for damage or removal costs incurred should the tree or its parts fall onto your property. (For more information on this issue, see chapter 11, Landscape Insurance and Tax Breaks.)

Preventing Backyard Wildfires

According to FEMA, wildfires burned nearly 10,000,000 acres in 2006, more than tripling the burn area of a decade earlier. As droughts grow more prevalent due to climate change and housing developments spread deeper into woodlands, grasslands, and chaparral, devastating wildfires are becoming more

A single wildfire can trash your property values. Courtesy of FEMA/Susie Shapira.

of a threat to landscapes during dry spells. Prevention has never been more important.

A Case in Point

After wildfires raged out of control around Santa Barbara, California, in 1990, destroying 500 houses, homeowners got serious about creating fire-resistant perimeters around their properties. When, to quote the local fire chief, "all hell broke loose" once again in the spring of 2009, the efforts of those prudent homeowners were credited with helping to keep the loss down to 77 burned houses, saving hundreds of others.

Thanks to extensive mandatory clearing of brush and flammable materials beneath trees within 100 feet of their house, and the use of a sprinkler system to soak down structures, Richard and Penny Martin were among the lucky ones. When the raging inferno rolled through, six of the nine houses in their canyon neighborhood burned to the ground, including those belonging to three of their closest neighbors. Penny recalls Richard saying, "What used to be in Technicolor is now in sepia." But the Martins did not even lose their wooden decks.

If you live in a fire-prone area where wildfires can erupt and spread with breath-taking speed, a fire-resistant landscape sometimes can be a matter of life or death for more than just your trees and shrubs. Here is a checklist of tactics that can help you reduce that considerable threat.

Open up Space around Structures

Maintain a fire-prevention zone within at least a 30-foot radius of your house and other structures. You need a buffer zone two or three times larger if you live on a slope or your property is exposed to winds. Any grass or specimen plants grown within this radius should be kept well watered at all times. Keep leaves, pine needles, and other flammable plant debris raked up.

Keep Flammable Plants at Bay

Crush tree foliage in your hand: if it is aromatic, it might contain resins that are highly flammable. Cedars, spruces, junipers, firs, and eucalyptus fit this category and should not be planted within a fire safety zone—if at all—in fire-prone areas. Large ornamental grass plants that go dormant and dry during winter also should be avoided.

Nix Wood

Avoid wooden fences, trellises, arbors, decking, and firewood within the fire-safety zone. Remove wood-chip, bark, or other flammable mulch from foundation beds, replacing these with stones or other nonflammable materials.

Get in the Gutter

Keep leaves and pine needles cleared from rain guttering and the roof.

Remove Ladder Fuel

For tall trees, remove low branches at least 6 to 18 feet from the ground to help keep grass fires from leaping up and igniting the crowns. Also remove any vines or Spanish moss growing in the tree.

Space Trees and Shrubs

Within the fire zone, space trees and shrubs at least 20 feet apart to help keep fires from leaping from crown to crown.

Plant Thick-Barked Trees

Thin-barked species such as maples and redbuds can suffer deep charring from wildfires, while the thick bark of species° such as elms and oaks helps to protect their vital underlying tissues.

A Case in Point

The California oaks on the Martins' acre of property are known for their thick, fire-resistant bark. That does not mean they are invincible—some of the oaks uphill from the Martins' house were gutted by intense flames. But though the oaks in the front yard were scorched and defoliated, they have a good chance of surviving.

Plant Native Species

Plants that are native to areas that are prone to periodic conflagrations are often more resilient when they come under fire.

A Case in Point

As a lifelong resident of the drought- and wildfire-prone West, Pablo Solomon has had more than one brush with hungry flames. At the end of one long, dry summer, a monster 3,000-acre wildfire roared past two sides of his property. Always mindful of wildfire danger, Pablo cultivates relatively fire-tolerant species, such as live oak trees that are native to his Texas Hill Country. And, "I try to keep an area mowed really, really short for about fifty yards around the house."

Prevent Lightning Damage

Lightning-protection systems are available for trees, just as they are for your house, if you are willing to pay the price. Protection for a large tree can vary, but often costs in the range of $1,500, installed. Do-it-yourself kits are available. But for safety's sake, lightning-protection systems should be installed and annually inspected by a professional.

Is your tree worth it? A large, well-maintained tree of a desirable species can be worth several times the cost of lightning protection. Also, the removal of a large, severely lightning-damaged tree will cost at least the price of a lightning-protection system. So you might want to consider having a big-ticket tree protected from lightning if:

the specimen stands tall enough above surrounding trees and structures to
    be attractive to lightning

the specimen contributes substantial value and appeal to your real estate

the tree is located within 25 feet of your roof, and your house is on a light-
    ning-prone elevation

For additional information on lightning-protection systems, see the resource
listings in appendix III. Or, check for contractors under Lightning Protection in
your telephone directory.

During the Disaster

In 1995, a century-old American elm survived the terrorist bombing of the nearby Alfred P. Murrah Federal Building in Oklahoma City. Then in 2007, the Survivor Tree, as the venerable elm came to be known, was struck by yet another potentially lethal disaster: a major winter storm coated its branches with tons of ice. As worried arborists looked on, its big limbs sagged lower and lower under weight that rapidly approached the breaking point.

When nature throws her worst at your big-ticket trees and shrubs, it is easy to feel overwhelmed, even helpless. But often there are things you can do immediately prior to or even during a severe-weather event to improve the chance that your threatened landscape specimens will survive whatever damage they might suffer. And in some cases, timely action can help your plants come through the crisis entirely unscathed.

Note: Ice, wind, and other extreme-weather events that strike unexpectedly, especially at night, can inflict major landscape damage even before you realize what has happened. To avoid being caught by surprise, it helps to become a "weather junkie," monitoring the latest daily and weekly forecasts. Your big-ticket landscape plants will appreciate your weather consciousness, and so will your property values.

But do not risk becoming a victim along with your landscape. In some extreme-weather conditions, even stepping outdoors can put your own safety at risk. During dangerous weather events, use good judgment as to whether you should attempt direct intervention to protect your trees and shrubs.

High Winds

Once high winds have set in, there is little you can do to mitigate the effects on your big-ticket landscape plants. If you have selected wind-resistant species, practiced preventive pruning, and provided sufficient water and space for specimens to develop sturdy roots and top growth, you have already done your best. For the most part, the rest is up to the plants themselves.

But if you have even a brief forewarning of a big blow, you might have time to make one or two helpful emergency moves.

Staking and Guying

Tethering a young or newly transplanted tree can help prevent uprooting. *Note: Trees less than one inch in caliper can break at the tether point, and so should not be staked.* But even some established specimens—especially those with root-space restrictions, or species having dense lollipop crowns such as Bradford pears—are vulnerable to uprooting in high winds when the soil is saturated. Emergency guying sometimes can help these trees maintain their grip. See the Flood section of this chapter for details and chapter 3 for general staking and guying guidelines.

Be aware that guying will not permanently solve the problem that caused the instability of a mature plant. When similar conditions return, so will the threat of toppling, as Michelle Wendt knows with her 12 toppled Bradford pears: "Every time it has rained heavily since, we have run to the business to check on the trees."

Emergency Cabling

In an emergency situation, weak forks and double trunks on small trees can be temporarily cabled for extra support by simply tying or strapping them together. This will not be as secure as professional cabling by an arborist, but as the saying sort of goes, "Any support in a storm."

Frozen Stuff

The biggest immediate danger from either ice or snow is the astounding resultant weight. As frozen stuff forms on branches, it provides a larger surface upon which additional ice or snow can accumulate during a continuing storm. And because ice is much denser than snow, only a fraction of an inch of ice accumulation can cause major damage.

Caution: Extreme Danger! A landscape filled with badly storm-damaged trees

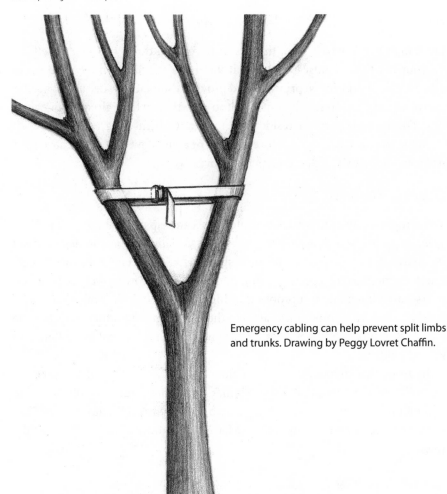

Emergency cabling can help prevent split limbs and trunks. Drawing by Peggy Lovret Chaffin.

is fraught with all the perils of a minefield coupled with aerial bombing. As ice and snow accumulate, even relatively small tree branches can take on hundreds of pounds of weight. And when an ice-coated limb fails, it comes down with the force of a falling safe. Avoid standing directly beneath limbs that are burdened with frozen stuff.

Ice Removal

There are two schools of thought when it comes to removing ice from trees and shrubs. Most experts recommend against attempting to break off ice buildup because damage to brittle branches during the process is virtually unavoidable. But when a specimen approaches *terminal ice load* (the point where major limbs can no longer bear the ice weight), breakage of smaller twigs and branches can be a relatively minor sacrifice compared to the loss of a major part of a tree.

Extreme Measures: Deicing the Survivor Tree

As the Survivor Tree at the Oklahoma City National Memorial approached terminal ice load during the catastrophic 2007 ice storm, Mark Bays, urban forestry coordinator at the Oklahoma Department of Agriculture, Food and Forestry, and a team of trained arborists swung into action. Armed with long telescoping poles, they began gently tapping ice from the ends of the tree's outermost branches, where the heaviest ice loads accumulate. As the ice fell free, the limbs gradually began lifting. They repeated the operation once more when additional ice accumulated, saving the treasured tree from serious damage.

But when a severe ice storm strikes, do not expect to find an arborist to deice your trees or shrubs. Every arborist in your area will have his hands full dealing with damage that is already taking place. For do-it-yourselfers, deicing efforts should be considered only as a last resort when major limbs are drooping under the weight of ice as they approach terminal load, and should be executed with extreme caution:

- Small specimens no more than 15 feet tall are the best candidates for nonprofessionals to tackle. Even if you have the equipment to work higher than that, unless you have experience handling long, unwieldy poles, you could end up doing more harm than good.
- Wear heavy clothes, eye protection, and, if possible, a hard hat.
- *Do not stand beneath ice-weighted limbs.* A large ice-laden limb can easily weigh more than half a ton.
- Watch your footing: the ground will be slippery, and maneuvering a long pole can throw you off balance.
- Do not use a ladder or climb into the tree. Whatever you cannot reach from the ground is not worth the risk.
- Ice buildup is heaviest on the proliferation of smaller branches at the ends of limbs. Use a long pole (whatever you have, from PVC tubing to the extension pole from a lopper) to gently tap the outer branches. You will break some twigs or branches, but the main objective is to prevent the failure of major limbs or the splitting of a fork. As the ice falls away, you should see burdened limbs begin to lift.
- Repeat this process throughout the storm if ice accumulates again.
- Wait for the weather to clear before repairing the breakage you cause.

Some sources recommend that you hook a water hose to a hot-water faucet (presumably on your household water heater) and spray heavily ice-laden trees to melt away ice. But if the water is too hot it can scald the specimen—and if it

Ice buildup on branch tips. Courtesy of Paul A. Mistretta, USDA Forest Service, Bugwood.org.

is not hot enough it can freeze to branches and add to their ice load. In addition, shooting large quantities of hot water into the frigid air can create serious ice problems for neighboring plants. And bear in mind that you will be creating a hazardous skating rink as the water freezes on the ground.

Snow Removal

Shrubs can be suffocated or crushed by deep drifts or plowed snow and need immediate relief. Also, evergreens and deciduous trees and shrubs that have not lost their leaves in the fall are particularly vulnerable to snow buildup that can distort or break branches. Not much can be done about heavy snow loads in tall specimens, but you can reduce buildup on shrubs and smaller trees:

- Use a shovel or a snowblower to clear around the perimeter of a buried shrub or hedge if necessary.
- Snow-burdened specimens already have all the weight they can handle, so avoid doing anything to add to the downward pressure. Use an upward motion with a broom to sweep away snow that is stressing or distorting branches.
- For higher branches, use a pole to gently lift a branch to jiggle off its load. Begin by unburdening lower branches first and then work upward. Otherwise, you will add to the existing burden on the lower branches by dumping more snow from above. *Again, do not stand beneath burdened branches.*

Anticipating Problems

In heavy-snowfall regions, I recommend that you consider ahead of time where your plowed snow will accumulate or be pushed: make sure there is a designated area that will not be affected by the plowed snow pile. This area can be considered in the landscape design process initially, but also should be given consideration when inheriting a property. If a contractor plows your driveway, consult with him ahead of time to ensure that lines of communication have been established. The day of a four-inch snowfall is not an appropriate time to discuss this issue!

Dean Hill

Emergency Cabling

As with wind emergencies, weak forks or double trunks of small trees might be saved from splitting under burdens of frozen stuff by temporarily tying or strapping them together. But this needs to be done prior to their acquiring a heavy load of ice or snow.

Bent Evergreens

If the weight of snow is bending out of shape arborvitae or other evergreens that have upright habits, gently remove the snow and tie up the branches with wide strips of cloth until a thaw sets in. Of course, this is manageable only with relatively small-scale specimens. Do not try to tie up ice-coated branches, which are likely to break when bent back toward their proper stance.

The Scoop on Deicing Chemicals

Rock salt and many other chemicals commonly applied to icy sidewalks and roads can damage or kill neighboring landscape plants, as well as pollute soil and waterways. There are measures you can take to help minimize salt damage to your landscape:

- Hose off road salts that splash onto curbside trees and shrubs as soon as possible. Better yet, do not plant specimens within splash distance in the first place! Road salt is more than just a surface problem: within the splash zone (usually up to 15 feet from the road) salt can build up in the soil to levels that are lethal for even salt-tolerant species.
- Use ice-melting chemicals to keep ice from building up on surfaces rather than to melt existing ice. If you must use these chemicals on walkways, apply them *before* the storm arrives. After a storm strikes, you should first shovel and sweep away the buildup before applying deicers. Yes, this

involves lots of backbreaking work, but that is the price you must pay for not taking preventive measures by applying deicers before the storm.

- Apply the thinnest possible layer of deicing agent.

Knowing what chemicals you are dealing with can help you make informed choices:

- Worst: Sodium chloride (rock salt) and potassium chloride require friction (such as passing car tires) to activate. When used on walkways, these chemicals will pollute the adjacent soil without providing the desired deicing.
- Next-to-worst: Calcium chloride and magnesium chloride do not require friction to activate, but work only down to 20 to 25 degrees Fahrenheit. Commercial ice-melt products often contain mixes of calcium, magnesium, sodium, and/or potassium chlorides.
- Good-but-bad: Urea is often used as a "natural" deicer because its high-nitrogen content creates heat and also serves as a fertilizer. But the serious pollution that urea runoff creates in waterways makes it an unwise choice for the environment. And since deicers are spread on hard surfaces, substantial runoff is inevitable.
- Better: New nonsodium deicing products are coming onto the market, including IceClear (corn-based with potassium acetate) and Safe Paw (amide with glycols). Unlike chlorides, the latter will not irritate pets' paws.
- Safest: Abrasives such as coarse sand and kitty litter can be sprinkled atop the ice to provide traction without harming pets' paws, valuable landscape plants, the environment, or your wallet. They do track indoors—as do many chemical products—so you will need a doormat.

Drought

Unlike most other types of extreme-weather events, drought conditions develop and progress at a relatively slow pace. This usually allows you time to employ a range of creative measures to help save your stressed trees and shrubs. But because most specimens do not show drought stress until they are already in dire straits (and sometimes not until they are well beyond rescuing), a drought is best attacked with vigor as dry conditions set in rather than after waiting for warning signs of trouble.

Prioritize

If water rationing is in force or appears to be in the offing, concentrate on keeping your big-ticket trees and shrubs alive. Turf grass, annuals, and nonwoody perennials can be replaced relatively quickly and cheaply. But if your 35-year-old Caddo maple dies of thirst, it will take 35 more years to grow another one that size!

These trees and shrubs are most vulnerable and should be given highest priority:

new transplants
specimens that have suffered damage, infestation, disease, or other stresses
    in recent years, reducing their ability to withstand additional stress
trees or shrubs with restricted root systems
specimens growing near heat-reflective surfaces
plants already showing stress symptoms such as leaf wilt or yellowing, or
    leaf drop

Deep Soak

A single deep watering that soaks feeder roots 6 to 18 inches deep is more beneficial to a tree or shrub than 10 shallow waterings. This requires at least an inch of water per soaking.

As drought conditions take hold:

use a drip or slow-running hose to conserve water and avoid runoff from
    dry soil. Place the hose beneath mulch materials
remember that specimens grown near pavement, walls, or other heat-re-
    flective surfaces require more water than plants in less stressful locations
water out to the drip line, and five feet beyond for evergreens
water sandy soil more frequently than clay soil
water more frequently in hot and/or windy weather

See chapter 3 for a recommended watering schedule.

Adapt Plants

Water rationing can dramatically limit the amount of water that you can apply to thirsty big-ticket landscape plants at a time when they need it most. Fortunately, according to the University of California Cooperative Extension's Center for Landscape and Urban Horticulture, field studies show that during drought conditions most established specimens can survive on 20 to 40 percent less supplemental water than is ideal.

But rather than reduce the amount of water applied at each soaking, gradually extend the period between waterings so specimens can adapt to the new regimen. For example, if you have been watering your trees every week, stretch that schedule in stages to every 10 days. *Note: Do not extend the periods between supplemental waterings for new transplants, which require soaking at least two to three times weekly.*

Water-management specialist David A. Goldhamer at the University of California, Davis, points to extensive research showing that plants can take months to make the adjustment to drier conditions. So by monitoring long-term, seasonal weather forecasts issued by the U.S. Weather Service, you can sometimes anticipate potential drought conditions well in advance of when they actually set in. This can allow you to begin water-reduction measures early in a drought cycle, providing specimens the time they require to adjust as much as they can to the new regimen.

Reduce Crown

In extreme drought conditions, when water supplies are limited, a tree or shrub's moisture needs can be somewhat reduced by thinning its crown. Remember, the operative word here is *thin*. Remove any weak or relatively spindly branches, but do not top trees! No matter how extreme the drought, do not remove more than a third of the crown or the plant might lose too much of its ability to photosynthesize.

In addition, avoiding the use of fertilizers near root zones can help to regulate the crown sizes of specimens during a time of drought stress.

Reduce Plants

Cut down on competition for moisture by reducing the number of plants around your choice trees and shrubs. Again, prioritize: choose high-value specimens over cheaper-to-replace annuals, nonwoody perennials, and lower-value nonspecimens.

If the competition happens to involve fairly high-value shrubs, and transplanting is an option, consider moving some plants to a roomier location rather than simply removing and discarding them. The best time to do this varies regionally, but in most areas it is in early spring. But whether the transplanting is done in spring or at a less advantageous time, make sure you closely adhere to the watering regimen recommended for transplants in chapter 3.

Shrink Lawns

Turf grasses present serious competition to specimen plants for precious water and nutrients. To eliminate that drain on diminishing water resources, remove lawn grass at least from within the drip line of a tree, preferably well beyond that. The less lawn you have to maintain, the more water you can spare for your big-ticket plants.

Proper thinning of the crown does not include topping! Drawing by Peggy Lovret Chaffin.

A Case in Point

In search of a low-maintenance landscape that would require less water and fewer chemicals, Lynn and Norm Ginsberg had the front yard of their Encinitas, California, property converted from turf grass to native plants that are ideally suited to their dry, Mediterranean-like climate. Instead of soaking a high-main-tenance lawn once or twice a week, they now water Englemann oak, manzanita, mountain mahogany, and other native plants "only five or six times a year."

The reduction in water bills can be astounding. According to Greg Rubin, owner of California's Own Native Landscape Design, Inc., which installed the Ginsbergs' native landscape in 2001, "the biggest problem we have is people trying to water these landscapes too much." Where turf grass is said to require an inch of water weekly (especially to maintain a putting-green appearance throughout the growing season), native landscapes can get by with a quarter inch of supplemental water every two weeks during extended dry periods.

Mulch Beds

Mulch reduces evaporation of precious soil moisture and keeps the root zone cooler during the hot conditions that usually accompany summer droughts. Use shredded leaves or a wide variety of commercial mulch products ranging from bark chips to ground corncobs. In a pinch—though it will not win you prizes for aesthetics—you can even use shredded paper, covered with straw to keep the paper from blowing away.

Note: Look for natural mulch materials that are produced in an environmentally sustainable manner. For example, some commercial cypress-mulch operations have caused severe destruction of cypress forests. On the other hand, mulch made from invasive trees such as Australian pine or, in the West, eastern red cedar actually creates a useful product from trees that are overpopulating themselves beyond all reason. Sustainable mulches can also come from tree trimmers in your area, though these mulch products sometimes can be too coarsely shredded for attractive landscape beds.

Do not build a volcano cone of mulch around a tree. Apply materials two to four inches deep, beginning a foot from the trunk to avoid causing trunk rot, and extending at least to the drip line. Mulch materials applied deeper than four inches can suffocate soil by interfering with the free exchange of oxygen and other gases. Plus some trees may send new feeder roots into the mulch. And a cone of mulch dries out faster than the soil underneath because of the steep angle of the volcano, which sheds water and causes added stress during droughts.

Avoid Nitrogen

Nitrogen fertilizer encourages rapid growth that increases a plant's demand for water. Therefore, high-nitrogen fertilizer should not be applied during drought conditions regardless of whether specimens are showing stress.

Adopt Low-Cost and No-Cost Watering Techniques

Even when water rationing is not an issue, providing ample supplemental water for thirsty specimen plants can do ugly things to your water bill. But watering costs can be reduced in a number of ways:

1. Rain harvesting. An inch of rain runoff from 100 square feet of roof surface can more than fill a 50-gallon container presto quick. A tree needs 10 gallons of water per inch of trunk caliper at each soaking. So during dry spells, especially when water rationing is in effect, harvested rainwater can mean the difference between life and death for your trees and shrubs. A wide choice of rain-collection containers is available, including many sizes of tanks, cisterns, and bladders, as well as 50-gallon rain barrels. (To find out more about rain collection systems, search online, or check listings in appendix III.)

2. Redirected rain gutters. Flexible rain-gutter downspout extensions can divert runoff from roofs to collection areas, tanks, rain gardens, or specific plants.

3. Gray water. Buckets of used water from the shower, bathtub, or kitchen sink can provide hundreds—even thousands—of gallons of cost-free water for landscape specimens during dry spells. While you might not save a large established tree with your bucket brigade, you can certainly keep young transplants or shrubs alive with this method.

4. Gray water deluxe. Some municipalities permit the piping of gray water directly to the landscape from your washing machine, kitchen sink, or other household sources. Obviously, direct piping can result in major savings. But do contact your city code-enforcement office to make certain this is allowed in your area before getting this ambitious. (Arizona has the most liberal regulations, so far.)

   If you do pipe gray water to your landscape:

use biodegradable soaps and detergents, and never use gray water containing bleach or water that has been softened with sodium-based systems
preferably, pipe gray water to a cistern or holding tank where it can be diluted with rainwater, especially if it contains detergents
do not pipe hot water directly to plants or you will risk scalding roots
monitor soil-moisture levels at the end of the pipeline daily to make sure you are not drowning landscape plants

Flood

Persistent soil saturation deprives plant roots of oxygen, destabilizes their anchoring, and creates soil conditions favorable to lethal root rot. So remember: flooding is flooding whether you must deal with Hurricane Katrina–scale inundation or simply experience chronic saturation of foundation beds from roof runoff. Without prompt action, your valuable landscape specimens could be in mortal peril.

In the case of inundation, there is little you can do while the disaster is in progress beyond waiting until the water recedes. But when persistent rains or melting snow create saturated soil conditions for extended periods, there are a couple of emergency measures you can take to save threatened trees and shrubs.

Emergency Rain Guttering

Within just minutes, the roof of your house can produce tons of runoff—hundreds of gallons of water—from a single heavy rainstorm. If your property is graded properly, the majority of this sudden overabundance will flow away from the house toward lower-lying areas or into storm drains. The remainder soaks into the soil, where the excess gradually drains away. But when rains persist over long periods, saturation can cause serious problems for plants, especially in poorly drained soils or where grading near foundations is inadequate.

Putting in an emergency call to a contractor to have rain guttering installed on roof eaves, allowing for runoff to be channeled away from the house, can rescue threatened specimens when unrelenting rains keep foundation beds waterlogged for weeks on end. Do not expect a contractor to install guttering during a rainstorm, but be aware that persistent rains often come in waves, and installation can take place during the pause between downpours.

Guying

Top-heavy plants are in danger of tipping in waterlogged soil, especially if roots are restricted, and when exposed to winds and/or burdens of frozen stuff. By providing emergency support, you can help stabilize trees and shrubs that might otherwise lose their grip on terra firma.

Guying works best on relatively small-stature species such as Bradford pears. Anchoring large trees is a job for a professional arborist, if it can be effectively accomplished at all.

When anchoring specimens in soggy soil:

- Be sure to drive stakes deeply enough through the mud to firmly imbed them in solid ground. Place stakes at a distance far enough from the tree so the tethers will be at a 45-degree angle when attached to the leader at the lowest tier of branches.
- Provide strong anchoring on three sides.
- Do not anchor trees to fences or other trees. If a tree is in unstable ground, so might be everything around it.

Even in cases where anchoring is impractical, be alert to the fact that prolonged saturation of soil can make trees unstable and therefore potentially dangerous, especially on sloping ground or in windy conditions. A single gust might be all it takes to cause tipping. So it is unwise to leave your heirloom birdbath or the family wheels within striking distance of a threatened specimen.

Into the Trenches

Heavily snow-laden trees and soggy soil can be a hazardous mix, particularly when roots are constricted. Some years ago, I encountered just such a situation when snow flocked a 40-foot blue spruce alongside my driveway. Sunlight broke through the clouds, turning the quiet neighborhood into a dazzling winter wonderland even as the snow began to melt, turning the soil into mush. That night a second storm blew in on a gusty north wind, dropping yet another heavy load of snow: the next morning we found the spruce toppled across the driveway, having narrowly missed a car.

Sandra Dark

Removing Mulch

Mulch works well in dry conditions, but during wet spells it holds in moisture and prevents soggy soil from drying out. So keep mulches pulled back beyond the drip line until drier conditions return.

Anticipating Problems

"My tree is standing in water!"

Well, if your tree's an older tree, say forty to sixty feet tall, then I would guess that it probably has been through something like this before, and survived. If the tree is younger, then unfortunately it becomes a case of the wrong plant for the wrong location—assuming that it isn't a water-loving species such as bald cypress.

Right plant for the right spot is my motto. Mother Nature has a way of culling the herd! Planning ahead, intelligent design, and making educated choices are paramount. Impulse buying at a nursery is not!

Dean Hill

It's all too true: when soggy conditions are a frequent problem, your best/cheapest/easiest solution might be to stop fighting Mother Nature and simply replace the imperiled tree or shrub with a more suitable plant.

Wildfire

Let's assume that you have already implemented the fire-prevention measures suggested in chapter 3, including creating a safe zone in your landscape. If wildfires approach your property, and you have time to safely take additional action, you can also do the following.

Water the Perimeter

Soaking the grass, trees, and shrubs within your safe zone will help keep flying embers from igniting fires at ground level. Because wildfires are usually accompanied by dry winds, fine sprays can evaporate before the water does any good. So use sprinklers or hose attachments that distribute full streams or large droplets of water.

Clear Debris

Rake up and bag leaves and pine needles inside the safe zone. If ornamental grasses have gone dormant, cut them down and remove the dry, flammable cuttings.

Lightning

During an electrical storm? Don't even think about it!

Assessing the Damage

However nature has chosen to run amok in your landscape—from breaking a single limb out of your prized Shumard oak to trashing every major specimen on your property—the aftermath can look and feel devastating to you. But first impressions can be deceiving.

Sometimes the damage to a tree or shrub is not as serious as it first appears; at other times it might be far worse. Regardless, keep in mind that cleaning up the debris, making emergency repairs or alleviating stress factors, and restoring your weather-assailed landscape specimens to big-ticket status is a step-by-step process. Each step you take will carry your landscape and real estate values closer to recovery.

Depending on the degree of injury that your trees and shrubs have suffered, the cleanup process alone might take anywhere from hours to days, even weeks. But once you are past that hurdle, full restoration of your landscape to a point where the damage is no longer obvious requires time for injured specimens to recuperate or replacement plants to grow. And this can take months or years.

To chart the quickest, easiest route through the process, you need to know exactly where you are before recovery begins and where you want to be in the end. With a carefully focused road map for what you need to do and when it needs to be done, you can avoid a great deal of wasted time and effort, unnecessary expense, and costly mistakes.

And this is no small thing: having a clear plan for recovery can give you a sense of control in the face of chaos.

In the wake of any destructive extreme-weather event, your first step should be to make a careful assessment of the damage that your landscape has suffered. Creating a complete checklist of damage—from the toppled hackberry tree to minor branch breakage on the photinia shrub—enables you to set priorities regarding how best to clean up the devastation, rescue injured specimens, and heal your wounded property values.

What's more, understanding what needs to be done can help keep you from being taken to the cleaners by so-called experts who either do not know what they are doing, or are downright charlatans out to prey on desperate disaster victims.

Is All Damage Obvious?

Not always. Sometimes, serious to severe underlying damage can show up in relatively subtle ways, or might not become evident until months or even years later. So while inspecting landscape specimens, watch for such telltale signs as:

cracks in the bark, which might indicate underlying structural damage to limbs or the trunk
wobbly specimens (possible root damage)
sagging limbs (possible structural damage)
stressed plants that might not completely leaf out, or that appear to be struggling

You can judge the severity of the damage by using three rankings. Class 1 damage includes life- and property-threatening emergencies:

limbs in contact with power lines
buried utility lines uprooted by toppled trees
severe structural damage (including damaged or extensively exposed roots) that might cause a tree to collapse or topple
dangling limbs or treetops
damaged limbs fallen on structures or threatening windows, air conditioner units, vehicles, etc.

Warning! When Class 1 damage is evident, use extreme caution as you survey your landscape. Even when the extreme-weather event appears to be over, Class 1 injuries with all their inherent instabilities remain a disaster-in-progress.

Class 2 damage includes plant-threatening emergencies:

failure of one or more major limbs
loss of more than a third of top growth

Danger! Trees in contact with power lines. Courtesy of FEMA/Michael Raphael.

split single or double trunk
crushed shrubs and small trees
partial or complete uprooting
severe bark damage
flooding
foliage wilting or changing color

Class 3 damage includes aesthetic disfigurement:

broken limbs and branches that amount to a third or less of the top growth
loss of the leader
moderate bark damage

With your detailed checklist in hand, and the damage prioritized by class, you can begin making prioritized decisions on how best to deal with stress and injuries to your big-ticket trees and shrubs.

Class 1: Dealing With Life- and Property-Threatening Emergencies

In the immediate aftermath of any destructive extreme-weather event, your primary concern should be to make yourself and your property safe.

Limbs on Power Lines

Do not go near a tree that is in contact with power lines, or a power line that is on the ground. Even if the power is off in your house, the outside line could still be alive.

What to do: Report the danger to your power company immediately. Until the line is cleared, remain indoors.

Power lines on the ground can be deadly. Courtesy of USDA Forest Service—Forest Health Protection—St. Paul Archive, Bugwood.org.

Utility Lines Uprooted by Toppled Trees

Even when large landscape specimens are planted outside the rights-of-way for underground utilities, they commonly extend anchor roots into areas where water, natural gas, electrical, and other lines are buried. If such a tree topples, its roots can tear out the utility lines, creating an extremely dangerous situation.

What to do: Report the damage to the affected utility company immediately. If you cannot reach the utility company at once, do not delay: call 911. Severed natural gas lines are especially dangerous and can cause deadly explosions; evacuate the area as quickly as possible.

Severe Structural Damage That Might Cause a Tree to Topple

A tree that has lost several major limbs, shows cracks in the bark, or is leaning (indicating root damage) might be structurally unsound. And if you can see serious damage, there might be much more that is not visible to your untrained eye. Whether the damage is evident or not, structurally compromised limbs can fall at any moment.

What to do: *Do not walk beneath damaged trees.* Large trees that might be structurally unsound demand the prompt attention of a professional arborist. Do not attempt to clean up debris from under the tree until the specimen has been inspected and made or declared safe. Pruning or otherwise trying to repair a large and possibly unstable tree is not a job for a do-it-yourselfer.

If you watch an experienced arborist working beneath a structurally unsound tree, you will see him make a chain-saw cut, then look up into the tree—make a cut, then look up—until the entire tree has been made secure. Unstable trees are in constant danger of collapsing under their own weight.

Dangling Limbs and Treetops

Following a storm, always look up! Inspect tree canopies with care. Dangling limbs and treetops that come crashing down without warning can be especially lethal if you have not even noticed they are up there.

A Case in Point

The morning after a destructive thunderstorm rolled through her Pelham, New York, neighborhood, Lisa Collier Cool counted herself lucky: though a huge tree had toppled onto a neighbor's house, uprooting water and gas lines, Lisa's own property appeared to have come through unscathed.

But a few hours later she noticed several branches on her lawn: "I looked up and saw the entire top of a fifty-foot-high oak dangling precariously upside down some twenty feet off the ground."

What to do: Those dangling treetops are known as "widow makers," and not without good reason. Dangling limbs and treetops are jobs for a professional arborist. You should not attempt to climb into a tree to cut out or dislodge large, dangling tree parts! A trained arborist can remove the dangerous wood safely and trim the wound so it will have the best chance to properly callus over.

Damaged Limbs on Structures or Threatening Windows, Air Conditioner Units, Vehicles, Etc.

Besides posing a danger to passersby and pets, a large limb can cause serious and costly damage to property if it should fall.

What to do: Contact a certified arborist at once. The cost of having a large limb removed by a professional will be less than the expense of repairing damage caused if the limb falls on your air conditioner unit or crashes through your dining room window. Plywood barriers and tepees can help protect threatened objects from damage while you wait for the arborist if you can install them without endangering yourself.

If the limb or tree has already fallen onto your roof or vehicle, crashed through a window, or otherwise damaged structures, take photos before the debris is removed. Also contact your homeowner's-insurance agent. Your policy might cover all or part of the cost of removing limbs or trees from structures or vehicles, plus the cost of repairs to the damaged items (all less the deductible). For more on this, see chapter 11, Landscape Insurance and Tax Breaks.

Class 2: Dealing with Plant-Threatening Emergencies

Valuable specimens that have suffered severe damage require prompt care. In some cases, emergency measures can save a tree or shrub that, if left untreated, might eventually deteriorate to a point where it has to be removed.

Failure of a Major Limb

Trees can usually survive the loss of one or two major limbs if the overall damage is not severe and proper repairs are made. A traumatic amputation inevitably leaves a stump that must be removed and sometimes a ragged bark wound that needs to be repaired before pests and disease organisms can invade.

What to do: Call in a certified or registered consulting arborist. Besides his ability to safely remove the limb and repair the wound, an arborist can inspect the entire tree for other hidden instabilities. Also, if the limb failure caused a major wound such as a deep tear involving underlying tissue in the trunk, a professional can help you decide whether the specimen is worth trying to salvage. For more on this, see chapter 7, Rehabilitate or Remove?

Stubs will die back, providing food and entry points for fungi and other harmful organisms. Courtesy of Joseph LaForest, University of Georgia, Bugwood.org.

Note: Even during an emergency visit, make sure the arborist removes the stubs along with the broken limbs. This way the tree wound can begin to callus over and *you will save the cost of a return visit by the tree trimmer.*}

Loss of More Than a Third of Top Growth

A tree or shrub that was healthy prior to being injured usually can survive the loss of up to a third of its crown. When the loss approaches half, survival becomes iffy. In most cases, loss of more than half of the top growth will prove to be fatal, at least in part because the relatively few remaining branches might be unable to generate enough foliage to nourish the specimen through its difficult recovery period.

What to do: Contact a certified or registered consulting arborist when any specimen suffers the loss of more than a third of its top growth. A trained professional can best judge the degree of damage, which might not be as bad or irreparable as it appears. Then if survival is deemed likely, and the specimen is judged to be worthy of the effort, the arborist can make necessary repairs. Do not even consider having a tree topped!

Note: In some cases, even an expert cannot easily determine the likelihood that a severely damaged specimen will survive. For example, a specimen that has been subjected to flooding or drought might not reveal its true condition for months or years following an extreme-weather event. This complicates the decision as to whether a salvaging attempt should be made, especially if the specimen is a highly desirable species or occupies a particularly useful or aesthetic place in the landscape. For more on dealing with this dilemma, see chapter 7.

Split Single or Double Trunk

A single trunk that splits almost always leaves a tree structurally unsound and is a recipe for removal. Likewise, when one side of a double-trunk tree splits off, you are left with half a tree that has a low likelihood of long-term survival. But here too, if the traumatized tree serves an important utilitarian or aesthetic purpose, such as protecting a shade garden or balancing the architecture of your landscape, you might feel it is worth trying to save.

What to do: If you want to attempt rescue, contact a certified or registered consulting arborist immediately. In some cases, especially with a young tree, split single or double trunks can be brought back together with a mechanical support system.

If a split double trunk cannot be braced back together, you will need to decide whether the remainder of the tree is worth trying to save. Whether it has even the slimmest chance of survival might depend on how much damage the split has done to the remaining trunk. If you do decide against removal of the entire tree for the time being, an arborist can cut away the fallen section and clean up the wound to help reduce the threat of pests or diseases invading the crippled plant, a crucial first step in its lengthy struggle to survive.

Crushed Shrubs and Small Trees

During extreme-weather events, it is not uncommon for shrubs and small trees to be crushed by neighboring trees, wind- or flood-borne storm debris, or heavy snow.

What to do: If you can do so safely, remove the debris or snow that is responsible for the crushing. But if the debris is from a nearby tree that appears to be unstable, first contact an arborist, who can make the site safe.

Once the crushed specimen is fully exposed, determine if the tree or shrub appears to be salvageable. Is most of a tree's crown intact? Can the shrub be restored eventually by cutting it back to undamaged wood? An arborist can help you make this decision; or review both Class 1 and Class 2 conditions.

If you deem the specimen worth saving, prune broken branches back to the nearest lateral branch. Do not try to manicure the misshapen plant at this time. It needs all of its remaining branches and leaves to regain its strength. Wait to see how much it fills in again on its own during the next few months or, in the case of fall or winter damage, the following spring.

Partial or Complete Uprooting

When it comes to surviving full or partial uprooting, size and age are of the utmost importance.

A large, mature tree or shrub that has been completely uprooted cannot survive the shock of losing most or all of its vast and vital feeder-root system. Even if a large tree could withstand such a loss, the likelihood is slim that heavy equipment and manpower would be available to quickly get the specimen upright and replanted, an absolute necessity in any uprooting incident.

A smaller, younger plant (less than 10-inch trunk caliper) can sometimes survive if at least one-third of its root system has not been dislodged.

It is important to determine why the plant tipped over during adverse weather conditions. If the cause was some unsolvable problem such as *Cytospora* canker (see chapter 8), previously severed roots, or restricted root space, the plant will uproot again in the future, and removal is the only permanent solution.

But with prompt emergency care, otherwise healthy young trees and shrubs—especially those planted within the past year or two—often can recover from the shock and produce new feeder-root systems in time to survive.

What to do: Quick action for uprooted trees or shrubs can save the plant:

- Cover the exposed roots immediately with wet cloths or moist soil to keep them from drying out.
- Dig down deep and wide enough to make room for all the dislodged roots. Do not try to twist them into a too-small space.
- Bring the plant upright and reset the roots in the hole. Backfill the hole with soil to the same level as it was before the uprooting, firming it in as you go. Water it thoroughly unless the soil is already saturated.
- Stake or guy the plant (see chapter 3) on three sides to hold it in position until roots can reanchor themselves.
- Remove only broken branches. The custom of reducing top growth to bring it into balance with root loss simply adds injury to injury, and is increasingly considered "old arboriculture."
- Follow the watering regimen for a newly transplanted specimen: soak the feeder-root zone three or four times a week, or daily in warm, dry conditions.

- Do not apply fertilizer. Nitrogen boosts crown growth that throws the top-growth-to-root-system ratio still further out of balance, making the root-damaged plant even more top-heavy and vulnerable to tipping. Nitrogen also interferes with the plant's recuperative process: diverting energy from root regeneration to top growth reduces rather than increases the plant's chances of survival.

Deciding when it is safe to remove tethers can be a difficult call. In general, supports should remain in place for at least 6 months, but no more than 12. If the plant shows continued instability at the end of that time, it might never develop sufficient root anchorage to hold it in place in windy conditions. Your only practical alternative will be to remove and replace the specimen.

Severe Bark Damage

The bark of a tree or shrub serves as its tough outer skin, protecting the softer underlying phloem, the vascular tissue that transports nutrients produced by photosynthesis in the leaves. When a tree has been completely girdled—the bark and phloem stripped away in a continuous band around the circumference of the trunk—the entire vascular system is severed.

A girdled specimen will die unless immediate action is taken, and often even then. But a significant specimen might be worth the effort.

What to do: In some cases, scions of live bark and underlying tissue can be grafted onto the tree to bridge the girdled area. If these grafts take hold, transportation of nutrients can resume. Such bridge grafting also can be useful in a case of partial girdling, to prevent part of a tree from dying.

The difficulty is in finding the fairly rare expert who actually knows how to accomplish a bridge graft. You can try calling certified arborists on the outside chance that you will find one with experience in this highly specialized and exacting operation. You also might check with tree nurserymen or urban foresters in your area.

Whatever actions you attempt, timing is critical. If the girdling occurs during the growing season, a wait of just a few days will doom whatever chance the specimen might have had to survive.

Flooding

Many species can tolerate flooding for days, even weeks, without incurring permanent damage—pines are a notable exception. To find out how tolerant your landscape specimens are to flooding, check appendix I or contact your local Cooperative Extension office.

But regardless of how well a species takes to water, soil that remains saturated

Water marks left by a 1997 flood in Grand Forks, North Dakota. Courtesy of FEMA/Michael Rieger.

for periods beyond a tree or shrub's natural tolerance level can put the plant in mortal danger. Even repeated short-term saturations can dim a specimen's chances for survival if it does not have time to fully recover between recurrent flooding episodes.

What to do: Once floodwaters subside, remove any debris that has washed into or against plants. If silting has occurred, carefully remove the silt from the plant's root zone (unless the silt has been in place long enough that roots have already grown up into it). Repair any damaged limbs or torn bark, or call an arborist if injuries are extensive or require climbing.

In cases where specimens were not actually standing in water but the soil has remained saturated for an extended period, try to remedy the situation. This might require the installation of rain guttering on roof eaves or otherwise channeling water away from the site.

Then wait for the specimen to give some indication as to how it is faring. Flood-damaged plants can take many months to either perk up or give up the ghost. In the case of fall or winter flooding, wait to see whether the specimen leafs out the following spring. Meanwhile, do not apply fertilizer!

For guidance on the long-term care of flood-damaged plants, including what to do about saltwater invasions in coastal landscapes, see chapter 8.

Foliage Wilting or Changing Color

Unlike colorful fall foliage displays, off-season or unexplained changes signal that a tree or shrub has already reached an advanced stage of stress *right now*. Every moment counts if the specimen is to be rescued.

Foliage warning signals can be triggered by one or more of a number of lethal culprits, including drought, flooding, construction damage, disease, and infestation, any of which can obstruct a plant's vital life processes. Sometimes the cause can be a combination of stressors, such as when flooding drowns roots and provides inviting conditions for a variety of fungal diseases. *Note: Plants that have been defoliated by high winds usually will leaf out again, either from secondary buds later in the growing season, or in the case of late-season defoliation, the following spring. If leaves fail to appear in the spring, the plant has died.*

What to do: The most urgent order of business is to determine exactly what is causing the foliage to wilt or change color. If drought conditions prevail, that is most likely at least a contributing factor. Make sure the tree or shrub's feeder-root zone is deeply soaked on a regular schedule. (See chapter 4 for guidelines on watering during droughts.)

If the cause is not immediately evident to you, then do not delay: call in a certified or registered consulting arborist, or contact your local Cooperative Extension office for assistance in diagnosing and treating the problem. If the specimen is diseased or infested, treatment should begin as soon as possible. In extreme cases, you might need to remove the ailing plant altogether before the problem can affect neighboring plants in your landscape. (For more information on dealing with postdisaster diseases and pests, see chapter 8.)

A Case in Point

An intense, prolonged dry spell coupled with blistering summer temperatures can put tremendous stress on landscape specimens. So when more than a thousand mature pine trees suddenly turned brown and died in landscapes throughout Norman, Oklahoma, most homeowners just naturally blamed the ongoing drought.

But the local Cooperative Extension agent pointed a finger at the primary culprit causing the pine die-off: pine wilt nematodes. These tiny organisms often infest mature pines in the area's pine-inhospitable climate, clogging their vascular systems and interfering with the transportation of water and nutrients. The ongoing drought only added to the stress so that, instead of the pines dying over a period of years, they all succumbed in the course of a single summer.

Class 3: Dealing with Aesthetic Disfigurement

A tree or shrub can sustain a moderate amount of damage that, while it might take away from the plant's appearance, poses no immediate threat to its survival. In some Class 3 cases, repairs can wait for weeks or months, but should be made in a reasonably timely manner (usually that season) for the sake of the specimen's health, as well as for the aesthetic aspect of your real estate.

Broken Limbs and Branches That Amount to a Third or Less of the Top Growth

Damaged limbs that do not threaten a tree or shrub's structural integrity or pose a real or potential danger to life or property can still affect the plant's appearance, as well as its value as a specimen. This is especially so when the damage alters a plant's natural shape. *Note: If there are no branches left on a substantial stretch of the central leader, the tree cannot fill back in that area. Such extensive, permanent disfigurement raises the question of whether you will want to keep the tree. (See chapter 7, Rehabilitate or Remove?)*

What to do: Prune damaged limbs back to the nearest lateral branch or to the trunk, being careful not to damage the branch collar. (For proper cutting technique, see figure on page 53.) When the pruning entails climbing into the tree or using a tall ladder, your safest choice is to hire an arborist.

If damage is fairly extensive, do not attempt to reshape the specimen all at one time; restoring its natural shape might require a gradual pruning regimen spread over several seasons. Pruning more than is necessary at this time only adds to the number of wounds that the plant must heal from the initial damage, further sapping its energy reserves.

Loss of Leader

A tree usually can survive the loss of its leader if damage to the remainder of the crown is not too severe. But the loss of the leader will permanently affect a mature specimen's natural shape and appearance—especially for pyramidal species such as pin oaks—which can make a difference in the tree's aesthetic and monetary values to your landscape.

What to do: Contact a certified arborist to make repairs. With young trees, another top branch sometimes can be trained as a new leader. Barring that possibility, an expert often can reshape either a young or mature tree so that it will eventually grow back into a pleasing form. Though a plant's redesigned form might not be the classic shape of its species, it can still serve aesthetic or functional purposes in the landscape without the cost of removal, or the time and expense involved in starting over with a new plant.

Moderate Bark Damage

Any untreated bark wound, great or small, be it from loss of a limb or mechanical damage, can leave a plant vulnerable to invasion by harmful organisms, and so should be repaired promptly.

What to do: Use a sharp knife to trim away loose or ragged bark, shaping the wound into an oval with rounded ends, not points. Be careful not to slice any deeper than necessary.

Prune torn bark in an oval shape, so the wound can begin to callus over. Drawing by Peggy Lovret Chaffin.

Do not use paint, tar, or other wound dressings, which can interfere with the healing process. (The exception to that rule: studies have shown that wound paint can help protect oak trees from oak wilt if that fungal disease is prevalent in your area.) When the edges of torn bark are properly trimmed, the wound should callus over completely; this can take from one to several growing seasons depending on the size of the wound.

What If My Tree Has Fallen onto a Neighbor's Property, or Vice Versa?

It depends.

In most cases, if the tree was healthy before it fell, the part that lands across the property line "belongs" to the property onto which it has fallen. On the other hand, if the tree was unhealthy—and this might need to be determined by an arborist—it belongs in its entirety to the property on which it grew. The same holds true if only limbs fall onto adjoining property. But this covers only the issue of who owns the debris and is legally responsible for its removal, as well as for any damages to structures that it caused; it does not address the emotional issue.

In the wake of any natural disaster, as the magnitude of the damage soaks in, emotions can run high. So how you assess the situation and deal with a tree that has fallen across borders can have long-lasting effects on neighbor-to-neighbor relationships. Whenever possible, it is helpful if neighbors can think of (and deal with) toppled cross-border trees not as "mine" or "yours," but as "ours."

What to do: First, if the fallen tree is in contact with utility lines, has uprooted buried utility lines, or poses an immediate danger to people or structures, follow the guidelines above for Class 1 emergencies. If and when it is safe to deal with the fallen tree:

- Assess who "owns" the part of the tree that has crossed your property line. If you have past photos of a neighbor's unhealthy, unstable, unkempt tree, that helps your cause. Lacking prior pictures, if the fallen tree clearly has a rotten trunk or limbs, take photos of that condition now. *Note: If your tree has toppled across borders, this is yet another example of why maintaining healthy, vigorous trees can be a cost-effective strategy.*
- In the case of a tree that was healthy and well maintained prior to toppling onto your property, you will be responsible for removing the part of the tree that you now "own." You and your neighbor might be able to save on expenses if you hire the same tree service to remove the entire tree and split the cost. In a best-case scenario, your neighbor might even be generous enough to foot the entire bill.

- If you have the equipment and skill to clear away the tree yourself, try to team up with your neighbor on the effort, and split the cost of hauling away the debris if that is necessary. (For more on tree removal, see chapter 7.)
- In negotiating the removal of a cross-borders tree, bear in mind that your neighbor is as stressed as you are over the devastation. An ounce of diplomacy can pay off handsomely in long-term neighborly relations.
- Before removing the debris, contact your insurance carrier to find out if your homeowner's policy covers any of the cost of tree removal. If so, be sure to save all receipts. (See chapter 11, Landscape Insurance and Tax Breaks.)

What If My Tree Is Scorched by Wildfire?

Fast-moving wildfires often scorch tree bark without damaging the vital phloem tissue beneath. But slow-moving fires can linger long enough to char deeply, especially if the specimen is a thin-barked species such as redbud or maple.

What to do: Scrape the bark to find out how deep the charring goes. If charring is shallow and not extensive, the specimen has a good chance of survival.

If charring extends past the bark into the underlying phloem tissue, contact a certified or registered consulting arborist who can assess the specimen's prospects of survival. Or simply adopt a wait-and-see approach to find out whether the tree shows vigorous growth in the coming growing season.

Note: In either of the above situations, maintain a regular watering schedule and eliminate as many stressors as possible during the recovery period.

But if charring is deep and encompasses all or most of the trunk, the tree is a goner and should be removed.

What If My Tree Is Struck by Lightning?

All lightning strikes are not created equal. Assess the degree of damage to your tree by determining which of three possible paths the electrical charge took.

Through Central Heartwood

When this is the route, the tree explodes.

What to do: If lightning has shattered the specimen, engage a tree service to clear away the debris, or do it yourself. For guidelines on removing a tree, see chapter 7. *Note: Lightning strikes are always fatal to pine trees.*

Through the Phloem Layer beneath the Bark

You can tell lightning has gone this way when the bark has separated from underlying tissue, often peeling away in long strips.

What to do: If bark has separated from underlying phloem tissue (especially if this is extensive), contact a certified arborist to evaluate the injuries, assess the tree's overall health, and make necessary repairs. (For do-it-yourselfers: trim away hanging strips of bark. You can use galvanized shingle nails to secure loosened bark to the tree.)

Along the Exterior Bark

Here the bark might be scorched, but has not separated from the tree. If only the surface of the bark is scorched, the tree probably is not in danger.

Into the Breach

When you're dealing with any moderate to severe trauma to trees and shrubs, a certified or registered consulting arborist can be your landscape's best friend. To learn what you need to know before hiring an arborist or any other specialist to deal with extreme-weather events in your landscape, keep reading.

Experts to the Rescue

Plants have an amazing capacity to survive, and sometimes they can recover from what at first might appear to be horrific injuries. The century-old elm at the Oklahoma City National Memorial is a prime example. Having endured a marginal life of neglect in the asphalt desert of a downtown parking lot, the tree was defoliated by a massive bomb blast and charred by burning vehicles. But one year later, it grabbed the spotlight as new leaf buds burst open. From that unexpected splash of greenery amid the scars came its name—the Survivor Tree.

Following any disaster, be it man-made or an extreme-weather event, there are many potential survivor trees out there, all in desperate need of emergency care . . . and patience.

After a catastrophe, seriously injured and stressed trees and shrubs cannot simply resume life as usual. Like any patient, they require an extended period of carefully monitored rest and recuperation to get over the shock and to callus over their injuries. So before you make a final decision regarding the ultimate fate of a once-valuable but now badly damaged specimen, there are times when it is wise to bide your time, giving the plant an opportunity to show you whether it has what it takes to continue playing with the hand it was dealt.

But being patient does not mean you should just stand by and expect a tree or shrub to properly mend itself without assistance any more than you would expect a badly broken bone to properly heal itself without a trip to the emergency room. Even if a specimen does manage to survive its injuries on its own at least for the short term, vivid evidence of trauma such as broken limbs, badly torn bark, or areas of deadwood can remain visible for many years, if not permanently. This can devalue your landscape and the curb appeal of your property.

Even worse, harmful organisms can invade through open wounds, or the weakened and stressed plant can attract opportunistic pests. So a big-ticket specimen that might have been restored to its position as a valuable asset with a pleasing appearance and robust health can end up looking forever maimed, or be lost altogether because of "health complications."

Proper emergency measures by experts can help rescue a badly damaged or threatened specimen that might otherwise die. As for the cost, where valuable trees and shrubs are concerned, immediate costs need to be measured against the long view. By rescuing your big-ticket landscape specimens, you can avoid the cost of removing and replacing them, as well as the long wait for replacements to grow to comparable size. In the process, you help to preserve both the value and market appeal of your property. So hiring the right *qualified* experts is an investment that can end up actually saving you money in the long run.

Can I Do It Myself?

Many emergency measures involved in recovering a battered landscape from an extreme-weather event—and most preventive measures—can be handled by a do-it-yourselfer. But first you need to take careful stock of your abilities, as well as your limitations.

In some cases, physical fitness is an issue: repairing extensive damage to a large tree or shrub, or removing the specimen altogether, is always strenuous, labor-intensive work. So are many other projects that might be necessary or desirable to help prevent or mitigate extreme-weather damage. These might involve building a pond, rain garden, bog, or water garden to alleviate (or take advantage of!) a chronically soggy area of the landscape, or installing an underground cistern to collect rainwater during drought conditions.

Also, coping with damaged or stressed trees and shrubs requires varying degrees of equipment that can range from something as simple as a water hose or pruning shears all the way up to a chain saw and tree-climbing equipment. Most specialty and heavy-duty machinery, including bucket lifts, can be rented. But unless you are experienced with their use, the risk to your safety can be substantial. Even experienced arborists can have rare but hair-raising accidents.

When To Do It Yourself

For safety's sake, all Class 1 and many Class 2 emergencies (see chapter 5) should be dealt with by experts. In general, stick with an expert when:

major limbs are involved
a tree needs to be felled
a tall ladder or tree climbing is required
a chain saw is involved, especially if you are a novice

Caution: A chain saw is a dangerous tool even in experienced hands; combining one with an inexperienced operator and a badly damaged tree that requires climbing can be a recipe for disaster. One rule of thumb is to never use a chain saw above shoulder height.

All this said, many landscape-disaster recovery measures are well suited for the dedicated do-it-yourselfer if:

- You have appropriate equipment. Depending upon the form of extreme weather that has assailed your landscape, this might range from lopping shears and manual tree saws to a stump grinder or snowblower.
- You can reach damaged limbs with a tree saw or a pole lopper, and you are willing to educate yourself as to proper pruning techniques. Improper pruning can be as bad as or worse than no pruning at all. Some basic pruning tips are provided in this book, but preventive- and repair-pruning guidelines can vary depending upon the natural growing habits of different tree and shrub species. Instruction sheets from your local Cooperative Extension office can be very helpful. And check out the comprehensive pruning books listed in appendix III.
- In the case of infestations—a not uncommon problem when plants are stressed or injured—you have the knowledge to identify the invader. And you are sufficiently familiar with Integrated Pest Management methods to design and execute an effective treatment program. (See chapter 8, Intensive Care.)

Basic Safety Rules

For your own safety when cleaning up major landscape damage, always:

- Look up. Constantly. As mentioned before, damaged limbs can come crashing down out of trees without warning. If branches are on the ground beneath a tree, do not take it for granted that they are the last that will fall. Remember, do not go near large, unstable trees until a professional has made the area safe.

Unstable trees are extremely dangerous. Courtesy of Sandra Dark.

- Look down. When trimming or removing limbs, always be aware of where they will fall, especially if people, pets, the family car, or your favorite birdbath are nearby.
- Do not mix power tools with ladders or climbing.
- Use eye and hearing protection with chain saws, snowblowers, and other power equipment.
- Clean up as you go. If the job is substantial, alternate between making and clearing piles of debris. This varied routine will help keep your muscles from becoming overstressed. And rather than feeling overwhelmed at the end of a grueling day, you will have a better sense of accomplishment.

Danger Underground!

Learn where all the buried utility lines are located on your property. Although underground utility rights-of-way are supposed to be kept clear, trees and shrubs are often unknowingly planted within or near them.

In addition, several buried lines (electricity, digital cable, etc.) probably run to your house from the main right-of-way near the edge of your property, not all of them necessarily following the same path. Natural gas and water/sewer lines are usually buried deeper, but erosion or a grade change might have left them closer to the surface. So before dealing with stump grinding, tree or shrub planting, trenching, rain-garden construction, or any other subterranean endeavor, call 811 or link to www.call811.com online to have your lines marked.

Lines are marked with spray paint and/or flags, and the marks are usually good for at least 10 days. If you lose track of markers or they wash away before the invasive aspects of your landscape project are completed, call and have the lines marked again.

What Type of Expert Do I Need?

The type of damage that your landscape has suffered or that you hope to prevent will determine what kind of expert you might need. Because extreme-weather events can be complex, such as combining flooding with damaging winds, you might require more than one type of expert to deal with either prevention or the aftermath.

The cost of hiring an expert can vary depending on your location, the type and extent of work required, and conditions that might be unique to your property or specimens. These conditions might include such diverse things as difficulty of access, the size and condition of a damaged tree, or the configuration of house eaves that need rain guttering to divert water away from the foundation.

Certified or Registered Consulting Arborist

A trained arborist can provide vital emergency care for weather-injured landscape specimens, diagnose and treat diseases and infestations, and give educated advice.

In addition, a certified or registered consulting arborist often can shape a damaged specimen to reduce the "uh-oh" factor of its appearance during the recovery period, a definite plus if your property is on the market. Also, a certified or registered consulting arborist can recommend preventive measures to help protect your valuable landscape specimens from future damage from extreme-weather events. These measures might range from thinning an overcrowded Japanese holly hedge along your back fence, to adding mechanical supports to a weak fork in your venerable burr oak, to replacing unsuitable specimens with species that are more tolerant of extreme-weather events or salt pollution.

Developing a working relationship with a trustworthy arborist before disaster strikes can benefit your landscape in much the same way that having a family doctor can be to your long-term advantage. An expert arborist can evaluate your landscape specimens and help you make informed decisions about preserving, restoring, improving, and managing their health and value. And just as a trusted family doctor will be there for you, that arborist will be there for your landscape if disaster strikes. (See appendix III for a list of professional arborist associations.)

Note: A registered consulting arborist (RCA) is one step up from a certified arborist (CA), having received more training in arboriculture. But there are far fewer RCAs, so finding one in your area, especially in an emergency, might not be possible.

The fees charged by a CA or RCA can vary widely, depending upon the arborist's experience, the type of work you need done, and your locale. An arborist might charge an hourly rate, generally from $65 to $200 or up per manhour, or might quote a flat fee for a specific job. The low end of the scale would be for standard pruning and maintenance jobs, with higher rates applying to emergency work and consulting.

To remove a large tree, expect to pay from $800 on up depending on the degree of difficulty, while small trees might be dealt with for as little as $150. The cost of pruning a damaged tree can begin as low as $65 and rise into the high $100s, based on the size and condition of the specimen. When multiple trees or shrubs are involved, the per-tree cost often can be negotiated down. Do get quotes from more than one arborist, time and circumstances permitting.

Landscape Architect

A landscape architect can help you evaluate the damage and, in collaboration with your arborist, determine what all of your options are for restoring—and possibly even improving upon—the function, aesthetics, and real estate value of your landscape. *Note: A landscape architect is licensed; a landscape designer is not.*

Instead of focusing entirely on decisions that need to be made immediately, a landscape architect will consider long-range (and potentially costly) conditions that often get overlooked in a time of emergency. For example, perhaps neither you nor your arborist is aware that your damaged hackberry tree has provided erosion control for a very long time and removing it could cause significant runoff onto a neighbor's property. Therefore if the tree is not a surefire goner, a landscape architect might recommend spending money now to try to save it rather than potentially having to pay damages to your neighbor later.

A landscape architect also can help you make long-term choices and decisions that can enhance the design and value of your landscape as well as boost its ability to withstand extreme-weather events. In both cases, the overall value and marketability of your property can benefit. (See the list of professional associations in appendix III.)

The cost for services is around $70 to $100 per hour, or a flat rate based on that hourly rate for a complete project.

Rain-Gutter Contractor

Simply having rain guttering installed on the eaves of your house can remedy chronic flooding of foundation beds or nearby plantings caused by persistent, voluminous roof runoff. A skilled contractor can analyze the drainage around your house and design an efficient gutter-and-downspout system, possibly including above- or belowground downspout extensions, which will carry runoff well away from the foundation.

For a small section of guttering with downspouts to remedy a soggy foundation bed, the cost might be around $200 to $300. Guttering an entire house can cost $1,000 and up, depending on the roof size and configuration. Prices vary, and so does quality.

Shop around to make sure you are getting the best price for quality materials *and* workmanship. Cheap, poorly installed rain guttering can take away from the eye appeal of your real estate and will not stand up to nature's worst. Adding insult to injury, a nonexpert contractor might not properly analyze the drainage needs of your property and therefore fail to solve the problem.

Do-it-yourselfers: You can purchase rain guttering at a home-improvement center and install it yourself at a substantial savings. But be aware that installing guttering so it drains properly and looks good is not as easy as it might seem, especially if eaves are more complicated than a simple straight line. And if you want seamless guttering, you will need a professional with special equipment.

If you do opt to do it yourself, choose only quality materials, and study the process thoroughly before you begin. Some home-improvement centers offer minicourses on rain-gutter installation. Sign up!

Rainwater-Collection Contractor

Systems for collecting rainwater for use in the landscape are a growth industry, with "green" contractors proliferating across the country. If there is no such contractor in your locale, you might find a "green" plumber who has the experience to install an efficient rainwater-collection system for your property.

Your options range from 50- to 150-gallon plastic rain barrels and bladders all the way up to 1,500-gallon and larger above- or belowground concrete cisterns. The more ambitious the collection system, the more experienced and skilled the contractor should be. Search "rain-collection systems" online, and check out the American Rainwater Catchment Systems Association listing in appendix III. Some rain-gutter contractors also now install aboveground collection systems.

Another beneficial resource is a landscape architect who can look at your total excess-water issue and make recommendations on where the drainage should be placed to alleviate future damage. He also will look for opportunities to store and move water without causing problems in your neighbors's yards and downstream. And during an emergency, the landscape architect might have valuable contacts with rain-collection contractors who can help out in a speedy fashion.

As with any serious undertaking involving a landscape, collaborating with a knowledgeable landscape architect and a contractor with a "green" or "sustainable" designation can complete the circle, ensuring that the new water-collection features are integrated in such a way as to maximize their value to your landscape while minimizing their utilitarian appearance.

As for cost, if you already have rain guttering on your roof, installation of a 50-gallon rain barrel can run around $300 to $400. For do-it-yourselfers: a 50-gallon rain barrel can be purchased for less than $100, and the installation does not involve rocket science, so you can save handsomely, especially if you install multiple interconnecting barrels. The cost of installing a more ambitious system such as an underground cistern can run into thousands—even tens of thousands—of dollars. But there is a rain-collection system to fit almost any budget and do-it-yourself skill level, so shop around and educate yourself before making your choice.

French-Drain Contractor

A French drain is basically a trench filled with gravel, usually with a perforated PVC pipe near the bottom, designed to carry excess water away from a poorly drained area. In some cases, French drains can help dry out persistently flooded areas around foundations that result from faulty grading or runoff from uphill property.

Note: Do not simply take the word of the French-drain contractor that he is accustomed to working around trees and knows how to protect roots! Before permitting trenching anywhere near valuable trees or shrubs, consult with a certified arborist or a landscape architect to ensure that feeder-root systems will not be severed.

The least you can probably expect to pay for a French drain about 75 feet long is around $800. If tree or shrub roots are an issue, add to that the cost of consulting an arborist or landscape architect. Do-it-yourselfers, for no great investment, can purchase perforated PVC pipe, a load of gravel, and a level to measure the grade, then either dig the trench by hand or rent a trencher. But be forewarned that even with trenching equipment the work is arduous even to install a fairly short French drain, especially in stiff clay soils. And for the sake of your valuable specimens, you still might need to consult with an arborist or landscape architect. After all, you do not want to end up damaging the very trees or shrubs that you are trying to rescue.

Is Hiring an Expert Worth the Money?

Let's go back to value: a healthy, mature tree of a desirable species and location can be worth from $1,000 to $10,000 or more. And if you lose a tree or a mature shrub or hedge, a replacement might require a generation or more of growth to match its stature as a functional, aesthetic, and financially valuable component of your landscape. So an expert who can help prevent damage to your big-ticket landscape specimens, or restore their health and appearance following an extreme-weather event, can be a highly cost-effective investment. But there are experts, and then there are *so-called* experts.

So make sure that you find the real deal. Do not risk being taken to the cleaners by inept so-called experts or by outright scam artists who, like roofers after a hailstorm, inevitably converge on communities that have been hammered by disasters. These charlatans can end up causing lethal damage to injured trees and shrubs that could have been saved—and they will charge you for the harm they do!

Are All Contractors Created Equal?

No! Just because a contractor has a chain saw and a truck does not mean he has the knowledge and skills to properly prune or treat your valuable landscape specimens. Even some established local tree services that do not employ certified arborists have been known to top trees. Likewise, the ranks of rain-gutter installers, and other contractors as well, have steep gradations of expertise that range from consummate professionalism to serious incompetence.

You should be particularly cautious about hiring contractors after a major natural disaster involving your entire community or region. In times of greatest need, unscrupulous predators charge desperate property owners exorbitant fees for substandard work that often does more harm than good. Or they might demand payment up front and not do the work at all.

And not all contractors charge the same for their services, even for the same quality of work. So get more than one estimate, and compare the contractors' qualifications, references, and materials. Your final choice should be based upon:

experience (how long the contractor has been licensed or certified)
quality of work (do not hesitate to check out the contractor's recent clients)
quality of materials used
cost

When all of these factors are weighed together, the cheapest contractor might not necessarily be the best choice—but then, neither might the most expensive.

Get It on Paper!

Before hiring any contractor, be sure to get the following on paper:

- Exactly what the contractor plans to do. For example: "Install 50 feet of guttering on the north side of the house, with one downspout and one 10-foot expansion diverter" or "Prune damaged limbs from the red oak in the side yard and remove the debris from property."
- The total, itemized fee, including all materials. If an hourly rate is quoted, a "not to exceed x amount of dollars" phrase should be included in writing.
- When the work will begin and when it will be completed.

"Expert" Danger Signals

These are warning signs to watch for when shopping for any contractor:

- The "expert" has no license or other credentials. For example, a tree trimmer is not a certified arborist, or does not have an arborist on staff, or cannot even recommend one!
- The "expert" is not insured for personal injuries, workmen's compensation, or damage to your property. *Note: If the expert works for a company, make sure he or she is actually on the job for the company and not moonlighting. Moonlighting workers are not covered by a company's insurance policies.*
- The "expert" has come knocking on your door and is not local. This does not always signify that the expert is not legitimate or capable. Crews of out-of-state certified arborists often converge on areas stricken by major natural disasters, but so do charlatans. If an expert is not local, make sure you see certification documentation. And if an expert claims membership in a professional association such as the International Society of Arboriculture, go online or call the organization for verification. *Caution:*

Sometimes, an out-of-state "expert" will use the name of a local company, with or without permission, when soliciting business in a disaster area. Steer clear of any supposedly local expert who is unable or unwilling to show you local credentials such as licenses, permits, insurance documentation, etc., especially if he is driving a rental vehicle or one sporting an out-of-state license tag.

- The "expert" has no business cards, logo-bearing invoices, or other professional materials showing a business address and phone number. The contractor should also have a business checking account and a Federal ID number.

- The "expert" is reluctant or unwilling to provide a written, itemized, signed description of work to be done, including total charges and start and finish dates. A firm promise to provide this later is not good enough. Do not allow any work to begin without first obtaining this document.

- The "expert" cannot provide a list of local clients whom you can contact as references. And do call them! But also bear in mind that no contractor in his right mind is likely to give you the names of unsatisfied customers.

- The "expert" requests payment in advance. In some cases, a contractor might request an advance payment, often a third to half of the total cost, to ensure that you will not back out after the materials for the job have been purchased. But agree to an advance payment only if the contractor is a well-established local or national company having a solid reputation. Never pay in advance for the entire job. A 30 to 50 percent down payment is standard operation procedure for contractors. *Note: Charlatans commonly request advance payment for materials, then neither the materials nor the contractor ever shows up for the job. Some will even tell you they will take care of everything and you won't even have to pay your insurance deductible! So if in doubt about whether you should trust a specific expert's integrity, err on the side of caution, especially if the contractor is unknown to you and you are unable to contact past clients.*

- Complaints against the "expert" have been filed with your local Better Business Bureau or district attorney's office. Also be aware that a lack of complaints is not always a safe sign, especially if your community has just suffered extensive damage by an extreme-weather event. In that case, property owners who have had bad experiences with a contractor simply might not have had time to file complaints yet.

- The "expert" recommends topping a tree. Do not take it for granted that an "expert" will do the right thing. You should clarify right up front what you do not want done, as well as what work you do want. And, "I do not want my trees to be topped" should be at the head of the list. (Likewise, never allow a contractor to use climbing spurs on a tree that you want to save!)

How Do I Find a Reputable Expert?

There are three basic ways to locate trustworthy experts who can help you rescue and restore your landscape following an extreme-weather event or help prevent damage and stress to your big-ticket trees and shrubs before disaster strikes.

The Telephone Directory

Experts who advertise their services in the Yellow Pages are more likely to be established professionals in your community with local reputations to safeguard. If their training, credentials, or experience (such as "certified arborist" or "licensed contractor for 17 years") are not listed in the ad, be sure to ask about them when you call.

Just because a contractor's advertising claims he has been in business for 20 years is no guarantee that he follows currently accepted professional practices. For example, some so-called landscape designers recommend tree or shrub species that are not suitable for a location. So "experienced" does not always mean "knowledgeable." And regardless of a contractor's good intentions, unsuspecting clients can end up paying dearly for the "expert's" lack of up-to-date training and education.

Professional Associations

Many professional associations have public directories of their memberships that enable you to locate an expert in your area. To obtain membership in such an organization, a professional usually must provide proof of a specified degree of training and/or experience in the field, which can vary depending upon each group's requirements. See appendix III for a list of professional associations. *Note: Do proceed with caution. Some associations are little more than paid directory listings, and membership in one of these is not necessarily a good indication of skills, qualifications, or reputability.*

Asking Around

Friends, neighbors, and co-workers often are able to recommend trustworthy arborists, landscape architects, rain-gutter contractors, or other experts with whom they have had positive experiences. In addition, these same referring parties can fill you in on an expert's work habits and fees.

Equally as important, these "been there" acquaintances can steer you away from experts who have failed to deliver satisfactory work, overcharged, or otherwise resulted in a negative experience.

Don't Experts Have Long Waiting Lists Following an Extreme-weather Event?

Oh, yes. And the more destructive the disaster, the longer the waiting list is bound to be. But you might be able to jump to the head of an expert's list (or at least move higher on it) if one or more of the following conditions apply.

You Were a Previous Customer

Experts who have trimmed your trees, installed rain guttering, or done other work for you in the past will almost always put you ahead of new customers during an emergency situation. So having had preventive or maintenance work done on your landscape or structures often can pay off with faster service after a natural disaster.

You Know a Valued Client

When disaster strikes and you have had no firsthand prior experience with a desperately needed expert, nothing opens doors faster than a referral from a valued client. Call friends, relatives, neighbors, co-workers—anyone you can think of who might be able to provide such a referral. And do not be shy about dropping names.

You Can Demonstrate a Clear and Present Danger

When calls come pouring in, experts prioritize. Therefore, if your emergency involves a tree that has fallen onto your house, or some other situation that seriously endangers life or property, an expert is more likely to move you up on the list.

When you call for assistance, be very clear about the degree of your emergency. But do not overdramatize. If a harried arborist rushes to your property expecting to find part of your house crushed beneath a mighty oak only to find a few branches leaning against an eave, he might well move promptly to higher-priority clients and never return.

Also keep in mind that quality work and a correctly completed project are worth the wait. Just because you are anxious to have a problem taken care of, you might rush to hire the first contractor who answers your call—only to suffer in the long run because you did not wait for the right one.

How Can I Save Money, Even with an Expert?

Let me count the ways!

Do the Grunt Work Yourself

Experts charge for their expertise—then charge extra for the work that can be done by anyone with a strong back. You can save money by providing the strong back. For example, once the arborist has finished the sawing and lopping, you could cut up and dispose of tree or shrub debris. (If limbs are too large for your hand tools to manage, have the arborist cut them into suitable lengths.) Or you can take down old or damaged rain guttering prior to having new guttering installed.

If a fee already has been quoted for the entire job, be sure the contractor adjusts his charges in writing to reflect any work that you intend to do yourself. And if you inform the contractor up front that you will do the grunt work, make sure he is not charging his usual all-inclusive fee anyway.

Recycle

If you have a way to haul it, old metal rain guttering can be sold to scrap-metal companies. The limb your oak tree lost in the big windstorm can be turned into firewood. The trunk of your downed walnut tree might have lumber value. If these trees were not diseased or infested, small branches and twigs can be shredded into useful mulch.

A Case in Point

In Washington, D.C., in June 2009, a storm knocked down a 70-year-old European linden on the White House lawn. The tree was turned into mulch for White House landscape beds.

Get a Volume Discount

When hiring an expert, check to see if nearby neighbors need similar work done. Sometimes a contractor will lower the overall bid for a batch job.

Get Competitive Bids

If time and the scope of the disaster permit, shop around, compare prices, and talk with previous clients of the contractor. *And do not be afraid to negotiate.*

In the process, make sure inferior materials will not be used. As the saying goes, "You get what you pay for." While you do not want to get scalped, neither do you want your landscape and real estate values to suffer because of your misplaced frugality. Quality materials, from rain guttering to the new replacement tree in the backyard, tend to be more appealing to the eye *and* more durable in the face of extreme-weather events.

Design for Do-It-Yourself

When working with a landscape architect or any other contractor to repurpose, renovate, or restore your landscape, ask that as many do-it-yourself elements as possible be included in the project. These elements should match your construction or gardening skills and physical abilities. Most people are quite capable of planting small trees and shrubs or removing areas of turf grass to create spacious beds for specimens. But if you have more advanced talents that can be employed in the landscape, let them be known!

Use Local Services

Does your community routinely pick up yard wastes, including small branches? If so, you can save an arborist's hauling fee by trimming and bundling small branches to the required size (usually about four feet in length) and simply placing them at the curb. See chapter 7 for more on ways to reduce debris-hauling costs.

How Do I Know if a Tree or Shrub Is Worth Rescuing?

When nature throws a fit in your landscape, experts truly can come to your rescue. But whether you hire a pro, or opt to do the rescue-and-recovery work yourself, an extreme-weather event can leave you with serious, often time-critical decisions to make regarding your big-ticket trees and shrubs. First and foremost among those decisions is whether you should try to save a specimen at all or choose to remove it and start over. So read on.

Rehabilitate or Remove?

When your landscape has been hammered by sudden high winds, crushing ice or snow, floods, lightning, the slower torture of prolonged drought, or any other destructive force, you might be left with valued trees and shrubs that are obviously damaged. But as often as not, deciding whether you should try to rehabilitate a badly damaged specimen or simply remove and replace it is not an easy call to make.

Even if the injured tree or shrub is potentially salvageable, whether you will *want* to make the effort can depend upon a combination of factors. These include the plant's age, its general health prior to being damaged, its contribution to the overall landscape design and purpose, and its aesthetic, utilitarian, and sentimental worth both to you personally and to your real estate values.

To begin with, if prior to the damage you had your landscape specimens appraised for their replacement value and for their contribution to the overall value of your property, you already have an expert assessment of which plants are high value and which are not. Or perhaps, based simply upon your own observations of your landscape, you had already developed firm opinions as to the importance or expendability of specific trees or shrubs. In either case, should a plant in the expendable category be seriously damaged, you might assume that you can simply proceed with having it removed from the landscape.

Take a moment for a second look.

Let's say that your seemingly expendable silk tree was damaged by a late spring storm. Before that fateful event, it was ailing, decrepit, misshapen, or in a bad location; it might even be the wrong species for your region or growing conditions. Almost invariably, such a plant is a sad thing to see.

But sometimes a nonspecimen that is expendable for all of the above reasons might serve a vital purpose in the landscape. (This also might be the case for a desirable specimen that has been severely injured.) For example, your silk tree might protect a shade garden from blistering afternoon sun or provide crucial erosion control along a slope. So simply removing the plant might cause serious collateral damage or require a potentially costly and time-consuming redesign of the landscape.

And remember that any time you replace a mature tree or shrub, you will have to wait years or even decades for a new plant to grow to match its size.

Whenever a borderline rehabilitate-or-remove issue arises, a certified or registered consulting arborist can offer expert advice as to whether a tree or shrub might be restored as a utilitarian or aesthetic element of the landscape. The arborist can also provide skilled emergency and long-term treatment for the damaged, sick, or infested plant, maximizing whatever potential it has for recovery and future usefulness.

In addition, a landscape architect can advise you as to the possible long-term ramifications of removing a tree or shrub that occupies a significant place or purpose in your landscape. If removal is ultimately deemed necessary, he can recommend suitable replacement plants or landscape-design changes that can help to mitigate the loss.

A snap decision is seldom necessary. Unless a tree is dangerously unstable, do not feel that you have to leap into a decision. Take whatever time you need to investigate your options before making the best choice for your landscape and overall real estate.

What If My Property Is on the Market?

All other considerations as to whether you should try to save a plant might be trumped by whether your property is, or soon will be, on the market. Even assuming that the plant is believed to be salvageable, the restoration of a seriously damaged tree or shrub can take several years, with no ironclad guarantee that the process will succeed. Therefore, depending on the prominence or importance of the specimen in your landscape, you need to determine whether its "uh-oh" factor in the curb appeal of your property now is less or greater than its restored value will be later.

When your property is up for sale, the species and vigor of badly damaged trees and shrubs might influence your real estate's marketability even if it does not necessarily decrease the asking price. For example, a potential home buyer might be apt to overlook the temporary unsightliness of a high-value species such as burr oak or Japanese laceleaf maple. But a disfigured Bradford pear or some other short-lived, low-value species might be less likely to receive such a pass. In that case, you could be better off removing and replacing the damaged plant.

If you do choose to try to rehabilitate a big-ticket anchor plant while your property is on the market, hiring a certified or registered consulting arborist is an especially good investment. Expert pruning and treatment can minimize the unsightliness of the beleaguered specimen while it is on the road to recovery. And if an extreme-weather event has damaged landscapes throughout your neighborhood or community, an injured tree or shrub that clearly has received expert treatment is likely to have less of a negative factor for prospective buyers.

When Should I Absolutely Remove a Tree or Shrub?

Choosing to remove a valuable (and valued) anchor plant from the landscape is always a momentous decision, as it should be. Although time and expert care can heal many seemingly devastating wounds, damaged plants generally should be removed if:

- More than 50 percent of a tree's branches have been destroyed, or 30 percent for pines. Some species of shrubs also fit into this category, though many can survive near-total debranching.
- The trunk is split. In rare instances, split trunks can be repaired by an arborist. But only a very high-value tree would be worth the effort and expense with no clear-cut guarantee that the specimen would ultimately survive.
- The specimen is badly unbalanced by the loss of at least 70 percent of its limbs on one side. When all or most major limbs have failed on one side, that space will never fill back in.
- The specimen has suffered severe root damage.
- The tree is interfering with overhead utility lines and cannot be downsized without severe mutilation.
- Any pine has been struck by lightning—or any other species has been shattered by lightning or has lost more than 30 percent of its bark.
- The cause of the damage cannot be mitigated. For example, a flood-prone area of the landscape cannot be properly drained, or a curbside specimen cannot be protected from splashed road salts infiltrating the soil every winter.

In addition, a tree or shrub might not be worth the effort and expense of trying to save if it is at or near the end of its normal life span, is badly located, serves no important aesthetic or utilitarian function in the landscape, or was not in prime condition before being damaged.

Can an Endangered Shrub Be Moved?

Yes, if it is not too large. Actually, almost no shrub is too large to be transplanted if you want to hire an expert and heavy equipment. But unlike trees, which can take decades to mature, many shrub species can be grown to substantial size within a relatively short period of time, so removal and replacement is usually a cheaper option.

But if you have a modest-sized shade-loving shrub that is suddenly exposed to hot sunlight—or some other specimen that would thrive better in a different location—you can hire an arborist to transplant it for you.

For do-it-yourselfers:

- Though the best time to transplant shrubs varies regionally, in most areas it is best in late winter or early spring, just as buds begin to swell.
- In the new location, prepare a hole large enough to accommodate the root ball of the transplant.
- Tie up the lower branches of the shrub to make digging easier.
- For large shrubs, use a sharp spade to dig a trench all the way around the shrub, going at least 18 to 24 inches deep. For shrubs less than shoulder high, simply make an unbroken spade cut in the soil all the way around the plant. The trench or spade cut should be two-thirds of the way out to the drip line.
- Undercut the roots beneath the shrub. After all roots have been severed, move the plant out onto a tarp by levering the root ball, not pulling on the trunk. If the root ball is not too heavy, lift the plant in a wheelbarrow for transport; otherwise, you might have to drag it to its new location atop the tarp.
- Settle the shrub into its new hole to the same depth as it had been growing in its previous location. Do not bend roots to make them fit a too-small hole! Backfill the planting hole with soil and water thoroughly. Do not add compost, peat moss, or fertilizer to the hole; research shows that transplants do better without soil amendments.
- Maintain the watering regimen recommended for any new transplant (see chapter 3).

Are Big, Old Shrubs and Trees of Greater Value?

Not necessarily. Regardless of how big and old a low-value species becomes, it will never become high value. In fact, just the opposite: each tree or shrub species has its own natural life span, and once it becomes a geriatric case, its monetary-to-sentimental value ratio can shift dramatically. (This is true of even high-value species.)

A specimen that is well past its prime is particularly at risk during extreme-weather events, and once it has been injured it is even more vulnerable to future damage, pests, and diseases. So the effort and cost of trying to restore an Old One, especially if it has been poorly maintained in the past, becomes an issue of diminishing returns.

On the other hand, exceptional specimens of great historical or emotional value, such as the Survivor Tree at the Oklahoma City National Memorial, deserve a great deal of consideration. And while the old sugar maple in your front yard might not draw admirers and well-wishers from around the world, the fact that it was planted by your grandfather on his wedding day could make it priceless to you and your family. In that case, if the tree has been well maintained through the years, you probably will want to make every effort to save it.

Should I Get More Than One Expert Opinion?

No two medical doctors will necessarily agree on the proper treatment for a badly injured or ailing patient; the same holds true for arborists prescribing treatment for your valuable trees and shrubs. While experts have the training and experience to make educated judgments on how best to deal with your wind-battered basswood tree or ice-shattered elm, the ultimate decision is yours to make. So if you have any reservations at all about going along with an expert's recommendations, by all means opt for a second or third opinion.

A Case in Point

Keith Newcomb thought the big old hackberry overhanging his driveway had a lot of character. So when two large limbs failed, he called in two different tree services to take a look at the damage. One expert tried to sell him on cutting down the tree, predicting that it was going to die anyway. "The other one," Keith says, "was telling me all the wonderful things I could do to save the tree's life without having to engage his services to cut it down." In the end, Keith chose to have only the two failed limbs taken out, a decision that seems to be working out well: "The rest of the tree is doing great."

Even with heroic efforts, a badly damaged specimen cannot always be saved, but once it has been cut down there is no going back. So if a tree or shrub with aesthetic, utilitarian, or even sentimental value has any chance of being restored, you might want to opt for treatment rather than removal. After all, if it is not able to regain its former vigor, it can always be removed later.

Is It All Right to Delay My Decision?

For a damaged or stressed tree or shrub, the gift of time can be its salvation—or its worst nightmare. Though your decision as to whether to remove a specimen often can wait, treatment for damage, disease, or infestation should begin at once.

Stressed plants are particularly vulnerable to an array of villainous organisms that commonly attack weakened victims and find easy access through untreated wounds. So the longer you wait to repair damage—or in the case of drought stress, to supply life-sustaining water—the greater the likelihood that your decision whether or not to attempt restoration will be taken out of your hands.

Most plants try to live if they can. But the fact is, even an expert cannot always tell for certain exactly what is transpiring within the hidden world of a tree or shrub's root system or interior tissues. So a damaged specimen that does not at first look seriously threatened might in fact be in dire straits, while a plant that initially appears to be in bad shape might still retain the vigor to eventually overcome its injuries.

Even if a large, structurally stable tree does die (a process that can take months or even years) it usually will not pose a danger until it begins to decay and fall apart. Therefore, assuming that all necessary emergency repairs and treatments have been made, and the tree or shrub is structurally safe, you might want to hold off on long-term decisions as to the fate of a valued specimen if:

- You have nothing to lose. Perhaps your property is not currently on the market, or the injured specimen still serves a useful function.
- The damage occurs during the dormant season. Cold weather reduces the immediate threat of disease and infestation and allows you to wait and see how well the specimen produces new growth in the spring.
- The specimen exhibits at least modest signs of vigor in the weeks and months following an injury that occurs during the growing season. The flame-scorched and battered Survivor Tree defoliated by the April 1995 terrorist bombing in Oklahoma City produced some secondary leaf growth that summer. But the 100-year-old American elm did not show real leafing vigor until the spring of 1996.

- The specimen was in good health prior to being damaged. A healthy, robust plant is better able to muster its natural defenses to withstand or recover from traumas. This is one of the major payoffs for practicing preventive landscape care (see chapter 3).

What If I Choose to Rehabilitate a Specimen?

Be patient. The decision to try to save a badly damaged tree or shrub and restore its value entails a long-term commitment. A mature specimen might have taken decades to grow to its recent big-ticket stature. Following an injury, your maple tree or holly hedge will require at least a few years to callus over its wounds, recoup its reserves, and fill out its shape with new growth.

In general, the rehabilitation program for a landscape specimen progresses in three stages.

Stage 1: Emergency Treatment

This involves dealing promptly with any damage that either poses a people-or-property danger or threatens the life of the specimen, such as:

removing broken limbs
repairing torn bark
reducing drought stress
replanting and staking uprooted specimens

See also chapter 5, Assessing the Damage.

Stage 2: Secondary Treatment

This nonemergency care is for conditions that do not immediately threaten the life of the specimen, including:

1. Restoration pruning to reshape crushed or otherwise disfigured specimens. In some cases, this can take place weeks or even months after the initial damage occurred. For example, if a summer windstorm damaged your crabapple tree, nonemergency restoration pruning might wait until late the following winter, just before bud swell. Restoring the shape of a badly damaged plant might require a series of prunings taking place over two or more successive pruning seasons. (For more on this, see chapter 8, Intensive Care.) Restoration pruning for large specimens should be left to a certified or registered consulting arborist. Besides having an expert eye for how a particular species should look and knowledge of how a plant will grow after specific cuts are made, a trained arborist is

best able to judge whether a specimen can ever be properly restored. A pruning-savvy do-it-yourselfer with sharp snips, loppers, and tree handsaws can usually manage restoration pruning of shrubs and small trees. But keep in mind that improper pruning can be worse than none at all, spoiling the looks of a specimen for years to come, if not permanently. Besides knowing where to make cuts, you also must know how much is enough and how much is too much. You also need to know the proper pruning season for a specific species. Two good pruning books are listed in appendix III, and you can also obtain basic guidelines at your local Cooperative Extension office.

2. Monitoring for evidence of hidden damage (such as a sagging limb) that shows up well after emergency repairs have been made.
3. Removing turf grass from the drip zones of stressed specimens to reduce competition for water and nutrients.
4. Mulching plants and maintaining a regular watering regimen.

Stage 3: Long-Term Treatment

For a moderately to seriously damaged specimen, this can take years. In order to regain robust health during that time, the plant will require a rehabilitation program that might include:

1. Pest-control treatment for infestations that often occur while a plant is in a weakened condition.
2. Disease-control treatment for plants that are invaded by harmful organisms through open wounds or via stressed root systems. *Note: Early detection of both pest and disease attacks is crucial. These "secondary infections" can be as lethal as pneumonia striking after the flu.*
3. Fertilizer, but *only if a soil test indicates a nutrient deficiency.* And do not use high-nitrogen fertilizer near woody anchor plants for several years after damage has occurred! High-nitrogen fertilizer will trigger a burst of leaf production and twig growth that a damaged specimen can ill afford to support while it is trying to recover. Also, the additional weight and wind resistance of this added growth can make a root-damaged tree even more unstable in high winds. Instead of fertilizer, top-dress plants with an inch of compost from the drip line outward to improve the soil and increase the beneficial microbes.
4. An extended multiyear pruning program designed to gradually correct structural imbalance and/or eventually restore the damaged specimen's desired shape.
5. Careful soil-moisture maintenance to ensure that the production, transportation, and storage of vital nutrients remain continuous.

Any tree or shrub that has suffered significant damage requires long-term care during its recuperation. So if you opt to not remove a tree or shrub—at least for the time being—be prepared to give it special attention in the weeks, months, and even years ahead. (For an extensive discussion of long-term treatment measures, see chapter 8.)

What if I Opt for Removal?

Do-it-yourselfers take note: safely removing any large tree is dangerous work requiring the special skills and equipment (including climbing or use of a crane) of a professional.

But cutting down the specimen (usually a section-by-section dismantling operation) is only the beginning. Once the tree's crown and trunk are on the ground, there are other issues to deal with such as stump removal, hauling away the debris, and what to do with the new empty space in the landscape. These same issues apply if you opt for removing a large shrub or hedge.

Removing a Big Tree

This involves substantial risks. During removal, large trees in confined spaces can fall on and damage nearby structures and landscape plants—both yours and your neighbor's. Trees growing near power lines are particularly hazardous to remove.

If you choose to do the work yourself, you are legally liable for any and all injuries to persons or property that might occur. (For liability information, see chapter 11.) So a major mishap could end up costing you far more than if you had hired a professional. An experienced, reputable certified or registered consulting arborist has both expertise in mitigating risks and insurance to cover any mishaps.

Hiring a Pro

Besides being dangerous, the dismantling and removal of a large tree—especially one that damage or disease has left structurally unsound—is labor-intensive work. Even if you choose to do much of the removal work yourself, *you* should at least hire a trained professional to get the crown and trunk safely on the ground.

Make sure that your contractor:

- Has proof of insurance against property damage as well as workmen's compensation for injuries that might be incurred during the operation.

Certified arborists are skilled at climbing safely. Courtesy of Sandra Dark.

- Has expertise in tree removal. Ask for references. *Note: In a pinch, you might get by with an experienced and insured tree cutter who is not a certified arborist. But this can raise the risk that you might be hiring an "expert" who does not adhere to safe work practices, which can actually increase the risk to your property.*
- Has the equipment necessary to cut down the tree and remove it from your property (assuming that you do not intend to do the latter yourself).

The actual tree cutting is done either by climbing the tree or by using a crane or bucket crane. With the climbing method, the arborist climbs into the tree with safety lines and a chain saw and cuts the major limbs, either lowering or drop-ping them to the ground. After that debris is cleared away, the trunk is felled and then cut into manageable chunks for removal. In this way, the complete dismantling and removal of a large tree can take from one to two days, depend-ing on the stability of the tree and the size of the crew.

The crane method might be required for safe removal of a very large tree, or a big tree growing in a confined area or close to power lines. This is especially the case when the tree is structurally unstable or there is insufficient clearance at the site to permit convenient debris removal. A crane parked in the street in front of a house can reach over the roof to the backyard and help stabilize the tree during the cutting process. This can help ensure that it will not fall onto nearby structures or cause further landscape damage. The severed tree parts then can be lifted safely and easily out of the yard.

Many arborists also use bucket cranes to lift them to treetop levels for prun-ing operations so they can work safely without actually climbing into an at-risk tree.

Most people blanch at the prospect of having to hire a crane on top of other tree-removal costs. But when a large, unstable, or inconveniently located tree is involved, a crane can greatly speed up the removal process. Therefore, your overall costs might be no higher than if the arborist had to climb up and care-fully prune, dismantle, or remove the tree the hard way.

The cost of removing a tree will depend on its size, location, and condition, all of which affect the degree of difficulty and danger in the work. The removal of a large tree can run anywhere from $1,000 on up to $20,000, usually exclud-ing stump removal, with small trees starting as low as $150.

Fees can vary widely even within a community, so get more than one quote if possible. Refuse to give a price if a service asks what you are prepared to pay: insist that the tree service quote you its fee for the removal. And remember, do not be afraid to negotiate. If more than one or two specimens are involved, a little quibbling might save you hundreds, even thousands, of dollars.

The quoted price should include both cutting down the tree and hauling away the debris. If you plan to dispose of the debris to cut costs—either hauling it yourself, or putting it out for municipal pickup—the fee should cover cutting the limbs and trunk into manageable sections and lengths, unless you have the tools and energy to do that as well.

Stump-grinding fees are usually quoted separately. If you intend to deal with the stump yourself, request that it be cut as low to the ground as possible. This will speed up its decomposition if you opt for a natural process, or reduce the grinding time if you rent a stump grinder.

Avoiding Collateral Damage

A tree can weigh somewhere between 35 and 75 pounds per cubic foot, depending upon the species, and around 80 percent of that weight is in the trunk. So felling a large tree trunk can cause serious soil compression, possibly resulting in damage to the roots of surrounding plants. Likewise, trucks and other heavy equipment that are driven off paved areas to pick up the debris can cause compression damage to septic tanks or sewer pipes as well as root systems of plants along their paths.

So by all means clearly mark areas in your landscape that are "no go" zones for the tree-felling operation, and discuss these with the tree-cutting crew. To reduce soil-compression problems, a tree might need to be lifted from the site with a crane. And rather than drive heavy vehicles into the landscape, use two-wheel handcarts to transport sectioned limbs and trunk segments to a paved area for pickup. (Even then, adhere to no-go zones for the handcarts to minimize soil compaction.)

For more information on avoiding collateral damage to valuable specimens, see chapter 3.

Reducing Hauling Costs

Debris-removal fees can be substantial when a large tree or hedge is removed or when an entire landscape has been devastated by an extreme-weather event. Tree services usually quote fees that include debris removal, but those fees can vary widely depending on the volume of plant materials, the distance to the dump site, whether the contractor has to pay a dumping fee, and the man-hours involved.

But there are alternatives that can help you reduce or even eliminate hauling costs:

- Call firewood vendors. Depending on the desirability of the tree species, some vendors will haul away logs for free, leaving only the smaller branches for you to deal with. In some cases, the firewood vendor might even cut large trunks and limbs to size. *Note: When community-wide devastation of trees has occurred, the sudden overabundance of wood generally causes the bottom to fall out of the firewood market, leaving vendors much less likely to be interested in your logs.*
- Put out a Free Firewood sign. Stack logs near the curb and watch them disappear. You can help along the process by having the logs cut to firewood lengths. *Note: Actually selling firewood from your residence might require a permit.*
- Take advantage of yard-waste pickup. If your community picks up yard

waste, you might be able to dispose of large amounts of debris by placing it at curbside. Find out what the rules are. There might be a limit on how much you can place at the curb each week. But even if it takes a few weeks or months to complete the process, the cost is covered by your monthly waste-pickup fee.

- Check on major debris removal. If your locale has suffered a massive ice storm, flood, or other extreme-weather event resulting in widespread devastation of landscapes, chances are good that your community will hire a firm to undertake the mammoth task of debris removal. The company is commonly contracted to pick up everything from small branches to cut-up tree trunks. In some cases, crews will even trim broken limbs on street-side trees. Call city hall or your community action line to find out if such a plan is in the works. If so, be patient: getting crews and equipment on-site can take a few weeks. Taking advantage of a citywide program usually involves some form of placing your debris within a certain distance of the curb. For liability reasons, debris-removal crews generally are not allowed to bring equipment onto your property beyond the right-of-way. But often, the debris does not even have to be bundled. In this way, you might be able to dispose of your tree and shrub debris, including major logs, at no cost to you.

Into the Trenches

When an ice storm destroyed or damaged tens of thousands of trees in my community, the city hired an out-of-state disaster-recovery firm to manage the titanic job of clearing away and disposing of more than half a million cubic yards of vegetative debris. Working swiftly to bring order to chaos, the crews made three separate sweeps through town with a variety of heavy equipment, including grappling hooks, scoops, and giant debris-hauling trailers.

On the first sweep, they picked up tangled mountains of branches from next to our driveway and at curbside. The second sweep relieved us of tons of logs that had replaced the earlier batch. The third sweep picked up major chunks of tree trunks that had been rolled and wheeled to the curb. In addition, the normal city yard-waste pickup took 30 industrial-size bags filled with small twigs. The entire debris-removal process took six weeks, but the cost was covered by municipal funds, a major FEMA grant to the city for disaster mitigation, and our monthly city waste-pickup fees. Though all of that involved our tax dollars, we were not hit by direct hauling fees on top of all our other recovery expenses.

Sandra Dark

Debris-removal crews bring in equipment to remove large logs. Courtesy of Sandra Dark.

Stump Grinding

Once the trunk and limbs of a tree have been cleared away, you are still stuck with the stump. Unless you plan to use the stump as a quaint garden table or carve it into a seat (in which case you should have instructed the tree cutters to slice off the trunk at an appropriate height), getting rid of the stump is going to require money, your personal sweat, or time for nature to take its course.

Bringing in a professional stump-grinding contractor is the most cost-effective way to quickly rid your landscape of one or two unsightly stumps. Commercial stump-grinding equipment can chew away stumps to a depth of up to a foot belowground, often allowing you to plant a replacement tree in the exact same location.

If your tree had a lot of surface roots, you should have those ground off along with the stump. Sometimes this can cause major disruptions to surrounding lawn, but in some species, such as Bradford pears, those left-behind roots can produce annoying root suckers for many years to come.

Contractors commonly charge from $3 to $5 per inch of stump diameter, with a $50 to $100 minimum. For more than a tree or two, the cost of grinding additional stumps usually goes down; if it does not, get in there and negotiate! The stump is not going anywhere, so you have plenty of time to shop around

Large trees leave large stumps that must be removed. Courtesy of Sandra Dark.

and get estimates from more than one contractor. *Note: Before grinding a tree stump, dial 811 or link online to www.call811.com and request that the buried lines on your property be marked. Trees and shrubs are often planted near or over underground utility lines, and aside from the serious danger posed by chewing into or vibrating loose a line—especially natural gas—you could end up paying the cost of repairs. So in the future don't plant trees where they could damage the underground infrastructure.*

For do-it-yourselfers: you can rent a stump grinder for around $100 to $250 per day, plus a home-delivery charge if you are unable to haul the machine yourself. Operating a stump grinder is well within the capabilities of most hale and hardy do-it-yourselfers. And when multiple tree stumps are involved, considerable savings can be had. Here are the basics:

- A 10hp grinder is suitable for small stumps, but you will need at least a 25hp machine for stumps that are two feet or more in diameter. Make sure the grinding blades are either new or freshly sharpened. Dull blades are fairly useless.

- Grinders work best on hardwood stumps and can be much less effective on moist, freshly cut softwood stumps.
- Before starting the job, clear the work area of all rocks, bricks, bed borders, and other hard objects that can dull the machine's blades.
- Keep pets and children indoors.
- Stump grinding is loud, messy work, with wood chips flying everywhere. So be sure to wear both eye and hearing protection and protective clothing.
- The grinder should come with operating instructions, but do get at least a brief tutorial from the rental store so you will know what you are getting into. Basically, you set the toothed grinding wheel over a stump, then pull and push the machine back and forth. As the surface of the stump chips away, you keep lowering the wheel until the grinder has gone as deep as it can.
- Pat yourself on the back for having had your arborist cut the stump as close to the ground as possible, thus minimizing the tedious grinding process.
- When the grinding is finished, rake up the chips, of which there will be a substantial amount if the stump was large. You can either bag them to be hauled away, or if the tree was not diseased or infested, begin the process of turning them into compost by mixing them with manure. Extensive guidelines on various ways to compost are available online or through your local Cooperative Extension office. Or the chips can be used as mulch in planter beds and on garden walkways.
- Finally, fill the vacated hole with screened garden soil in preparation for either planting a new tree or otherwise restoring the site.

Natural Stump Removal

If the tree stump does not occupy a prominent spot in the landscape—and you have the patience—nature is quite capable of removing it through the natural process of decay. The upside of this method is that it will cost you nothing; the downside is that you will have to wait up to five years for the stump to rot away. Still, there is a certain symmetry to this method since it completes a process that was, after all, begun by an act of nature.

On the other hand, if five years stretches the limits of your patience, you can speed up the decomposition:

Step 1: If you had the trunk cut as low to the ground as possible, you have already helped to speed up the process of natural stump removal.

Step 2: Drill holes several inches deep and a few inches apart across the entire surface of the stump, or have the arborist make crosscuts over the surface with a chain saw.

Step 3: Cover the stump with manure or compost, and top with mulch. Keep this moist to encourage the activity of decay-generating micro-organisms. Do not be surprised to see mushrooms growing from the stump—fungi are a natural part of the decay process. To help camouflage the site, you can set out potted plants, a bench, or other yard accessories on your neatly mulched bed. You could also bring in topsoil to create a mounded bed over the stump for growing flowers or vegetables. Pro-spective buyers probably won't even notice that a tree was ever there.

Step 4: Check the stump from time to time. As the wood decays, you should be able to knock off chunks with a sledgehammer or loosen them with a pry bar. If the stump is kept moist, the entire decay process might take as little as two years for the cost of no more than a bag or two of manure and mulch.

Intensive Care

Even when an extreme-weather event is history and the damaged plants in your landscape have received emergency treatment, they are far from being out of danger.

Once broken limbs are removed, torn bark is repaired, and other first-aid measures are taken, your specimens might look as if they are well along on the road to recovery, but the entire scope of the damage they have suffered might not be apparent yet. After all, a thick layer of bark can conceal all manner of problems, and other potentially lethal injuries and threats can lie hidden underground in the vital root system. Between seen and unseen injuries, seriously stressed trees and shrubs can take years to fully recover.

During that extended period of recuperation, plants can be highly vulnerable to additional extreme-weather events and other stressors, including opportunistic pests and diseases that attack in times of weakness. You can give your big-ticket specimens their best possible chance of survival by providing them with long-term special care.

Long-term care differs from postdisaster emergency measures in numerous ways. Emergency treatment deals with such immediate issues as broken branches, bark damage, uprooting, and other traumas. On the other hand, long-term care aims to boost a specimen's immune system and help it recover from injuries that threaten its long-term survival, as well as to enhance its ability to withstand damage from future extreme-weather events.

And without long-term intensive care, all the effort and expense that you threw into emergency treatment in the immediate wake of disaster might end up being wasted.

The needs of a recuperating landscape can be complex, especially when damaged or stressed plants represent a variety of species and growing conditions. So when the marketability, value, and/or sentiment attached to your landscape and real estate are at stake, you can benefit from seeking expert advice on tailoring a long-term intensive care program for your hard-pressed trees and shrubs.

A certified or registered consulting arborist can custom design a long-term-care program for your big-ticket landscape plants from the soil on up to the topmost branches. This can include such elements as making sure that nutrient and moisture needs of each convalescing plant are met; establishing a multi-seasonal pruning schedule aimed at restoring a severely damaged specimen's stability and form; and treating any infestations or diseases that might strike vulnerable trees or shrubs while they are in a weakened condition.

A landscape architect can identify and recommend remedies for problems that could be the primary cause of—or simply contributing to—the stress or damage experienced by your recuperating trees and shrubs. These problems might include poor soil drainage, severe root restriction, soil compaction from foot or vehicular traffic, or a landscape plan that has not taken into consideration the individual needs of its plant species.

But with or without expert help, the well-being of your abused specimens begins and ends with you. With any postdisaster landscape recovery program, it is vitally important that you first try to identify the long-term intensive-care needs of your stressed plants, and then develop a comprehensive game plan to meet those needs.

Where Should I Focus Attention First?

The most vital part of a tree or shrub's physiology is its vascular system, beginning at the fragile, hairlike tips of its feeder roots and extending via layers of tissue beneath its bark all the way up through the stem to the buds and foliage in its crown. Stem damage, flood, drought, or any other condition that impedes the flow of water and nutrients up and down these channels can result in the death of all or part of the specimen; at best, its growth might be stunted for a season or more.

Given time, a plant that is not too severely damaged can grow branches to replace those lost during a storm as well as regenerate roots to replace those lost to drought, flood, or partial uprooting. But to accomplish this feat, the plant must regain and maintain its vigor and vitality.

In simplest terms, every plant in your landscape must have an adequate supply of water and nutrients at feeder-root level. And up at crown level, those same plants must produce enough foliage to keep photosynthesis, that great energy-producing engine, revved throughout the growing season. These two basic needs are crucial for the well-being of a healthy plant, and they are a matter of life or death to a recovering one.

The Central Issue of Water

The need to meet the soil-moisture requirements of your big-ticket specimens cannot be overemphasized. Without an ample supply of water from either natural precipitation or supplemental watering, a stressed plant cannot properly and efficiently photosynthesize, much less transport the nutrients that are absolutely necessary for its healing process. (See chapters 3 and 4 for supplemental watering guidelines.)

To help ensure that your recuperating specimens receive sufficient water, you also might:

1. Install a rain gauge. Locate the gauge in an open area well away from taller objects in order to obtain the most accurate reading possible. When your property receives less than an inch of rainfall over a seven-day period at any time during the growing season, apply supplemental water. *Note: Should the seven-day dry spell occur following a period of heavy rainfall, check the soil before watering; if the soil balls in your fist, hold off watering for a few more days.*

2. Mark rainfall days and amounts on a calendar. This will help you track rainfall patterns so you can tell when your property appears to be entering a dry period that might develop into drought conditions. In that case, take drought-management measures recommended in chapter 4.

   As an alternative, you might check local weather websites to find out how much rain or snow your area received, but that isn't always an accurate measure of how much has fallen in your own yard. Some local television stations have weather subscriptions that can provide you with accurate data on precipitation amounts in your neighborhood.

3. Maintain a winter watering regimen. In all but the southernmost subtropical regions of the country, trees and shrubs go dormant during winter, but their roots continue to grow and function throughout the year. So in the absence of regular precipitation, keep up a monthly watering schedule for your anchor plants, especially evergreen specimens, throughout winter when the ground is not frozen. *Note: evergreens need to continually move water through their vascular systems, which is why*

harsh winter winds can kill a rhododendron or other sensitive broadleaf evergreen. An extra layer of winter mulch and a burlap wind protector are great and easy tools to use to protect your evergreens from drying out in winter.

Do Injured Plants Need Special Fertilizing?

First, let's get one thing straight: *healthy, mature trees or shrubs virtually never require supplemental fertilizer at all.* If the soil were deficient, the plant would not have been able to grow into a healthy specimen in the first place.

That said, an injured or stressed plant can be helped or harmed by supplemental fertilization, depending on the conditions. Knowing when to fertilize—and when not to—will help ensure that you do no harm in the process.

You should never fertilize a stressed specimen just to "give it a boost." A plant's natural response to stress is to conserve its resources by slowing its growth. Applying growth-stimulating fertilizers at such a time is like giving body-building steroids to a hospital patient in need of bed rest.

Any specimen that has experienced root damage from flood, drought, uprooting, or any other cause should not be fertilized until its roots have had time to regenerate, which can take several years for large specimens.

Likewise, refrain from fertilizing a specimen that has suffered crown or stem damage. Fertilizing will trigger a surge of growth that can be detrimental to its recovery and even result in additional damage from winds.

A long-accepted belief has been that infested trees can benefit from supplemental fertilizer. But studies at the Ohio Agricultural Research and Development Center and elsewhere indicate that this practice might actually cause infestations.

And here is why: a stressed plant produces defensive compounds that help it to resist harmful pests. But research by entomologist Dan Herms, who has extensively studied the physiology and health of landscape trees, shows that diverting a tree's energy to rapid growth might slow its production of those natural defensive compounds.

Fertilizing a tree or shrub's root zone can also enhance the growth of weeds and turf grass that will compete for water and nutrients. This unwanted collateral growth can partially or completely negate the benefits of fertilizing.

However, a specimen grown in soil that is seriously deficient in one or more nutrients can benefit from an application of fertilizer. Meeting a plant's nutrient needs in such circumstances can improve its pest and disease resistance as well as its ability to overcome stress or injuries.

But—and this is a big *but*—just because an area of soil is deficient in one nutrient does not mean it is deficient in all vital elements. If you add nutrients that already are in adequate supply, you will only create another nutrient imbalance that did not exist before.

So never take a shotgun approach by using an all-purpose fertilizer. Have your soil tested so you will know which specific nutrients are wanting, as well as what specific quantities to apply. In addition, the test might reveal that your soil's pH level is too high or low, which can interfere with a plant's nutrient uptake.

How and When to Fertilize

If a soil test reveals nutrient deficiencies and/or a pH imbalance, the lab results might include recommendations for amounts of specific amendments to apply to correct the problem. If not, your Cooperative Extension agent can assist you in determining suitable amendments and their application rates.

In the absence of a soil test, you should not feed injured or stressed landscape specimens without expert advice from a certified or registered consulting arborist.

Note: Do not use lawn fertilizers to feed trees and shrubs. The nutrient needs of turf grasses are very different from those of woody plants, and the high-nitrogen content of most lawn fertilizers can cause harmful growth spurts in damaged specimens. So keep lawn fertilizer away from the entire feeder-root zone of a damaged tree or shrub at all times, but especially throughout the course of its recovery.

If fertilizing woody plants is deemed necessary, the best time to make applications is either during the first flush of new growth in spring (before turf grass greens up) or in the fall from October to December. There is a lag time between the application of fertilizer and the tree or shrub's response, so results from fertilizer applied in the fall will show up in spring growth.

The amount of fertilizer to apply is based upon the total square footage of the feeder-root zone to be covered. To estimate the size of this fertilizer zone:

- Measure the radius of the plant's drip line—the distance from the trunk to the far outer reach of the plant's canopy. (For example, let's say the drip-line radius of your tree is 10 feet.)
- Add half-again more to that radius to take in additional feeder roots that extend beyond the drip line. (This makes the fertilizer-zone radius 15 feet.)
- Determine the square footage of the entire feeder-root zone to be fertilized by first multiplying the radius of the area by itself ($15 \times 15 = 225$ square feet). Then multiply that number by 3.141592. (707 square feet; round that off to the nearest hundred and voila, you end up with 700 square feet).

Following the recommendations from your soil test or Cooperative Extension agent, apply the proper amounts of nitrogen, phosphorous, potassium, or other nutrients evenly over the entire feeder-root zone. Begin two or three feet from the trunk for a mature tree and closer for shrubs or new transplants.

Note: Injecting fertilizer into the soil should be done only by a certified arborist who is experienced with this sort of treatment. If the drill holes are just inches too deep, soil injections can easily miss feeder roots and go to waste. Injecting directly into a tree—which hasn't been scientifically proven to work—will cause additional wounds that an already stressed plant might not have the energy reserves needed to callus over quickly, if at all, leaving the specimen even more vulnerable to invasive pathogens.

The Hazards of Overfertilizing

Never apply more than the recommended amount of fertilizer. Excessive fertilization is like overdosing on vitamins: what was intended to be beneficial can end up doing great harm.

Besides causing pollution of groundwater, ponds, and streams from runoff, excess phosphorus (P) and potassium (K) actually can act as a salt. In an attempt to dilute the saltiness, the soil will draw water out of the plant, causing wilting that will not always be helped by applying water. Unfortunately, the excess P and K will remain in the soil for a long period until they gradually leach out.

Better Roots with Mycorrhizae?

Mycorrhizae (pronounced my-keh-RYE-zee) are root-colonizing fungi that have formed mutually beneficial relationships with specific plants over hundreds of millions of years. These fungi, which 90 percent of plants need in order to thrive, can help your specimens produce more feeder roots, which is particularly advantageous when a tree or shrub has suffered root damage.

The tiny threads (*hyphae*) that mycorrhizae extend into the soil increase a plant's uptake and storage of water and soil nutrients by as much as a thousand times, thereby enhancing a specimen's health and well-being while reducing or even eliminating the need for fertilizers.

A wide variety of these tiny fungi might colonize your landscape soil and are especially beneficial to plants that have been stressed or damaged. Unfortunately, fragile mycorrhizae tend to die out in poor soil, in landscapes where fungicides or other chemicals have been used, or when soil has been tilled or compacted. Digging or tilling can destroy miles and miles of interconnecting hyphae, along with the fine feeder roots to which they are joined.

Most mycorrhizae are plant specific (meaning they grow only on a selected species of host plant) and cannot live if soil pH varies more than a point or two from the optimum range for their host plant. But ample decaying matter (common in natural woodlands, where mycorrhizae are in abundance) can eventually bring high or low soil pH toward the level favored by most plants, and also serves as food for root fungi.

You can make your landscape soil hospitable to mycorrhizae and a host of other beneficial microorganisms by applying two to four inches of compost, composted wood chips, shredded leaves, or other organic matter over the root zones of plants. Keep mulch materials a foot away from tree trunks and the bases of shrubs to avoid bark damage. And resist the urge to apply more than four inches of mulch; thicker layers can suffocate the soil.

A Long-Term Pruning Program

In the immediate aftermath of an extreme-weather event, broken limbs and deadwood need to be removed and other emergency treatments performed on damaged specimens. But beyond that, when it comes to postdisaster pruning, Indiana-based registered consulting arborist Jud Scott takes the view that less can be better: "In theory, a tree is like a battery—it only has so much energy. And a storm-damaged tree is already expending energy trying to callus over wounds and wall off fungus or any kind of bacterial attack. So to do any kind of excessive pruning is just another drain of energy."

However, additional pruning is necessary if more weakened branches fall in the weeks and months after emergency repairs are made. And there are some more dos and don'ts for postemergency intensive-care pruning:

- Do remove any stumps that were left during emergency pruning so the wound can begin to callus over.
- Don't make cuts strictly for manicure purposes if the plant has already suffered serious crown loss.
- Don't use wound paint or sealants except on oak trees, and only then if oak tree wilt is a problem in your area.

For a specimen left badly misshapen by a storm, restoration pruning can wait until the tree or shrub has had a chance to begin healing from its original trauma. How long that should be can depend upon the species and the severity of its injuries. For example, if a specimen has already lost a large percentage of its crown, removing more branches will further reduce its foliage, possibly to the point where the plant can no longer produce sufficient energy through photosynthesis to survive. In this case, restoration pruning should wait until the following year—maybe even the year after that.

When it comes to restoration pruning, the larger the tree, the more you need a certified arborist, both for the arborist's expertise and for safety's sake. Making wrong cuts can turn what could have been temporary unsightliness into permanent disfigurement. And ask hospital emergency-room staffers: following an extreme-weather event that has damaged large trees, victims of do-it-yourself tree-pruning accidents are all too common.

But for do-it-yourselfers who have adequate skills and tools, and who know not to overstep limitations, here are some important considerations.

Take a Moderate Approach

If the removal of a large amount of top growth is required to restore the shape of a tree or shrub, try to extend the restoration-pruning schedule out over two or three growing seasons. Excessive pruning all at one time will only serve to place additional stress on the recuperating plant, possibly increasing its vulnerability to pathogens.

Control Water Sprouts

Epicormic growth, commonly known as water sprouts, are weak shoots that develop on the branches or stems of trees or shrubs. A sign of stress, these sprouts can be triggered by crown damage (including excessive pruning), drought, disease, or numerous other assaults. Unlike normal branches firmly anchored in

This cutaway shows how a normal branch was firmly anchored in the trunk of a tree. Courtesy of USDA Forest Service—Northeastern Area Archive, Bugwood.org.

wood, water sprouts are poorly connected, making them vulnerable to storm damage. Also, their rapid, prolific growth saps energy from the tree.

On the other hand, if your tree or shrub has been mostly defoliated by an extreme-weather event, the leaves on water sprouts can provide much-needed photosynthesis. In that case, you might want to leave water sprouts in place

Weak epicormic growth in tree one year after topping. Courtesy of Sandra Dark.

until normal branch leafing occurs, either later in the growing season from secondary leaf buds or the following spring.

Water sprouts can be removed at any time of the year. Early in their growth, you can easily rub them off with a gloved hand; later, you will need hand pruners. *Note: Because topped trees will never produce anything other than epicormic growth, removing water sprouts will kill the unfortunate tree sooner rather than later.*

Prune Dry and on Time

Avoid pruning plants while the bark is wet, and in most cases wait until late winter or early spring, just as buds begin to swell. The wound will begin callusing over during spring, reducing the chance that harmful organisms will invade. (An exception: for trees that bloom, always save pruning until after the flowers have faded.)

Should I Brace a Damaged Tree?

Double trunks and major limbs having weak forks are always in danger of failing in high winds or under heavy loads of frozen stuff. If a tree has already suffered damage, installing mechanical supports such as cables or braces sometimes can help prevent additional damage.

But mechanical supports are not an end-all cure for double trunks or weak forks. Though an injured specimen might live many more useful years with the help of bracing and/or cabling, it also might die within a year or so after supports are installed, especially if decay has damaged its structural integrity. Because an owner's decision to invest in mechanical supports, especially for a mature specimen, can be a roll of the dice in many respects, the choice should not be made without careful consideration of options.

And this is not a job for amateurs! No two trees grow or destabilize in exactly the same way, and both the tremendous weight and complex limb structures of large, older trees can present extremely complicated challenges. So designing an arrangement of mechanical supports for your specimen is a science that should be left to a trained arborist.

What to Look for in a Support System

Trees are amazingly dynamic structures that move with the wind, each limb swaying independently of its neighbors. Some types of mechanical supports hold limbs pretty much stationary, which can put enormous strain on the entire structure in windy conditions.

But in addition to that normal consequence of mechanical supports, inferior

Elm bracing to protect heavy branches. Courtesy of Paul A. Mistretta, USDA Forest Service, Bugwood.org.

or improperly installed support systems can cause severe damage to the very plants they are intended to protect. Braces that are too small can simply pull out of the wood, creating serious wounds. And ineptly installed cables can add additional stress to limbs or slice right through bark.

Though there are no current industry-wide standards for support systems, the American National Safety Institute (ANSI) has recommended standards—including the A-300 series of supports—that are generally accepted by tree-care professionals. If an arborist gives you a blank stare when asked if he is familiar with the ANSI system, you should find another arborist to brace your tree.

Because of the complexity of designing and installing a support system for a large tree—not to mention the expense—you might want to have more than one arborist analyze your specimen's specific problems.

A qualified tree-care specialist can provide you with one or more potential solutions. For example, an arborist might recommend a dynamic support such as the patented Cobra System for a tree species that cannot sustain bolts and other invasive attachments. (Cobra uses flexible bands that allow the tree to move more naturally instead of being held rigid by taut wire cables and braces.)

But the final choice will be yours to make, so you should obtain a full rundown of all bracing and cabling options suitable for your specific tree's condition before making your decision.

A basic bracing operation might cost $125 to $400; a simple cabling job can cost in the range of $150 to $200, depending on cable lengths. But that is the low end of the scale. Mechanical support systems for really large old specimens (and trees needing supports often tend to be just that) might require a complex combination of cables and braces, and can run into the thousands of dollars. *Note: Do not try to cut costs by installing do-it-yourself support systems for large specimens! Cables and braces should be installed by trained professionals and inspected annually or after weather events that stress the tree.*

When Specimens Look Sick: Dealing with Disease

Trees and shrubs that have been weakened or injured by extreme-weather events, construction, or other stressors—including weed whips or string trimmers—are vulnerable to a wide variety of diseases during their period of recuperation. Root systems damaged by flooding or drought are particularly susceptible to attack. And when root-rot fungi or other harmful organisms are already present in plants, injuries can enhance the ability of those pathogens to do damage.

When it comes to protecting your big-ticket anchor plants from disease, the best method is, as always, prevention. Just as with people, health and vigor provide trees and shrubs their best defense against attacks by harmful organisms. Even so, prevention alone is not always enough when nature pitches a major fit.

In a stressed plant, disease can quickly progress to a fatal condition if not promptly treated—assuming that there is an effective treatment. So any specimen showing signs of leaf curling or discoloration, oozing from the bark, fungal growths, or other abnormality should be assessed by a certified or registered consulting arborist. Your local Cooperative Extension agent also might be able to help you diagnose the problem.

Stressed or injured trees and shrubs are particularly vulnerable to invasive fungi. Here's just a glimpse of the threat.

Armillaria Root Disease

Commonly known as shoestring root rot, *Armillaria* most often attacks specimens that are stressed by drought and flooding, both of which deprive roots of oxygen.

Symptoms: White, threadlike fans of fungi beneath the bark (invisible unless bark has been removed); clusters of mushrooms that appear on or around the plant in late summer or fall; defoliation; shoot growth; crown dieback.

What to do: Fumigation of the root zone is possible in some soils, but treatment can have iffy results at best. *Armillaria* might be able to spread to neighboring specimens in crowded conditions, so removal of the plant is sometimes the best option. Because the pathogen has been known to survive on fragments of old roots and woody debris for more than a hundred years, replace infected specimens with native trees such as oak, willow, or black walnut, or shrubs such as rose of Sharon (*Hibiscus syriacus*), which can be relatively *Armillaria* resistant.

Tree fall caused by *Armillaria* root rot. Courtesy of Joseph O'Brien, USDA Forest Service, Bugwood.org

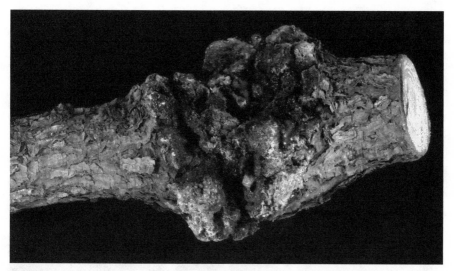

Cytospora canker on the branch of a spruce. Courtesy of William Jacobi, Colorado State University, Bugwood.org.

Canker Diseases: *Cytospora, Botryosphaeria, Nectria,* Etc.

These are triggered by a wide range of fungi that invade plants through openings in the bark caused by injuries or pests.

Symptoms: Discolored, sunken dead areas in trunks and branches.

What to do: These diseases are seldom fatal unless multiple cankers girdle the trunk. The best treatment is prevention of future injuries that can lead to additional invasions.

Pythium and *Phytophthora* Root Diseases

These so-called water molds can attack during or after floods, infecting many common landscape species including rhododendrons, azaleas, oaks, maples, pines, and fruit trees.

Symptoms: Leaf yellowing, trunk cankers oozing sap, stunting (including leaf size), and crown dieback.

What to do: Other than taking steps to increase the ailing specimen's vitality, little treatment is available once the plant is infected.

Note: Just as the health and vigor of a tree or shrub is its best defense against disease, so is building up the vigor of a stressed or damaged specimen often its best hope of fighting off or adapting to the presence of a disease. Most diseases tend to progress relatively slowly in trees, with pathogens taking as long as five years to bring about death. So if your diseased specimen is fortunate enough to survive, be prepared for a long battle. The alternative is to remove and replace the afflicted

Phytophthora collar rot on a young apple tree. Courtesy of William M. Brown, Jr., Bugwood.org.

plant. But you might want to put that option on hold until the struggle is obviously futile if your tree is high value or a sentimental favorite.

When Specimens Look Sick: Dealing with Pests

Harmful insects naturally gravitate toward stressed or injured plants, most likely attracted by the profusion of nutrients released by their already trauma-tized victims. Species such as oaks, hickories, birches, and pines are particularly favorite targets of trauma-related invasions, but any stressed specimen is at risk.

And as if opportunistic pests were not a bad enough tribulation by themselves, they often work hand-in-hand with diseases.

Pests and the specific tree and shrub species they attack are so numerous that they fill entire volumes that make up substantial sections of horticultural libraries. So do not be surprised if you encounter a sudden horde of bugs that you cannot identify. Certified and registered consulting arborists are skilled in the identification and treatment of pest infestations common to your area. You can also bottle up a sample bug and take it to your Cooperative Extension office for assistance in naming the culprit.

Stem Borers

Though most homeowners lack the training or equipment to effectively treat infestations in large specimens, there is one primary group of pests that you should keep an eye out for: stem-boring insects. Stem borers come in a seemingly endless variety that includes flatheads, roundheads, emerald ash, locust, elm, and shothole borers, to name but a few. They are divided into two groups: wood borers and phloem borers.

Wood borers tunnel into the heartwood of stems and branches, where they can cause structural weakness—a not uncommon cause of limb or trunk failure during an extreme-weather event. Phloem borers set up shop in the layers of

Distinctive D-shaped exit holes made by stem borers. Courtesy of Daniel Herms, The Ohio State University, Bugwood.org.

tissue just beneath the bark, where they play havoc with the plant's vital vascular system.

Symptoms: Look for entrance and exit holes in the bark. Entrance wounds are small and often ooze sawdust or sap. Exit holes are neat wounds in oval, D, or round shapes.

What to do: Pesticides are seldom effective against borers. To help prevent further infestation, clean up the tree and the surrounding ground, removing any deadwood or debris. Make sure mulch materials are not piled against the trunk. Build up the specimen's vitality with a regular watering regimen. If a soil test indicates deficiencies, make light applications of suitable fertilizers and/or top dressings of compost at the drip line and beyond over the next few years.

An Integrated Pest Management Primer

Integrated Pest Management (IPM) is all about prevention, as well as about identifying specific pests and combating them with their natural enemies, or *responsibly* employing chemicals that will cause the least harm to the environment. Employing IPM in your landscape is a key tool in both preventing and coping with harmful pests in your trees and shrubs.

IPM begins with prevention. This includes selecting native species, which tend to be more resistant to the local pests among which they evolved; locating these trees and shrubs on sites that are compatible with each plant's soil and sunlight/shade needs; and making sure each plant has an adequate supply of water and nutrients. It goes without saying that good landscape hygiene and maintenance practices also are important, including promptly removing fallen fruits or other debris and properly pruning plants to remove deadwood or clean up wounds.

Even with all of those elements in place, diligent monitoring for pests to ensure early detection is an essential part of IPM, especially when your landscape has been subjected to an extreme-weather event or other stress factors. Some pests such as tent caterpillars and webworms are easy to spot; others might make their presence evident with holes in leaves or bark, skeletonized foliage, or dripping sap.

Control of infestations can begin with mechanical means such as high-pressure water sprays (very effective on spider mites) or Tanglefoot®. Hand picking pests, such as plucking webworms from arborvitae shrubs, is among the oldest of IPM mechanical treatments. Children sometimes can be induced to become bug-plucking bounty hunters if the fee is sufficient to win over their enthusiasm.

If mechanical measures fail to do the trick, you can up the ante by introducing carefully targeted biological controls such as store-bought ladybugs, praying mantises, or other beneficial insects that prey on pests. Or you can attract your own native beneficials by releasing specific pheromone agents (basically, alluring sex hormones) into your landscape. These introduced biological controls will not work as preventives but must be introduced while the pest population is booming; otherwise the friendly predators, finding nothing to eat, will simply fly or crawl away to better hunting grounds.

Note: In times of stress, a bug-free landscape is wide open to invading pests, which tend to be more resilient and opportunistic than beneficial insects. By maintaining an insect-friendly landscape that is as chemical free as possible, you help to ensure a healthy balance of pests and predators, including bug-eating birds, bats, toads, and other wildlife.

When all else fails, the last resort of Integrated Pest Management is targeted, selective use of pesticides. *Bacillus thuringiensis* (Bt) stands at the low end of the pesticide scale. A safe, natural bacterial disease, Bt—which comes in different strains—is particularly effective against caterpillars and larvae, including mosquito larvae. Also, selected miticides and fungicides fit into IPM, although some fungicides can cause undesired collateral damage to bees and other beneficial insects.

The final step up in a war against attacking pests involves chemical pesticides. These should be chosen and used with extreme care, with the aim of causing the least amount of damage to the environment.

Contact your local Cooperative Extension office for information and advice on developing and employing an IPM program in your landscape.

What about Collateral Damage?

Sometimes the loss of trees and large shrubs can have a domino effect on the landscape, resulting in the loss of plants that have survived initial adverse conditions. For instance, the loss of a shade-casting maple tree might leave a bed of azaleas exposed to the withering heat of summer sunlight reflected off a brick wall. Or the loss of a large photinia shrub might expose moisture-loving ferns to desiccating summer winds. In these and similar cases, you have three basic options:

1. Provide temporary protection. For tender, exposed plants, trellises, screens, or other devices can provide protection until replacement trees or shrubs have time to mature.
2. Transplant vulnerable specimens. If the plants are not too large, move them to a new location where they will have necessary protection.
3. Remove vulnerable plants altogether. Replace them with species that can

withstand the altered conditions. If the plants are not too large to survive transplanting, you might find a neighbor or local park willing provide a suitable home for the evacuees.

Whichever route you choose, you should make your move before the vulnerable plants suffer damage. But in a pinch until more permanent arrangements can be made, simply draping a light-filtering sheet over a sun-exposed shade-loving plant during the heat of the day can make all the difference.

Salt-Saturated Soil or Plants

In coastal landscapes, hurricanes and tropical storms can leave soil and plants saturated with high levels of salt. This can be fatal to specimens, either quickly or over a period of months.

Salt spray, whether from wind-driven seawater or splashing from road salts, is especially harmful to plants. Because salt draws water out of the plant and causes "burning" of buds and foliage, the resulting desiccation interferes with photosynthesis. The longer sensitive plants are exposed to salt, the more harm they will suffer.

What to do: Wash down trees and shrubs with fresh water as soon as possible after exposure.

But salt-saturated soil poses a more difficult problem.

What to do: Once flooding has subsided—or winter salting of icy streets has ceased—and the ground has dried out enough to accept water once again, repeated deep soakings with fresh water can help wash salts deeper into the soil below root level. Heavy rains can help do this for you.

A Case in Point

When broken levees flooded New Orleans in late summer of 2005, trees were inundated with salt water for weeks. But after the floodwaters drained away, five inches of rain in the fall helped to reduce salinity in the soil so the city could begin replanting its drowned urban forest.

Many tree and shrub species such as live oak and inkberry are relatively tolerant of salt. (See appendix I for a partial species list.) If you have a coastal landscape, check with your local County Extension office or native-plant organization for lists of salt-tolerant species suitable for your specific landscape.

If your locale is subjected to salt-depositing storms on a fairly regular basis, and you have recently planted very salt-intolerant plants in your landscape, your best course of action is to be proactive: remove those unsuitable plants and replace them with salt-tolerant species.

What Else Should I Watch For?

The other shoe to drop.

Following a disaster, moderate-to-serious structural damage sometimes can remain hidden even from the skilled eye of an arborist. Months after you thought all necessary repairs had been made, a limb might suddenly begin to sag or an entire tree or shrub might take on a decided list. And evidence of flood damage often does not make itself evident until the year after the extreme-weather event.

This type of delayed-action response can come so long after the fact that the property owner might not even associate a sudden limb failure or the death of an entire specimen with a long-past storm, drought, or other assault. So even if your trees and shrubs initially appear to have withstood an extreme-weather event unscathed, they bear watching.

What about My Wildfire-Scorched Specimens?

The long-term prospects for your scorched landscape trees and shrubs will depend on a number of factors, including the severity of the burn; the species (sycamores, for example, are not well adapted to fire); and whether the specimen becomes infested with bark beetles or other pests following the injury (a distinct possibility).

Assuming that the charring of the tree or shrub is not too deep or widespread (see chapter 5), the best care you can give a burned specimen is an adequate supply of water and careful vigilance for pests. Beyond that, wait and see how the plant responds during the coming growing season before making a final decision as to whether the specimen is salvageable. Some native species in particular might astound you with their ability to rise from the ashes.

A Case in Point

In October 2007, a wildfire driven by 80 to 100 mph winds tore through Greg and Barbara Robersons' property in Ramona, California. Just two years earlier, the Robersons had opted for a native landscape filled with catalpa, honey mesquite, palo verde, coffeeberry, monkey flower, and many other drought-tolerant trees and shrubs. Only a handful of those plants did not suffer significant damage from the October fire.

Instructed not to touch a thing—just provide water—they left the charred landscape alone until the following March. By then, the scrappy native plants were showing "a tremendous amount of growth." Although the Robersons eventually had to replace "maybe a dozen plants" out of 250 or more, less than two years after the fire "you couldn't tell anything burned." By contrast, a neighbor lost the majority of his landscape, including palms and other non-native plants that he was still working to reestablish.

Such phenomenal regrowth is not uncommon among native plants that are adapted to fire-prone environments. As Greg Rubin, who has installed hundreds of native landscapes in drought- and wildfire-prone Southern California, points out, "Although the top growth was compromised, the root system and mycorrhizal biomass remain very much intact, thus providing the sustenance required for a voluminous, quick recovery." On the other hand, "often exotics, with their higher moisture content, are boiled to death at the root crown."

What about My Lightning-Struck Tree?

If most of the bark is intact, the tree has a fairly good chance of survival—assuming that it is not a pine, which has a near-zero rate of lightning-strike survival. Beyond emergency repairs to the bark, providing plenty of water, and regular inspection for pests, the best long-term approach is similar to that for charred specimens: wait and see how well the tree responds after the shock of a bolt from the blue.

When Is It a Lost Cause?

So you have done everything you were supposed to: you have called in an experienced arborist to make emergency repairs on your weather-ravaged trees and shrubs, and you have been diligently following an intensive-care program to help along the recovery process. But major branches in your ice-damaged oak continue to fail, or after what seems like a generous period of time your inkberry shrub still has not perked up from the drought.

Just how do you know when you are losing the battle to save a specimen?

a plant exhibits little vigorous foliage growth the spring after the injury
a plant appears to grow weaker despite your best efforts to boost its vigor
a tree begins to lose structural integrity, showing cracks in major limbs or the trunk, making it hazardous
a severely damaged or weakened specimen becomes badly infested or diseased

If in doubt, do not delay in obtaining a professional opinion, keeping in mind that a critically ill tree or shrub is less than an asset in your landscape: it is the horticultural equivalent of a rusted-out vehicle propped up on blocks in your driveway. And in some cases, you might need to remove the specimen quickly to avoid the spread of disease to neighboring plants. See chapter 7 for information on how to get rid of the plant, and chapter 10 for tips on how to choose and install a replacement that is more tolerant of local extreme-weather events.

Preserving "Heirloom" Plants

Some plants are priceless in the eyes of the world. The Survivor Tree at the Oklahoma City National Memorial and the chestnut tree outside the window of the Amsterdam attic where Anne Frank hid during World War II are international symbols of enduring hope.

But "heirloom" plants do not have to be famous in order to occupy important places in our lives. You might have a deep personal attachment to a lilac shrub grown from the latest of a succession of cuttings that have been handed down in your family for generations. Or perhaps research has shown that the post oak tree next to your garden shed was growing in that spot more than 100 years before your housing development was built.

In common terms, an heirloom specimen is a plant that has been cultivated in the same location for at least 50 years. But for the purpose of recovering or restoring your weather-beaten landscape, let's broaden that definition to include any mature tree or shrub that possesses a rich and colorful history, or that holds a special place in your own personal history.

But let's be clear about one point: unfair though it might seem, sentimental attachment holds no dollars-and-cents value in the marketplace. So no matter how profound your emotional connection might be to a landscape specimen, it is unlikely to translate into added value to your real estate beyond the plant's intrinsic appraised worth as a utilitarian or aesthetic element of your overall property, a figure best arrived at through a cooperative effort between a consulting arborist and a real estate appraiser.

The Survivor Tree, 100 years old and still thriving. Courtesy of Sandra Dark.

However, if your house is on the market, the age or life story of a particular tree or shrub might make your property more interesting to some prospective buyers. For example, a would-be buyer might be intrigued by the big hackberry tree that was planted the same year that your house was built, or the old southern magnolia that Elvis Presley climbed as a boy (you'd better have pictures!). In that case, a specimen with a colorful history can be a useful enhancement to your marketing toolbox.

But even if your heirloom plant never comes into play as an added point of interest for touring home buyers, it can warrant special consideration when it comes to ensuring its continued existence either in its present form or through future generations of itself.

How Do I Protect an Heirloom Specimen?

The methods used to help prevent an heirloom specimen from suffering damage or to restore the plant if it is injured are identical to those used for any other valued tree or shrub—except perhaps in degree: because heirloom specimens are irreplaceable in either a sentimental or historical sense, they arguably can be more deserving of extraordinary measures when threatened or damaged.

For example, you probably would not even consider having mechanical supports installed on your structurally unstable nonheirloom sycamore tree, but you might feel differently about shouldering the expense of bracing the hairline split in the trunk of your heirloom burr oak. Or when there is insufficient water to go around during a period of water rationing, you might choose to soak your heirloom holly hedge at the expense of less treasured elements of your drought-stricken landscape.

In such circumstances, "survival of the fittest" can take a backseat to "survival of the most loved"—and that means respecting needs that sometimes can be magnified by age.

During the course of its lifetime, an heirloom tree or shrub of advanced age has probably endured many extreme-weather events, as well as numerous manmade alterations to its ecosystem. More often than not, those alterations were undesirable if not outright harmful from the specimen's standpoint. But that does not mean the plant can continue to survive any and every disruption to its environment that is thrown its way.

Over any plant's lifetime, repeated injuries and stresses can weaken its immune system. Even if stressors have not been severe, a tree or shrub can become less able to bounce back from injuries as it slips into its senior years. So while being a good steward of an heirloom specimen involves tending to the basics, there also might be times when you need to go the extra mile to help ensure its continued longevity.

Roots are always a critical issue but never more so than with older plants. During many decades of growth, a tree or shrub without major restrictions will have extended its delicate feeder-root system far and wide, absorbing a nonstop supply of water and nutrients to store or pass on to its imposing top growth. The guardianship of that unseen realm, which might extend out two or three times the reach of the drip line, should be paramount.

Anything that threatens to compromise the root system (such as soil compaction, digging, competition from turf grass, and lawn herbicides) could spell the sad end of a grand old life.

Needless to say, construction projects anywhere near an heirloom specimen should be approached with extreme caution. But also be alert to potential collateral damage from activities farther afield. For example, you might notice that the new sunroom your neighbor added to his house causes runoff onto your property that could leave part of your heirloom holly hedge standing in water for extended periods during the rainy season. When changes occur near or uphill from your favored specimen, a landscape architect can help you analyze and, if possible, deal with potential problems before they become deadly ones.

Anticipating Problems

When it comes to protecting your landscape from outside runoff, landscape architects and civil engineers are committed to a zero-runoff scenario. Basically, what this means is that there should be no off-site occurrences that are detrimental to neighboring or downstream properties. So what happens when a severe weather event, neighbor, or unscrupulous contractor does create such problems on your landscape?

Let's say that a new drainage pattern sends water running across your property, threatening one or more of your specimen or heirloom trees. A landscape architect or designer is educated and trained to deal with this type of situation in any of a number of ways. For example, water might be redirected with a berm or some other form of earthwork. Landscape construction such as a French drain, retaining wall, or dry well also might be employed. But before any kind of corrective work is designed—much less begun—a landscape architect can analyze your property and plants to determine how best to protect critical root zones from construction.

Dean Hill

When far-flung environmental changes such as the construction of a new strip mall or the widening of a road are made that prove to be detrimental to your landscape, there are not always lifesaving remedies for your valuable plants. So it is better to raise your concerns about those changes while they are still in the development stage, at which point the plan might be altered to prevent damage that your landscape might otherwise suffer.

But before contacting a developer or showing up at a city-planners' meeting, you should have your potential problem analyzed by a landscape architect or engineer so you will have authoritative information to offer. You also might want to have your case presented by an attorney who is experienced in dealing with real estate issues.

An annual checkup is a must for an Old One. The advanced age of many heirlooms can leave them more susceptible to diseases, pests, and extreme-weather events, especially if they have been damaged or suffered neglect previously in their long lives. With a regularly scheduled inspection, a certified or registered consulting arborist can detect pathogens early, before damage becomes severe, which gives treatments a greater chance of success. The arborist might also spot structural weaknesses that, if not remedied, could needlessly shorten the life of a specimen.

An annual inspection might run between $75 and $175. In some cases a contracting arborist might perform this service at no cost, especially if you are a regular client.

How Can I Make Sure My Heirloom Specimens Live On?

Generally, if your heirloom plant dies, the monetary loss to your real estate is no greater than if any other tree or shrub of comparable size and quality gave up the ghost. And yet, the emotional shock of losing a favored specimen can be deeper and longer lasting.

But the loss does not have to be total. For countless generations since the beginning of time, nature's answer to death has been rebirth. Just knowing that the cycle of life has not ended for your treasured specimen—that you have living offspring from Great-Aunt Edith's lilac or that 200-year-old live oak—can help to ease some of your sense of loss.

Many heirloom trees and shrubs, from stately poplars to flashy forsythias, can be successfully cloned from cuttings or propagated from seeds as insurance against a possible future disaster. Saplings grown from the chestnut tree that Anne Frank gazed out upon from the window of her attic hideout during World War II have ensured that new generations will live on long after that aged, ailing, and revered tree is gone. *Note: Since this writing, Anne Frank's chestnut tree was felled by a storm in 2010.*

A Case in Point

In the months following the bombing of the Alfred P. Murrah Federal Building in Oklahoma City, no one put much thought into preserving the charred, defoliated American elm languishing in a parking lot across the street. Ignored in its field of asphalt, the 100-year-old tree managed to produce enough secondary leaves in the weeks and months ahead to endure yet another long, hot summer, followed by an equally unforgiving winter. Only when new leaf buds sprang to life the following spring, a full year after the blast, did people begin calling it the Survivor Tree. Only then did they begin thinking about its future.

Stephen Bieberich, who grows native trees and shrubs at Sunshine Nursery in Clinton, Oklahoma, stepped in to gather seeds and take cuttings from the Survivor Tree. Using specialized growing equipment, he produced a crop of seedlings the first year, and achieved the more difficult process of grafting identical clones from the cuttings. Sunshine Nursery has since grown thousands of offspring of the Survivor Tree.

When and How Can I Propagate My Heirloom Tree or Shrub from Cuttings?

That depends on the species and whether you intend to do the deed yourself or seek the assistance of a nurseryman who is proficient at the often complex process of growing trees from cuttings.

And let there be no doubt about it: though many shrub species are easily propagated from cuttings, cloning most tree species in this manner can be difficult. For one thing, some cuttings must be grafted onto rootstock that itself might take a year or more to prepare. And the grafting must take place at just the right time of year or it will not work.

But the beauty of growing a new plant from a cutting is that, unlike a seed-grown plant, you will produce an exact clone of your old favorite. You can do this by taking one of several types of cuttings, depending on the time of year.

If you are working with a nurseryman, he will probably prefer to take the cuttings himself. Why? Because cuttings need to be processed *quickly* if they are to have a chance of success, and the nurseryman will want to be fully prepared to move quickly. If you do take the cuttings yourself, be sure to coordinate the timing with your nurseryman. Closely follow instructions on how to care for the cuttings in transit; especially with softwood cuttings, the urgency can be as great as that for transporting a donor organ to a transplant patient.

What will this cost? Most tree growers (as opposed to nurserymen, who merely buy and sell nursery stock) rarely get requests to propagate heirloom plants. Therefore, there is no industry pricing standard. If they have developed a relationship with a customer, some growers will charge the regular price that they ask for a similar young tree or shrub in their nursery, adding nothing extra for the propagation. Others might base their charge on the degree of difficulty and time involved. *Note: Your chosen expert does not necessarily have to be professional. Through local horticultural organizations, you might find an experienced hobbyist who is adept at cloning woody plants.*

If you want to try propagating your favorite plant from cuttings, at least check with tree-growing experts in your area to find out if your chosen species roots readily from cuttings. (Most species do not, which is why an experienced grower or hobbyist is your best bet when it comes to cloning.)

Also be aware that older specimens with their less vigorous growth might be more difficult to propagate from cuttings than will be younger plants.

Spring is the best time to take softwood cuttings from birch, catalpa, elm, lilac, azalea, crape myrtle, boxwood, and many other woody ornamentals. When new growth is about six inches long, look for succulent, still-flexible stems that have matured enough to snap when bent.

Late spring to early summer is the time for semihardwood cuttings from your favorite crabapple, maple, or forsythia, to name a few. Select stems that have matured beyond the succulent, flexible stage but have not yet turned woody.

Winter to early spring is the best time to take hardwood cuttings from trees and shrubs such as eastern white pine, poplar, euonymus, honey locust, rose, and forsythia. Look for woody stems that have developed in the current year.

Some species of woody plants can be grown from all three types of cuttings: softwood, semihardwood, or hardwood. Your Cooperative Exchange agent can help you determine which type of cutting is best for propagating your specific species.

Note: Cuttings seldom root well when taken from plants that are water-stressed by either flood or drought, or that are suffering from either nutrient deficiency or overfertilization. Vigor is always a plus in the propagation process: the healthier the plant, the better the chance is that its cuttings will take root.

Taking Cuttings

For softwood and semihardwood, take 6-inch cuttings from the ends of stems, making the cut just below a node. Each cutting should have at least three leaf nodes.

For hardwood, make cuttings from 4 to 20 inches long. Each cutting should have at least two leaf nodes.

Cuttings taken from the uppermost part of the tree will provide better growth and are best made first thing in the morning (if reaching them is at all practical). The cuttings need to be handled with care and dispatch if they are to retain their full rooting potential. So pots and a sterile rooting medium (such as a half-and-half mix of builder's sand and milled peat moss) should be readied before cuttings are made.

1. Strip foliage from the bottom third of the cutting.
2. Remove flowers or flower buds. Better yet, take cuttings that have neither.
3. Dip the cut end into rooting hormone (available at garden centers) to increase chances of success.
4. Insert the bottom third of the cutting into the rooting medium. Getting the depth right is important!
5. Place pots in bright light, not direct sunlight, with high humidity and a temperature of 65 to 75 degrees. *Note: You can tent cuttings with clear plastic to help maintain humidity, but slit the plastic to allow the air to circulate—otherwise, mold problems can develop.*

Rooting can require three to six weeks, or even months, depending on the species. After a month or so, test by lifting lightly on the cutting: if it stays put in

Softwood (left) and
hardwood cuttings.
Drawing by Peggy
Lovret Chaffin.

the soil, roots are developing. Once roots develop, transplant the cuttings to containers filled with potting soil. Monitor the plants carefully while providing sunshine, water, and good air circulation.

As young plants develop, you can transplant them to gallon pots and sink them to their rims in a nursery bed outdoors until they are mature enough to take a permanent place in the landscape. Apply light mulch and maintain the proper watering regimen for transplants (see chapter 3).

For more extensive information on propagating trees and shrubs from cuttings, check under Recommended Reading in appendix III.

Can I Grow Trees and Shrubs from Their Seeds?

To quote eighteenth-century English writer Lewis Duncombe, "The lofty oak from a small acorn grows." But why limit your vision to just oaks? After all, maples, black cherries, pecans, viburnum, buttonbush, and many other species of trees and shrubs will grow readily from seeds.

Unlike woody plants grown from cuttings, seeds do not produce exact replicas of the original, especially if the species is hybrid or grafted. For example, papershell pecan trees are grafted onto native pecan rootstock. Therefore, because seeds from grafted plants revert to the rootstock, a seedling grown from a papershell pecan will grow into a native pecan tree. The same goes for the pits from any peach, plum, or other soft-fruit tree that has been grafted onto hardier rootstock. Also, grafted dwarf trees will revert to their standard-size rootstock. And of course, hybrid roses will not retain their desirable hybrid features.

So if you want a clone of a grafted tree or hybrid shrub, you should propagate the plant with cuttings rather than seeds.

The advantage of growing woody plants from their seeds is in the numbers: plants that propagate themselves from seeds often do so with abandon. Some can be downright pests about it, self-seeding offspring in lawns, garden beds, and even between cracks in sidewalks.

More often than not, growing woody plants from seeds is easier than growing them from cuttings. But producing seedlings can be slow going at first, especially when homegrown rather than nursery-produced. Planted in the spring, homegrown seedlings might grow just two to three inches tall by fall. But grown in a nursery with special pots and misting systems, the same plant might gain a height of two to three feet!

Besides the length of time required for most seed-grown woody plants to become large enough to take their permanent place in the landscape, there's the problem that some species produce seeds that are themselves notorious slow starters. For example, *Nandina* seeds might take an entire year just to germinate.

But rest assured that while some species are a challenge to propagate from seeds, oaks, pecans, maples, pines, camellias, and numerous other species can be grown successfully, and often quite easily, this way.

The ABCs of Growing Woody Plants from Seeds

Growing woody plants from seeds isn't like growing tomatoes and zinnias. It can involve weeks (even months) of preparation, and months (even years) of patience. But the result can be rewarding as you learn the language of growing mighty oaks and lush viburnum from scratch.

Seed gathering usually takes place in the spring, summer, or fall, depending on the plant species. Red-maple seeds mature in spring, while those of the southern sugar maple mature in the fall, as do acorns from those mighty oaks.

For trees and shrubs with fleshy fruits, seeds should be gathered when fruits are ripe.

Seeds gathered before they reach full maturity will not germinate. And fallen seeds gathered from the ground might be damaged by fungus, birds, lawn-mowers, or other hazards. So whenever possible, pluck mature fruits and seeds directly from the plant.

Seed viability varies widely by species. Some seeds are dormant and require preplanting preparation (see below) that can take place over a period of weeks or months after they are gathered. But many others—such as seeds from white oaks and silver maples, as well as those from fleshy fruits such as crabapples and persimmons—are not dormant and might remain viable for as little as two or three days after they mature.

Seed preparation begins the process. The seeds of many species are ready and waiting to sprout as soon as they mature and do not retain viability in storage. These should be planted right away, though some might require minor prep-ping. For example, seeds from fleshy fruits should be separated and air-dried before planting, and wings should be removed from maple seeds.

But other species produce seeds that are dormant, and these call for more extended effort. There are two basic types of seed dormancy, internal and ex-ternal, each requiring you to take a different approach.

Internal dormancy requires *scarification*—nicking or scarring the seed coat-ing—before seeds can germinate. This can be accomplished with coarse sand-paper or a knife, and is a must for seeds having very hard coatings. *Note: Do not scarify seeds until immediately before you are ready to plant them, or the seeds will lose viability.*

External dormancy requires *stratification*—exposure to cold temperatures for a specified period of time. In northern landscapes, this can be accomplished naturally by planting seeds directly in the ground at the time they are gathered.

In southern landscapes or when seeds are sown indoors, you can create a false winter by first soaking seeds overnight, then layering them in a plastic storage (not freezer) bag or container with moist (not wet) sterile vermiculite or sand. Refrigerate, but do not freeze, your bag of stratifying seeds, usually for three to four months. *Note: Some species might require shorter or longer strati-fication periods. Contact your Cooperative Extension office or research your tree species to find out its specific needs.*

Direct Planting

Nature knows best when to grow plants from seeds. If you sow tree or shrub seeds directly in a garden nursery area rather than in pots indoors, plant them at the time of year that they fall. Most planting-ready seeds will go ahead and germinate, producing transplantable seedlings that same season. Dormant seeds that need to stratify will do so over winter, and plants will emerge the following spring.

Plant seeds at a depth of no more than twice their diameter. Lightly mulch the bed and keep it evenly moist. Depending on the species, seeds planted outdoors will take anywhere from a few weeks to many months to germinate. Some species will sit tight for a year or more. So clearly mark the ends of rows lest you lose track.

To keep birds, squirrels, and other foragers from making a clean sweep of your planting site, cover the bed with screening or hardware cloth until seedlings appear.

Indoor Planting

Following scarification or stratification, tree and shrub seeds can be planted in pots filled with a sterile seed-starting medium, either store-bought or a combination of equal parts builder's sand and milled peat moss. Place the pots in bright light, not direct sunlight, and maintain a temperature of 75 to 85 degrees. Humidity is important, so tent the pots with clear plastic punched with holes to permit air circulation, and keep the soil moist but not soggy (professional growers accomplish this with misters).

Once growth appears, move the plants into direct sunlight or they will become weak and spindly. Do not place seedlings next to the glass on a sunny windowsill: sunshine through glass can produce withering heat even in winter. Set pots back from the window and monitor their moisture levels closely.

Whether planting seeds indoors or outdoors, keep in mind that even for professionals the success rate can differ from species to species and from year to year. So follow the example of Mother Nature: always plant many more than you want, thereby increasing the possibility that you will end up with a good selection of young plants from which you can choose the very best. The same holds true when propagating plants from cuttings.

Transplanting Seedlings

Tree and shrub seedlings are ready to be transplanted into larger pots once they have produced four true leaves in addition to the seedling leaves called *cotyledons* that appear initially. Take care to disturb the roots as little as possible during the process.

Before planting seedlings outdoors either in a nursery garden or directly into a landscape bed, harden them off for a few days in a shady location that is protected from desiccating winds. *Do not let their soil dry out!* Then transplant them in the early evening or on an overcast day. Apply a light mulch and follow the watering regimen recommended for transplants in chapter 3. *Note: Pampering young plants grown from stem cuttings or seeds during their critical first season outdoors will greatly enhance their chance of survival.*

How Long Will It Be before I Have a Landscape Plant?

Have patience. You will need to wait at least two years, sometimes several, before a homegrown cutting or seedling will develop into a plant large enough to take its place in the landscape. On the other hand, a nursery-grown clone or seedling from your heirloom plant is likely to grow to a useful size in a much shorter period thanks to the specialized equipment and expertise of the grower.

What If My Heirloom Specimen Is Already Destroyed?

If the specimen is fatally damaged or felled in a spring storm, you still might have a slight chance of propagating it if you act quickly. This is assuming that the plant was not diseased, drought-stricken, or otherwise in poor health before the storm. Even without storm damage, cuttings from unhealthy plants have a reduced chance of rooting.

Time is a critical factor in any attempt at emergency propagation. So you are unlikely to be able to successfully make arrangements for the process before time runs out if you do not already have a relationship with a professional or hobbyist tree grower. (Returning to the organ-transplant analogy: there is only a very narrow window of time during which the organ—in this case, plant material—can remain viable.)

If you want to give it a shot, contact your tree grower immediately—unless you choose to try rooting the cuttings yourself—to give him time to make preparations. Then take cuttings as described above. *During the growing season, this must be done before foliage wilts.*

Take lots of cuttings, because you will not have a second chance. Wrap the cuttings in a damp cloth to keep them from drying out while you either rush them to the designated tree grower or quickly prepare pots and rooting medium for a do-it-yourself attempt.

If the plant is a type of shrub that roots readily from cuttings, there is a chance that you might get a plant out of your emergency efforts. Successfully rooting cuttings from a fallen tree is a much longer shot. But if it is your only prospect of reproducing an heirloom plant, you might feel the attempt is worthwhile.

Nature's Own Seedlings

When emergency cuttings are not an option and you do not happen to have a batch of seeds stratifying in your refrigerator, you can always hope for the miracle of volunteer seedlings that might appear next spring.

Many species produce entire miniforests of volunteer offspring, often inadvertently helped along by squirrels and other rodents burying stashes of acorns, nuts, and seeds in the fall. If your heirloom plant is one of these, search regularly before mowing for seedlings that might sprout in spring or summer near the site of the lost tree or shrub. If you find offspring, simply transplant some of the most vigorous seedlings into an outdoor nursery site where they can safely grow.

How Else Can I Ensure That My Heirloom Specimen Lives On?

You can protect any tree or shrub only so far. When age or an extreme natural disaster looms, your best bet lies with the future generations of your heirloom plant—and your own generosity.

If you have the good fortune to own a tree or shrub that has historical significance, or you simply have a deep attachment to a specimen, propagating it while it is still in good health will establish those future generations. By spreading the offspring far and wide, you can help ensure that it will live on for at least another generation, and perhaps many more.

A Case in Point

The iconic Survivor Tree at the Oklahoma City National Memorial has become a multitude. Each year, hundreds of the treasured American elm's seedlings are handed out free at the memorial on the April 19 anniversary of the bombing. Other seed-grown offspring are available for purchase from the nonprofit American Forests Historic Tree Program (see Resources in appendix III). So descendants of this single old elm tree are now growing in parks, school yards, and residential landscapes across the country.

Start an heirloom nursery in a sunny back corner of your property where you can maintain new generations of offspring from your favored specimens, propagated by seeds or cuttings. Grow them in sunken containers to make transplanting easier and less traumatic for the plant.

When the young trees or shrubs outgrow the nursery, either move them to permanent locations in your landscape or donate them to parks, schools, or friends. Make sure you pass along the history of the tree or shrub's forebear as well as the plant itself. After all, that is what makes it special.

How Can I Replace a Lost Heirloom?

If your treasured tree or shrub cannot be propagated and no volunteer offspring have cropped up at the site, of course the old favorite is lost forever. So how can you fill that empty space when just another replacement oak or lilac would hold no historical or sentimental value at all for you?

One solution is to plant a descendant of some other historically significant specimen—and the choices can be breathtaking. For instance, American Forests, the oldest nonprofit conservation organization in the United States, offers more than 100 types of historic trees in its Historic Tree Program. These include direct descendants of trees grown from sycamore seeds that were taken to the moon and back in 1971; or of the 1,400-year-old Angel live oak, which is possibly the oldest living thing east of the Mississippi River; or of a weeping willow from Elvis Presley's Graceland; or of the Survivor Tree.

But keepsake trees and shrubs can represent more than just a single plant, place, or event—they can symbolize an entire revered species. On the pampered grounds of Balmoral Castle, the British royal family's summer getaway in Scotland, stands a stately sequoia tree that came all the way from a redwood forest in California.

To enhance the social stature of your "new heirloom" plant, you might wish to post a tasteful sign (which, of course, you will not nail to the tree) that proudly announces its heritage.

When shopping for the offspring of a historical tree or shrub, remember that the same rules hold true for them as for any other landscape plant: the candidate should be well-suited to your growing area—including the unique soil and microclimate of your specific landscape—and should be at least moderately tolerant of the extreme-weather events that are likely to occur there. Needless to say, transplanting an offspring of Elvis Presley's water-loving weeping willow to a drought-prone landscape would not be a smooth move.

Preserving the Loss

Standing by as a beloved tree is hauled away to a firewood lot or to the community landfill is an especially painful experience. But trees have sailed around the world in the keels of clipper ships and slumbered for thousands of years in the tombs of Egyptian pharaohs. With just a little imagination, lost trees can live on in many ways:

- Find a local woodworker to shape logs from your old cherry tree into bowls, vases, picture frames, or any number of other keepsake items that can be saved or used as meaningful gifts. (If the wood is particularly valuable, the woodworker might accept some of the logs as partial or total payment.)
- Oak, maple, and other hardwoods can be crafted into durable pieces of furniture suitable for handing down from generation to generation, becoming yet another form of heirloom.
- Large trees can be milled into lumber and used for construction projects on your property or donated to a good cause such as Habitat for Humanity. (The latter option might qualify for a tax write-off.)
- A gifted chain-saw artist can carve a tree trunk into anything from a soaring eagle to a totem pole to a rustic garden seat. *Note: An annual coating of wood preservative is a must for protecting outdoor carvings from the elements. Even so, their expected life span is usually around eight years. When deterioration sets in, the artwork should be moved under cover or indoors.*

A Case in Point

When a municipal sewer-line project in Norman, Oklahoma, killed a hackberry tree at James Maguire's front curb, he was not ready to let the 70-year-old specimen go to waste. Instead of sending the dead tree to a landfill, he hired a well-known chain-saw artist from Tulsa to carve the trunk into a statue of James's great-great-grandfather in his Civil War uniform. Because there was no existing photo of the deceased, the artist made the statue resemble James as closely as possible. The carving of the proud soldier, complete with rifle, became an instant landmark on busy Main Street.

Turning Lemons into Lemonade

An heirloom or keepsake tree or shrub can hold a special significance to you that far outweighs its intrinsic value. But the loss of any important specimen, regardless of its history or your emotional attachment, can substantially alter your landscape and at least temporarily damage the ambience and market appeal of your real estate as well as its overall value.

Even so, landscape disasters are not always entirely negative. While extreme-weather events and other landscape-trashing conditions can be costly and

A 70-year-old hackberry turned into a community landmark. Courtesy of Robert Dark.

traumatic, they can also create opportunities for positive change during the restoration process. For example, maybe you always wanted to grow vegetables, but you needed more sun. Well, now you have it. In the wake of a natural disaster, the best thing you can do is look forward.

Replacing the Loss

Violent storms, grinding droughts, and nature's grab bag of other extreme-weather events can be disturbing, at times even frightening. The loss of major trees and shrubs only adds to the shock. But losing one or more large landscape plants sometimes can end up being to your advantage by opening up opportunities that might not have been possible before.

A Clean Slate

A landscape that has evolved without a unifying design over a period of decades usually presents a complicated variety of problems. This is especially the case when property has passed through several hands. As each family puts its own personality into a landscape, the end result can be a hodgepodge of plants that defy both eye appeal and function.

Over the years, sun-loving shrubs or a heretofore-cheerful sunroom might gradually end up languishing in the shade as young trees mature into giants. Perhaps the deep-green foliage of a loblolly pine growing on the north side of your house now looks dreary against the dark brick and leaves your entryway in gloomy shadows. Or a big red oak has crowded against an equally large ash tree, causing both to take on misshapen forms.

And then a storm comes along and cleans the slate.

In these and many other cases, once the initial shock is over and you have a chance to survey your altered landscape more objectively, the loss of a large anchor plant might be viewed as a plus.

Landscape Updating

More often than not, a mature tree or shrub that was severely damaged or killed by an extreme-weather event was not in the best condition prior to its demise, whether because of age, poor maintenance, or disease. Or perhaps the specimen was reasonably healthy but happened to be of a ubiquitous species such as Bradford pear or red-tipped photinia, which you viewed as outdated or boring.

In these and a host of other scenarios, the loss of a major tree or shrub now can be your gain down the road as you plan your landscape restoration, not the least of which can be upping the value or marketability of your property. Even if you replace deceased plants with the same species, new cultivars and varieties often have higher replacement-value ratings and are more disease resistant, which can enhance both the worth and the enjoyment of your landscape and real estate.

Welcoming Change

I don't think anybody would necessarily go out and cut down a 300-year-old tree, or even a 40-year-old tree. But if a storm takes out that tree, then you definitely have the opportunity to inject some of your personal taste and personality into your landscape. Maybe you always wanted an American elm, as opposed to the red maple that was killed. Or you inherited a white-flowering crabapple and you always wanted a pink-flowering dogwood. Or you wanted a water feature but didn't have room. The loss of the tree has become an opportunity instead of a constraint.

Growers are constantly improving upon varieties. The American elm is a stellar example. As a young kid, I have fond memories of the arching branches of huge American elm trees providing a cathedral effect over the streets of Chicago. But in the 1960s and '70s, these trees were almost completely purged from major metropolitan areas by the ravages of Dutch elm disease. Now American elms are making a comeback as new introductions are being made, in large part because of the work of the Morton Arboretum in Lisle, Illinois.

Also, technology can lead us to plant materials that help solve modern problems. Trees sequester and store huge amounts of carbon, helping to alleviate problems associated with greenhouse gases. A recent study by Purdue University has shown that the American chestnut possesses inherent characteristics that cause it to absorb and store more carbon than most other trees. And breeders are diligently working to develop tree-species substitutes that do not suffer from anthracnose, emerald ash borer, and other modern ailments.

Dean Hill

As our lives evolve over the years, so can our landscape needs. Children trade in sandboxes and swing sets for basketball hoops, and then go off to college and lives of their own, leaving empty nests. Or we trade in busy careers for retirement, which allows more time for outdoor cookouts and gardening. But as our lives have evolved, shade trees have grown and grown, leaving no room for the desired patio extension, or no sunlight for the food garden that we have always wanted and for which we now have time.

Making major landscape alterations when mature trees and shrubs stand in the way can entail the horticultural equivalent of knocking down walls when remodeling a house: most homeowners simple cannot bring themselves to take down a 60-foot sugar maple tree to make room for a koi pond or swing set. So whatever stage your family might be in, the loss of one or more major specimens can provide just the opportunity you need to redesign your landscape to better fit your evolving lifestyle. And there is no better time to develop a holistic plan for your redesigned green space.

What Is a Holistic Landscape?

A holistic landscape combines form and function within the context of your geographical location (be it in a rural community or an urban environment), the architecture of your house, the character of your neighborhood, your current lifestyle, and your personality.

Whether your vision for your landscape involves a casual design or a formal sculpted look, taking a holistic approach does not necessarily require significant monetary, human, or natural resources. As an example: creating and maintaining an acre and a half of primped turf grass requires a substantial investment of money, toil, chemicals, and water, while the resources needed to grow a native prairie of the same size are at the opposite end of the spectrum.

Native plants that have adapted to your local soil and climate—including your common extreme-weather events—are an integral part of the holistic approach, along with such key elements as Integrated Pest Management, organic fertilizers, and perhaps even a rain-collection system.

A well-designed, well-maintained holistic landscape enhances your real estate values, meets your evolving lifestyle needs, and has the best chance to stand up to nature's worst tantrums.

The Importance of Design

The sudden loss of big-ticket anchor plants can leave your landscape with major holes that you probably had never anticipated. And just as probable, you will feel a powerful sense of urgency to fill those empty spaces.

Do not rush!

Replacement trees and shrubs require many years to mature, so waiting a few extra weeks or months while you carefully deliberate over the right species and placement will make no significant difference to their size in the long run.

When considering major replacements of specimens or changes in your landscape design, the best advice is to *get* advice. Taking advantage of a professional's expertise and experience can be the best and fastest way to find out what options are available so you can take advantage of the best of them. Whether you consult with a landscape architect or designer, or simply curl up with a stack of books on landscaping and arboriculture, the care that you put into planning every detail of the changes you want to make is an important investment in the future durability, value, and attractiveness of your landscape.

On the other hand, if you work in a vacuum without a precise, knowledgeable plan for restoring your damaged landscape, you will be susceptible to leaping at whatever quick fixes might come your way. In desperation, you might grab a likely-looking replacement tree from your local home-improvement center, only to discover down the road that your choice is just as vulnerable to the ice or drought or wind conditions that destroyed its predecessor—perhaps even more so. Or you might rush to fill the yawning empty space left by your toppled red oak with a similar species, never recognizing the opportunity to plant a dwarf peach orchard that could complement your food-garden hobby.

When destruction from extreme weather or some other specimen-killing event brings opportunity knocking, a comprehensive landscape design can serve a number of important functions.

Problem Solving

Perhaps the loss of a major specimen created potential erosion problems or eliminated shade for your house or a bed of shade-loving hydrangeas. Or your landscape was damaged by a flood or wildfire that could recur. Or the plants you lost were high maintenance, and you want replacements that will better fit your busy schedule and limited budget. Devising a comprehensive landscape design that will solve potential or existing problems before you stick a spade in the ground can save you both time and money in the long term.

Eye-Appealing Scale and Balance

How you arrange tree and shrub specimens is just as important to your landscape as the placement of your furniture is to the ambience of your living room: get it wrong, and the whole design looks and feels out of balance.

But unlike a couch or armoire that maintains its same dimensions as it ages, large landscape specimens can go from carry-me-home-in-your-arms size to

A well-designed landscape can be attractive, low maintenance, and tolerant of extreme-weather events. Courtesy of Greg Rubin/California's Own Native Landscape Design.

shade-the-entire-backyard stature as time goes by. The pint-sized arborvitae shrub that looked so cute at the nursery matures into a monster that eats your front steps. The young oak planted smack in the middle of your modest front yard makes the house look less significant with each passing year of growth. Unfortunately, there is no amount of pruning that can correct that skewed balance once the plants are established.

These and countless other mistakes can be avoided by not choosing or purchasing new plants until you have drawn up a comprehensive landscape design that takes into account their mature sizes.

Planned Evolution

The removal of large trees and shrubs opens up opportunities to redesign your landscape so it can be repeatedly adapted to serve evolving needs as children grow up or lifestyles change. The former site of a large oak tree might be the perfect location for a sunny play area that could easily convert to a food garden or mini-orchard once the kids outgrow their sandbox and slide. Or the landscape design can evolve in step with the growth of a young replacement tree as a sunny play area gradually transforms into a summer shade garden beneath the wide boughs of a maturing burr oak.

Lower Maintenance

With today's busy schedules, the trend is moving rapidly away from conventional high-maintenance landscape designs and toward more eco-friendly native plants and technologies. If nature has presented you with an opportunity to make wholesale changes, now is the ideal time to redesign your green space to conserve dwindling water resources, reduce or eliminate mowing, and cut back on the time you must spend on maintenance chores—while increasing the time you have available for enjoying your more carefree landscape!

Staged Installation

You and/or your landscape-design professional can devise a plan that enables you to install trees, shrubs, and other elements in stages over several seasons or years as your time and budget allow.

Because large specimens take a long time to mature, you will want to give them a head start on the rest of the landscape, so a staged installation usually entails planting the most important replacement trees and shrubs first.

Keep in mind that just because you hire a professional to help design your landscape does not mean you also have to hire him to do the actual work. In fact, you can request as many do-it-yourself construction and installation jobs in the design as you please, arranging for the professional to do only what is beyond your ability or desire to do. For example, to save time and sweat you might want to hire out the arduous job of removing turf from a large new tree bed, while you handle installation of the border and mulch, and even plant the new tree.

Can I Improve the Value or Marketability of My Real Estate with Replacement Plants?

In terms of value and eye appeal, nothing can fully take the place of a healthy 60-foot Shumard oak that was shattered by lightning or drowned in a 100-year flood—at least, not for many decades. But in most cases, a healthy specimen can weather the tempest without suffering fatal injuries. Trees and shrubs killed by extreme-weather events tend to be those that were either the wrong species for your climate, were being grown in stressful conditions, or were in less than peak form at the time of the disaster. All those conditions and more have been covered in earlier chapters.

But when the damage has been done and it comes time to choose replacement plants, yes, there are strategies that you can use to improve the eye appeal of your landscape as well as the value and marketability of your real estate.

Do Not Plant Cookie-Cutter Species

Home-improvement centers sell Bradford pears, red-tipped photinias, and other popular, usually inexpensive tree and shrub species by the truckload each spring. For the most part, buyers of these overused and often inappropriate plants get exactly what they pay for: a wallet-friendly thrill that wears like a pair of cheap shoes.

Opting for a higher-value species will give your landscape less of a cookie-cutter appearance. And if chosen wisely, the tree or shrub will stand up better to extreme-weather events, increasing the chance that you will not have to go out shopping for yet another replacement.

Do Select Larger Transplants

The larger the tree or shrub that you install, the sooner it will be of value to your real estate. A tree with a two-inch caliper, or a small shrub sold in a gallon container, is easy on the budget. But when compared to a tree with a four-inch caliper, or a large shrub in a five-gallon container, the smaller planting stock will initially appear minuscule in the landscape.

Still, there are tradeoffs: a younger tree will recover from transplant shock sooner, and will eventually catch up with the larger tree. So the size of plants you choose can be influenced by whether you are taking a short or long view.

Do Not Impulse Shop

Do your research before you hit the garden centers. Identify from one to three likely species of trees or shrubs (including the size and variety, such as "Siberian" elm or "Norway" maple) that would be suitable for a specific site and purpose. Then shop around to find the best quality and price for those species only.

If you fall in love with a plant that is not on your list, *wait*. Go home and carefully research the plant, including how it will fit into your landscape at maturity, before plunking down your money; otherwise, you might have the opportunity and cause to fall out of love with it after the plant has become an established part of your landscape.

Selecting Replacement Plants for Extreme Weather

Once a landscape has been trashed by an extreme-weather event, the natural response is to think, "I never want to go through that again"—especially if trees have compounded the damage by falling onto structures or vehicles.

A Case in Point

After Hurricane Katrina's winds and floods brought large trees crashing down on houses in New Orleans, many of the traumatized homeowners resisted replacing their landscape trees for fear that they too would eventually grow to represent a threat.

But trees are a major part of the intricate tapestry of natural rural and urban environments, of which we all are an inseparable part. Particularly in New Orleans, with its long tradition of tree-shaded avenues and magnolia-scented evenings, the restoration of its devastated urban forest is recognized by civic leaders and mental health experts alike as being a crucial element in the long and arduous process of restoring public peace of mind as well as regaining the city's unique identity.

On the other hand, extreme weather has an ugly way of repeating itself, and even what were heretofore considered to be 100- and 500-year weather events are occurring with greater frequency in some areas. This makes the selection of more durable and less weather-vulnerable replacement plants all the more important.

Before choosing a replacement tree or shrub, consider what types of extreme-weather events your community and region have experienced not just in the past 5 or 10 years, but for the past 25 years or longer. Old-timers still might be talking about "the great wind of '43" or "the drought of '52." Listen to them! Or if you are new to your area, check with your local Cooperative Extension office to find out about historical weather extremes. Or you might even talk with local television meteorologists, who are in the business of covering major weather events.

Let's say you find that your locale has a history of fairly placid weather except for frequent droughts. In that case, you can pretty much ignore issues of ice or flood tolerance and focus on finding replacement species that are drought tolerant. But if your area was subjected to limb-snapping heavy snow in 1979, destructive winds in 1982 and 1997, major ice storms in 2000 and 2005, record-setting rainfall in 2007—and last year's grinding drought killed your silver-maple tree—you will need to look for multitalented species that are best able to tolerate all of those conditions.

In addition, depending on its location, your choice might need to be capable of withstanding extreme-weather conditions created by microclimates that are unique to your landscape, such as extreme heat near a west-facing brick wall or deep snowdrifts against the north side of your house.

And last but not least, while meeting all those important weather-related criteria, your choice of tree or shrub should be appropriate to fill an aesthetic and/or utilitarian need in the overall landscape design as it matures.

When juggling all those balls, trying to make the right choice of plant for the right place, avoid simply taking the advice of so-called experts at a discount or home-improvement-center nursery. Chances are they will simply recommend one of the standard, often-inappropriate cookie-cutter species that they have on hand.

Because specimen trees and shrubs can have such long-term significance to the appearance and value of your real estate, talk with a true expert, such as:

a certified or registered consulting arborist
a landscape architect
your local Cooperative Extension agent
tree growers and nurserymen, especially those who specialize in species
    native to your area

These experts can help you compile a list of suitable plants from which you can narrow down the choices, depending on your needs.

Once you have chosen the most suitable species, your next most important step is selecting the best individual nursery plant. Look for a young tree with a straight stem that is thicker at the bottom than at the top, and a single, sturdy central leader. A shrub should have sturdy stems and be well shaped all the way around, rather than having a good side and a bad side. Evergreens should have full, healthy-looking foliage. *Note: Give the plant a little jiggle. If it feels loose in the container, it might be a holdover from last year that has been recently repotted. Also, heavily lopped-back stems are a dead giveaway that the plant is a holdover that failed to sell. These plants are often sold at low, low cost, but are not bargains at any price.*

Should I Look to the Short Term or Long Term?

Whether your property is on the market or soon will be can make a big difference in how you approach the issue of replacing lost specimens, especially important anchor plants. But first, there might be something you need to get over.

Let's call it the Phantom Tree. When a large specimen is lost, its presence can linger in your imagination for months afterward, like a giant hologram in the landscape. But if all traces of the unfortunate specimen have been removed, including the stump, the absence of even a major tree or shrub will not necessarily hurt the salability of your real estate. In fact, any prospective buyer probably will not even notice anything is missing.

Why? Because you are the only one who "sees" the hologram!

Face it: if prospective buyers are from outside your community, or even outside your neighborhood, they probably never knew the missing specimen was there in the first place. So for the short-term purposes of marketing your property, forget about the plant that was. You need only concern yourself with sprucing up the area where the missing tree or shrub once stood.

There are any number of ways that you can fill the footprint left by a large specimen, such as by installing a replacement plant on the same site, planting groundcovers, or filling the vacated bed with mulch and colorful annuals or perennials. Toss in a park bench or birdbath, and voila, in place of your missing shade tree you have a sun garden that looks like an established part of the landscape.

This sort of quick fix might be all you require for a long-term restoration as well. What you consider to be the proper décor of you landscape is, after all, a matter of taste and function. But a quick fix does not have to involve inappropriate choices when it comes to choosing replacement trees and shrubs.

In your haste to fill a suddenly yawning empty space, you might be tempted to pick a fast-growing species. Take a deep breath and back away from that temptation. Among the many downsides of the fast crowd is that many such species are highly susceptible to storm damage, their root systems often are invasive, and they tend to be so short lived that they might have to be replaced within as few as 15 or 20 years.

By contrast, slower-growing species tend to be structurally sturdier—making them more tolerant of extreme-weather conditions—and longer lived, and as a result often carry a higher replacement-value rating, making them a greater asset to your real estate.

But if you do opt for a fast-growing tree or shrub, at least make sure the species is suitable for your locale and soil and that it is tolerant of the forms of extreme-weather events that are most common to your area.

How Can I Correct Old Landscape Shortcomings?

The empty space left when one or more specimens are removed presents an excellent opportunity to solve problems that have kept your landscape from filling your functional needs or being the real estate asset that it could be.

If the size of the big sycamore tree overpowered your backyard at the same time its root system invaded your sewer pipes, you can fix that now by replacing it with a ginkgo or some other smaller, more orderly species. But your problem-solving prospects can extend well beyond just swapping out a tree or shrub. You can tackle a wide array of challenges.

Wet Areas

The easiest way to deal with a low-lying, chronically wet area of your landscape is to turn it into a rain garden. By embracing your miniwetland—which might include planting a bald cypress or other swamp-loving species—you can take advantage of your rain garden's ability to accept and hold runoff from heavy rains.

A landscape architect or designer can transform your wet spot from a negative to a positive, either by installing an attractive rain garden or by designing one that can be constructed by a do-it-yourselfer. (To find out more about creating a rain garden, check Resources in appendix III.)

Water Rationing

Permanent water restrictions are in the cards for property owners throughout much of the Southwest, and rationing is a periodic occurrence in many other

Coastal live oaks with an understory of native grass are tolerant of their region's extreme weather as well as being a good combination for promoting ecological health. Courtesy of Marion Brenner Photography/American Society of Landscape Architects.

parts of the country. The time has never been better for replacing trees and shrubs lost in an extreme-weather event with drought-tolerant species such as manzanita (*Arctostaphylos*) or chaste tree (*Vitex agnus-castus*).

At the same time, you might take the opportunity to replace water-guzzling turf grasses with less thirsty native plants, including native grasses.

Noise or Unsightly View

A carefully designed green barrier can filter street noise and block undesirable views while lending a sense of privacy and seclusion to your property. But a conventional spirea or photinia hedge is not necessarily the best solution because, as you might have discovered in the wake of an extreme-weather event, the loss of a single shrub in the row can cause difficult and costly replacement problems.

Welcoming Change

When faced with damage, I suggest that you take a hard look at what you want from your hedge. In today's American garden, a hedge is an excellent technique for providing a sense of privacy and seclusion with dynamic, living plants rather than with fences or walls. Unfortunately, besides its being a major maintenance undertaking, disease, pests, and severe-weather events can diminish or destroy its initial design intent if one or more of its components is damaged or killed.

If you are faced with such a situation, first ask yourself if the original intent of the hedge still exists. For instance, was the hedge designed to screen off a view of a neighbor's porch or a nearby road? If not, then perhaps the hedge does not need to be restored at all.

But if restoration is in order, you do not necessarily have to replace destroyed plants with the same material. Plantings are typically more interesting when grown in combinations, and the mix can reduce the monolithic look of a large hedge. For example, let's say you had an eight-foot-tall arborvitae hedge that has "lost a tooth." You might consider filling the void with a Black Hills spruce or a Colorado blue spruce. Or if you had a ten-foot-tall hedge of Japanese yew that suffered ice damage, you might consider using a southern or sweet bay magnolia, or even a grouping of Burkwood's viburnum.

The point is, take a look at the damaged hedge and reevaluate the situation. There are an infinite number of possibilities that can be explored in order to restore the function of the original privacy hedge.

Dean Hill

High Energy Costs

A landscape that substantially reduces the cost of heating and cooling a house is both a budget saver and a serious marketing tool. To achieve that, replacement plants need to be chosen with the summer and winter exposure of your house in mind.

For example, if your drought-killed spruce tree had shaded a sunny-side window throughout the year, you might replace it with a maple or other deciduous species that can provide shade during the heat of summer but allow sunlight in throughout winter. Or you could replace ice-damaged deciduous shrubs on the north side of your house with cold-hardy evergreens that provide natural insulation against frigid winter winds.

Drab Look

A mono-color (all green) landscape can look boring regardless of how lush and healthy it might be. In the aftermath of a landscape-trashing natural disaster, you have an opportunity to replace lost specimens with species that add splashes of color throughout the years.

Disease-resistant varieties of crabapple deck the landscape in pink blooms in spring. Numerous colors of crape myrtle put on a show all summer long and can be pruned into a multistemmed tree habit to reveal attractive peeling bark. For fall color, some deciduous species such as red oak, hickory, and sourwood are famed for their colorful foliage. And let's not overlook shrubs such as holly and *Nandina* that sport bright berries all winter—though *Nandina* is invasive in Florida and should be removed there.

Not Productive

For food gardeners, replacing one large tree with a mini-orchard can provide added value to the landscape by producing bushels of apples, peaches, oranges (in warm-winter areas), and other fruits. Dwarf and semidwarf trees fit nicely into most landscapes. Larger acreages can accommodate standard-size fruit trees as well as stately pecan, walnut, and other nut bearers. *Note: Dwarf trees often set their first crops within two or three years, while standards can take up to seven years to begin bearing. And nut trees favor deep soil.*

Too Urban

Even city landscapes can seem less so when butterflies, birds, and other wildlife populate the shrubs and trees. You can attract a surprising variety of critters by replacing lost specimens with tree and shrub species that provide forage and habitat for wildlife.

To create a wildlife-friendly landscape, it is important to lay out a continuous "stair step" of trees, shrubs, and groundcovers so birds, insects, and other wild things can move freely around your landscape without straying far from protective cover. If possible, connect your landscape layout with your neighbors' to extend the protective cover still farther.

When nature wreaks havoc in the landscape, nothing is more uplifting during the restoration process than the melodious trill of a songbird at dawn. But the loss of trees and shrubs can be devastating to local and migratory wildlife. Providing nesting boxes and feeding stations for birds that have lost some of their precious habitat can help to ensure their continued presence in your landscape while replacement trees or shrubs grow to size.

To bring the natural world back into your life, check out the many books available on how to create a thriving backyard wildlife habitat (one is listed in Recommended Reading in appendix III).

How Can I Keep from Repeating This Same Disaster?

The truth is that there is no foolproof way to totally protect your valuable landscape from the most extreme acts of nature such as powerful tornadoes, or monster winter storms that can crush even robust specimens under tons of frozen stuff.

But most extreme-weather events do not reach that level of destruction. And as we have seen, the best way to prevent a landscape disaster is to install tree and shrub species that are best adapted to withstand extreme-weather events common to your location—and then maintain those plants with proper watering, pruning, and other measures to keep them as vigorous and robust as possible.

With such preventive landscape design and maintenance, you can avert, or at least greatly reduce, damage from most extreme-weather events.

Are There Environmental Considerations?

Oh, yes. For example, if you plant an eastern red cedar in parts of the country where it has become a noxious pest of the highest order, you are only contributing to a rapidly growing ecological disaster. But if you plant noninvasive tree and shrub species that are native to your area, you will be increasing the extreme-weather tolerance of your landscape without the negative aspects inherent to exotic plants.

Plants that are pests in one area of the country are not necessarily so in another region. So before planting, always check with your local Cooperative Extension office to make sure that the species of your choice is not on a Noxious

Plants list for your area. This is especially important if you plan to mail-order trees or shrubs.

Potential Mistakes with Replacement Plants

By now, you already know most potential mistakes that you can make when replacing lost trees and shrubs. But let's review them in brief.

Wrong Species

Each tree and shrub species has its own desired range of growing conditions. If a plant is grown outside that range, it will be less healthy and robust, making it more vulnerable to extreme-weather events and pathogens that it might otherwise be able to withstand.

But some specimens that are grown under even the most desirable of conditions are just naturally more susceptible to damage from one or more types of extreme weather. So while matching a plant to your hardiness zone, soil, and landscape needs, also keep in mind its durability under your worst potential weather conditions.

Wrong Location

Just because a tree formerly grew in a certain location does not mean this is a good site for its replacement. In fact, it might not necessarily have been the ideal site for the original tree. Placing specimens in ill-chosen locations can actually reduce their value to your real estate and in some cases even damage the plants' health. For instance, growing crape myrtle so close to the house that air cannot circulate properly can result in chronic powdery mildew problems in humid conditions.

If you are not prepared to hire a professional to properly place your important trees and shrubs, at least study up on landscape design before breaking out your spade.

Wrong "Story"

Species such as dogwood and Japanese laceleaf maple are *understory* trees, meaning that in nature they flourish in the protective, mottled shade of taller trees. When planted in isolation on an open lawn, or against unshaded south walls where they are exposed to the reflected heat of the summer sun, they must struggle to survive during the hottest months. Likewise, *top-story* trees accustomed to unfiltered sunlight will languish if grown in the shade of larger specimens.

Wrong Size

When you spotted the cute little red oak sapling at the nursery last fall, its colorful foliage made it seem like a terrific accent plant for your smallish backyard. But given time to mature, the oak eventually will come to resemble Godzilla, distressingly out of scale with the rest of your landscape. Every tree and shrub that you introduce to your property should be chosen and located with its mature size and mature shape in mind.

Overhead power lines also should be a consideration. When New Orleans lost most of its urban forest to flooding from Hurricane Katrina, efforts were made to replace large trees such as old-fashioned magnolias that had grown into the power lines with smaller-stature species such as Japanese magnolias and crape myrtles. If you are given a choice, opt for trees that reach no more than 20 feet at maturity if overhead lines are an issue.

How Do I Properly Space a Young Replacement Tree?

If your sugar maple sent limbs crashing down onto your roof during a storm, the tree was growing too close to your house for safety. In that case, you have two options when installing its replacement: you can either plant a species that will be smaller at maturity, or you can plant another sugar maple–size species but locate it farther away from structures. To do the latter, simply:

- Determine the mature crown diameter of the selected tree species. To find this out, consult an arborist, nurseryman, or your Cooperative Extension agent or urban forester, or go online.
- Divide the crown diameter in half to get the radius, then measure that distance from your house to the proposed safe-distance planting site. If this positions the tree too close to a driveway, your neighbor's house, or other vulnerable structures, you might want to go ahead and opt for a smaller species.

Note: Often, an established tree or shrub can be trained to a somewhat smaller size with a regular pruning program. (You knew we would say it again: Topping the plant should never be a part of that program!) But annual or biannual reduction pruning can keep the specimen from attaining its appealing natural shape. And if the reduction is severe, it can cause serious stress to the plant, possibly increasing its vulnerability to extreme-weather events. So when selecting a species for a specific site, it is always better to match the plant's natural mature size to the space.

My New Replacement Trees and Shrubs Look Minuscule!

A young would-be specimen planted in the footprint of a fallen giant can seem to disappear in the landscape. But there are a number of things that you can do to make replacement plants appear more significant in their early years. Just remember that design is critical before the purchase is made and the first shovelful of dirt is excavated.

- Locate a young tree or shrub in a spacious planting bed filled with mulch, annual or perennial flowers, and a bench, birdbath, or other pieces of ornamental "furniture." As the plant grows, the extras can be gradually removed as they become less necessary for visual effect.
- Make the mulched planting bed the size of the *mature* specimen's future drip line. The tree will eventually shade out sun-loving turf grass anyway, and creating a large bed now will make the young tree appear more like a gem in its setting, reduce competition for soil nutrients and water, and eliminate the tree-stunting effects of some types of turf grass.
- If you want to downsize when replacing your 60-foot sugar maple or ash, but you still have its large footprint to fill, consider planting a grouping of 20- to 25-foot-tall dogwoods, hawthorns, or other smaller-stature species. Or a grouping of trees and shrubs, with the tallest in the center, stepping down to smaller species—an arrangement that also provides better wind resistance. Consult a landscape architect or designer, nurseryman, or Cooperative Extension agent for proper arrangement and spacing, as well as the best species options for your location.
- Simply invest in a larger replacement plant. A four-inch-caliper Shumard oak or an eight-foot-tall crape myrtle looks less minuscule right away and will reach substantial size years faster than a tree or shrub that you can bring home in the trunk of your car.
- If your budget allows, you might consider an even larger replacement that requires special equipment for transplanting such as a truck-mounted hydraulic spade and a backhoe. But expect to provide extra irrigation and care for several years to establish this tree, especially if there are droughts. *Note: There are no industry-wide standards for the cost of transplanting large trees, and the range can vary widely depending on supply and demand. So you need to survey established, reputable local tree services and compare costs, guarantees that the transplanted specimen will survive, and whether the service is insured against collateral damage to your property. Request references and check them out, bearing in mind that the service is unlikely to provide you with the names of unsatisfied clients.*

What If My Landscape Itself Is Minuscule?

Larger and larger houses are being built on smaller and smaller lots these days. Often these diminutive landscapes have not been professionally designed, and the trees or shrubs that the builder or previous owners planted have grown completely out of scale for the size of the property. So your destroyed 50-foot red maple might have turned glorious colors in the fall, but throughout summer it cast a deep shade that left your entire backyard looking gloomy and cramped. Now is your chance to open your landscape to the sun.

What's more, some landscapes can be too small to reasonably accommodate the expansive root systems of almost any tree, especially if the space is constricted by concrete patios, foundations, retaining walls, or other barriers. Indeed, the loss of your tree during an extreme-weather event might have been at least partially the result of restricted roots.

So before making a replacement choice that might tempt history to repeat itself, it is important to examine the soil-space potential, as well as to consider your specific needs.

Welcoming Change

Keep in mind that no matter how small the landscape, there is the perfect plant for your needs, and your job is to find out which one it is. The best place to start is by asking yourself a couple of questions.

Your first question should *always* be, "How tall do I want the tree or shrub to be ultimately?" The next is, "Do I want the plant to bloom or not?" Bear in mind that most plants that bloom also produce fruit—if that does not suit your purposes, be sure to look for fruitless varieties.

Next, you should be clear about what you want the tree to do. Provide shade for a patio? Provide protection and a food source for wildlife? Hold a tire swing? Block out a nosy neighbor? The more questions you ask yourself, the shorter your selection list will become.

Dean Hill

What If My Landscape Is Entirely Too Minuscule?

In small spaces, not all of your options necessarily include a tree. For example, a vine-covered pergola could provide just the needed amount of shade for a patio or entryway. Or a tall shrub tucked neatly against a fence or wall might provide bird habitat without requiring the space of a tree.

Healing a Bruised Bank Account

The care you put into selecting and protecting valued landscape specimens—and rehabilitating or replacing them in the aftermath of an extreme-weather event—is a vital part of maintaining the aesthetic appeal and overall worth of your real estate. But the health and well-being of your trees and shrubs prior to their being damaged can also make a difference when it comes to weather-related insurance claims and tax deductions, as you will see in chapter 11.

11

Landscape Insurance and Tax Breaks

If you wait until after your big-ticket landscape specimens have suffered severe damage before examining the fine print in your homeowner's insurance policy, you might be in for an unpleasant surprise. Most standard policies seriously limit coverage for trees and shrubs, if they cover them at all.

Sooner rather than later, you should discuss landscape coverage with your insurance agent so you will know what to expect should extreme weather wreak havoc on your prized plants. This is especially important if you live in Tornado Alley, the Ice and Snow Belt, or along a hurricane-threatened coastline. Likewise, it's crucial if your corner of the world is prone to wildfires or suffers from chronic drought conditions.

Prior Coverage Is Not Always a Reliable Indicator of Where You Stand Right Now

If you have changed your insurance carrier or moved from another state or region, do not take it for granted that your new homeowner's insurance policy will provide the same coverage as your former policy. Policies can vary markedly in their detail, so do specifically check out the landscape coverage whenever you move to a new location or change your insurance carrier.

But whether you are trying to plan ahead or a severe-weather event has already taken down the big pine tree in your front yard, you probably will want answers to a number of questions, such as the ones that follow.

How Well Does My Standard Homeowner's Insurance Policy Cover Landscape Losses from Severe Weather?

According to the Insurance Information Institute, a typical homeowner's policy covers weather-related landscape damage that is caused by fire or lightning. Period. Though coverage can vary depending on the carrier, payout is usually $250 per lost tree or shrub, with a maximum of $1,000 for the entire landscape. *Note: You are probably out of luck if the fire in your barbecue pit gets out of control and chars your honey locust tree.*

If frozen stuff, high winds, or some other extreme-weather event causes a tree to fall onto your house, your policy should pay to remove the tree from the house and repair structural damage to your abode—after you have paid the policy's deductible, of course.

On the other hand, if a tree or limb falls on your vehicle, the costs of repair or replacement of the vehicle are covered under the comprehensive portion of your auto insurance policy—assuming that you have comprehensive coverage—not under your homeowner's policy. In the absence of comprehensive automobile coverage, you are out of luck.

But if it was your neighbor's tree that crushed your ride and you have comprehensive coverage, your insurance carrier might try to collect damages from

Do you have the right insurance to cover a situation like this? Courtesy of Joseph O'Brien, USDA Forest Service, Bugwood.org.

your neighbor. If your carrier is successful, you could be reimbursed for the deductible that you paid.

Again, do not take anything for granted—check both your homeowner's and auto insurance policies to clarify exactly what coverage you do have.

But What about the Tree or Shrub Itself?

A basic homeowner's insurance policy will not cover tree or shrub repair, removal, or replacement costs. In effect, with a basic insurance policy, you have a small death benefit for your specimen—if that—but no medical or burial coverage.

Can I Get Insurance Coverage for My Big-Ticket Specimens?

For an additional premium, some insurance companies offer endorsements (also known as riders) to cover the landscape specimens themselves. Such endorsements can cover up to 5 percent of the insured value of a house. So if your house is insured for $500,000, the endorsement can cover up to $25,000 in damage to the landscape—but no more than $1,000 per tree or shrub.

Not all insurance companies offer endorsements covering landscape specimens, so you might have to shop around to find one. And such endorsements generally do not include flood damage. If you live in a designated flood-prone area, you will need to obtain a National Flood Insurance policy, available through the Federal Emergency Management Agency (see appendix III).

Annual premiums for landscape endorsements can range from $5 to $18 per $1,000 of coverage. Do the math: if you have five trees with an appraised worth of at least $1,000 each, insuring all five can cost around $50 to $180 per year. If all five trees were destroyed, you would receive a $5,000 payout, less the deductible. Even though the cost of premiums adds up year after year whether or not damage occurs, you might come out ahead with added coverage if:

- You have high-value, high-quality specimens that are key elements in the overall landscape design, and their damage or loss would cause a significant decrease in the fair market value of your real estate. Keep in mind that robust, well-maintained trees and shrubs that are pest- and disease-free commonly suffer far less damage than do weak plants—and plants that are in poor condition are not usually insurable. But no amount of preventive care and maintenance can totally protect a tree or shrub from a catastrophic ice storm, wildfire, or powerful hurricane winds.
- Your trees and shrubs serve an important utilitarian purpose on your property, such as erosion control, visual or sound buffering, energy

savings, or protection for a valuable shade garden. Should such specimens be lost, you might want to purchase the largest replacement plants possible in order to restore the hole in your landscape as quickly as you can. An insurance payment could help take some of the sting out of the costly cleanup and restoration effort.

- Your area experiences destructive extreme-weather events on a fairly regular basis. Your local Cooperative Extension agent or urban forester can be a good source of information on just how often large trees and shrubs in your community have been damaged by weather in the past.

But before opting for landscape insurance, you should find out the actual value of your landscape specimens. A certified or registered consulting arborist who specializes in valuating trees and shrubs can assess the health and vitality of your specimens and provide documentation of their replacement value. In addition, a landscape architect can evaluate the importance of each specimen to the overall landscape scheme, including its aesthetic and utilitarian importance. These assessments, coupled with an appraisal of your entire property, can determine what effect the loss of key specimens might have on the value or potential marketability of your real estate.

Even with all that information at your disposal, your ultimate decision as to whether you would benefit from adding landscape endorsements to your homeowner's insurance policy can be a roll of the dice. Weather is never predictable, and may be growing even less so as climate change continues to unfold. It's true that your landscape specimens could live many decades without suffering major damage from an extreme-weather event. But then again, tornadoes, hurricanes, floods, devastating ice storms and snowstorms, and drought-kindled wildfires have been known to strike the same areas over and over again.

So, as with any form of insurance coverage, the final decision as to whether or not taking out endorsements on landscape specimens is the right move for you might come down to peace of mind—and how you feel about the added premiums.

Can I Insure Just One Tree?

If you have a valuable specimen, say a ten-year-old cherry blossom, or a healthy tree that serves a vital purpose such as erosion control, some insurance carriers will offer an endorsement for that single tree. The endorsement premium is arrived at by assessing the age and condition of your tree and the cost of replacing it with something similar, though, of course, not with a tree of its maturity.

As long as you can document the value of your tree, there is no upper limit for an individual endorsement. So if you have a tree that has been valuated at

$4,000—or $40,000—you can get endorsement coverage for that entire amount if you can track down a willing insurance company and if you are willing to pay the premiums.

Are Landscape-Insurance Premiums Tax Deductible?

Nope. Not for homeowners, although business owners should discuss this with a tax expert since rules regarding deductibles are subject to change with the issuance of each new tax code.

Are Out-of-Pocket Landscape-Recovery Costs Tax Deductible?

The U.S. Internal Revenue Service sometimes does allow casualty-loss tax deductions for damage to big-ticket landscape plants if the damage or loss reflects a decrease in fair market value of the real estate as a whole, including the residence, land, and improvements.

There are two basic ways to come up with the figure as to how much the damage to your landscape has decreased your property values:

- You can have your entire property appraised for its fair market value following the damage, and compare that figure to a predisaster appraisal. *Note: If your property and its landscape have not been appraised for decades, this method might not necessarily provide an accurate reflection of how much worth the trees and shrubs had contributed to the overall fair market value of your real estate prior to their being damaged or destroyed.*
- Or you can use landscape cleanup and restoration costs, less insurance or any other compensation received, to estimate the decrease in the fair market value of your property. For this method, add up all the *landscape-only* cleanup and restoration costs resulting from the extreme-weather event, including tree and shrub repairs, debris removal, and plant replacement. These costs should be limited to the restoration of your landscape to its predisaster condition and no more. Any costs that increase the value of your landscape beyond its predisaster condition are not allowable.

If you intend to deduct the decrease in your property values incurred by landscape damage, you will need:

documentation of the original fair market value of your property
documentation of your property's postdisaster appraised value

On the other hand, if you plan to deduct expenses incurred in recovering from the landscape damage, you will need:

documentation of debris-removal costs

documentation of plant-replacement costs, including installation, to restore the landscape to its predisaster condition

Note: You cannot include the cost of any equipment purchased for the cleanup, such as chain saws, lopping shears, or brush shredders. In addition to the above documentation, you will need to declare any related payments you have received from your insurance carrier or other sources, such as for the removal of tree limbs from your roof.

Can I Deduct a Lost Oak Tree That an Arborist Appraised at $4,000?

Not directly—at least, not at the arborist's valuation. But if an appraisal of your entire property determines that the loss of your oak tree decreased the fair market value of your overall real estate, you can deduct the loss figure arrived at by the property appraiser.

So How Much Can I Declare?

When filing for landscape-related tax deductions, you will be declaring a casualty loss. According to the current U.S. Internal Revenue Service code, "total losses are deductible only to the extent that the total loss amount for the year exceeds 10 percent of adjusted gross income." Therefore, the damage to your residential landscape must involve a truly major loss to your overall real estate value, and your total itemized deductions for the year must be substantial (exceeding 10 percent of your adjusted gross income) in order for you gain a tax break from your disaster.

Also remember that tax codes change annually. To make sure that your landscape-damage deductions are allowable, and that you get the maximum permitted under the current code, take all documentation to your tax accountant.

What Proof of Damage Will I Need for Insurance or Tax Purposes?

Valuable landscape specimens are assets, just like your laptop computer or antique-watch collection. For both insurance and tax purposes, besides having your landscape appraised, you should break out your camera:

- Save photos of your big-ticket landscape plants every year or so. Plants constantly grow and evolve, so you will want to have a record of your landscape as near to predisaster as possible to compare with its condition in the wake of an extreme-weather event.
- If your neighbors have unhealthy trees that could fall onto your property, snap a few pictures of those too. And if one of those trees does eventually

fall, take long-range and close-up photos that clearly show any apparent wood rot or other signs of poor health.

- Immediately after a disaster strikes, photograph in detail all damage to trees and shrubs before the mess is cleaned up.
- If your property is flooded for an extended period—long enough to cause damage to specimens—take pictures before the water drains away.

File away your pre- and postdisaster landscape photos along with landscape appraisals, receipts for landscape repairs and restoration, and other documentation related to your property values. You might also include receipts for routine pruning and maintenance of landscape specimens as proof that they were well cared for predisaster. (These records are best kept in a safety deposit box or other off-site location where they will be secure from floods, fires, or other disasters.)

Your documentation could come in handy:

when making insurance claims, especially for specimens covered by endorsements

if the Internal Revenue Service questions a landscape-related tax deduction

if you need to go to court because your neighbor's rotten elm tree fell and took down your fence, two fruit trees, and the roof of your gazebo

How Long after My Landscape Loss Can I Wait to File for a Tax Deduction?

Casualty-loss claims should be filed with your income tax return for the year in which the damage took place.

Getting ahead of the Game

Both insurance and potential tax-deduction issues are best scoped out ahead of time. Then during the disarray that so often occurs when disaster strikes, you will know just how you should proceed with gathering documentation.

For example, unless you carry landscape endorsements on your homeowner's insurance policy, there is little point in phoning your insurance agent if your hickory tree blows over in a storm *unless* it lands on your house or some other insured structure. (But you will want to give your auto-insurance carrier a buzz if the tree lands on your vehicle, assuming that you have comprehensive coverage.)

And unless the demise of that hickory tree represents a substantial loss to the fair market value of your real estate—and even then, only if its loss and other deductions amount to more than 10 percent of your gross adjusted income—there probably is no point in badgering your tax accountant.

Note: Even if you do not believe your landscape damage is tax deductible, do save all related documentation and receipts. Then when it comes time to file your tax return, at least bring up the loss with your tax expert. As mentioned before, tax codes do change.

Self-Insurance

Another option to landscape insurance is to place the money you might have paid on premiums in a dedicated savings account to cover the cost of landscape-disaster recovery.

The Last Straw

From insurance claims to tax questions to the sickening wail of a chain saw, the devastation of an extreme-weather event can play havoc with your life—and not incidentally, with your emotions. The final chapter of this book might help *you* heal along with your landscape.

Healing the Heart

When nature unleashes her wrath upon your landscape, more than just plants, real estate values, and your bank account can take a hit. The loss of prized or cherished trees and shrubs can bludgeon you mentally and emotionally.

In extreme cases, violent-weather events can even result in Post Traumatic Stress Disorder (PTSD). And your natural disaster does not have to rank up there with Hurricane Katrina to leave you with PTSD. A major ice storm can bring tons of shattered wood crashing down with lethal force, the breakage sounding like cannon shots and making you feel as if you are in a war zone. And firestorms are horrifically Armageddon-like.

If a flood, hurricane, or other natural disaster is community wide or sprawls across an entire region, the scope of the destruction can be almost beyond your ability to comprehend. As one homeowner put it as he surveyed the devastation from an ice storm of catastrophic proportions, "It's like standing on the rim of the Grand Canyon. I just can't seem to get my mind wrapped around it."

Every major extreme-weather event begs comparisons. But no natural disaster in the United States within our lifetime surpasses the urban devastation wrought in New Orleans, Louisiana, by Hurricane Katrina in 2005. Boasting one of the greatest urban tree canopies in the country before the city's levees collapsed, some of its wards lost as much as 90 percent of their trees when flooding left them standing in salt water for two weeks. All the stately old magnolias were killed along Elysian Fields Avenue, a long corridor that stretches from Lake Pontchartrain down through the French Quarter, Gentilly, and the Seventh Ward.

The loss of even that many trees would seem to pale in comparison to the tragic loss of lives from that disaster. But whether along streets, in parks, or populating our own backyards, green and flowering trees and shrubs are a major part of the scenery of our lives. According to Jean Fahr, executive director of Parkway Partners in New Orleans, one of the things that hurt the most in Katrina's aftermath was the sudden "grayness of the city."

New Orleans is the most extreme of extreme cases. But from extreme-weather events great and small, countless landscapes across the country are regularly threatened with sudden grayness. Virtually every week, the evening news dishes up dramatic videos of natural disasters: wind-felled trees in New England; drought-abetted wildfires in the Southwest; overflowing rivers in the Midwest; hurricanes battering the Gulf Coast. In just one violent weekend in June of 2009, virtually every region of the country suffered some form of landscape-trashing extreme weather.

For those of us who do not have the misfortune of living in the affected communities, these events tend to be forgotten as soon as they drop out of the news cycle. But for locals who experienced the disaster firsthand and must deal with the aftermath, it is not that easy.

Damage to real estate values and marketability is just one disheartening consequence of an extreme-weather event. Along with the monetary cost of recovering a shattered landscape, a natural disaster can exact a toll that cannot be measured in dollars and cents. With the sudden, often savage loss of major specimens that might have been lovingly nurtured for many years, it is not uncommon for victims of major natural disasters to be plunged into a period of grief.

The empty space in the landscape that for decades, even generations, had been occupied by the grandfatherly stature of an old live oak tree or the graceful sprawl of an oleander shrub can find a companion emptiness within the homeowner. Because just as valued trees and shrubs are rooted in the textured reality of soil, so they can become rooted in an almost spiritual sense within us.

And their loss can feel visceral.

But whether or not you suffer actual grief, a severe storm might very well frighten the daylights out of you, and leave you with a lingering sense of anxiety.

The sound of big trees in their death throes, their limbs snapping and crashing to the ground under the stress of ice, snow, or high winds, can haunt you for weeks and months after the storm has passed. The fact that nothing can stop an extreme-weather event from recurring if the right conditions prevail hardly helps to calm your jangled nerves. Not as long as each new storm that rolls over your neighborhood continues to trigger a fresh adrenaline surge of anxiety.

Even when no serious attachment to the lost or damaged trees or shrubs exists, and you are not immediately worried about property-value issues, simply surveying a devastated landscape can be unsettling, to say the least. No one who has "been there" can deny that a single really bad extreme-weather event can create a god-awful mess.

But in the process of dealing with the physical lacerations to your landscape, you can also do things to help speed the healing of the psychological and emotional wounds inflicted on you.

Take Action

Aside from the obvious material losses, one of the worst aspects of a natural disaster is the pervasive sense that circumstances are beyond your control. At the outset, they very well might be. But you can move quickly to help alleviate that helpless feeling.

The best way to regain a sense of control is to take action: dive into the job of clearing away landscape debris, repairing damaged trees and shrubs, and removing plants that cannot be saved. If all or some of this work is beyond your physical abilities or expertise, the simple act of hiring qualified assistance can begin to move you forward out of the morass and into the process of restoring your peace of mind. *Note: Hiring inept "experts" or outright charlatans can end up driving your anxiety to new heights. So review chapter 6, Experts to the Rescue. Then take a slow, deep breath before making your calls.*

Once you actually begin taking action, what might have appeared to be an overwhelming scene of destruction can be transformed within a remarkably short period. Just clearing away fallen debris—bundling it at the curb for pickup or at least gathering it into piles—can start to bring order to the chaos. Having workmen on the site, or even being on their waiting list, can give you a sense that you are moving forward along a path that will eventually lead you out of the disaster.

In addition, taking swift and targeted action can help you overcome one of the most disturbing elements of a natural disaster: the fear that the destruction might not be over, and that the last limb might not yet have fallen. The sooner you can find an expert to stop the mulberry tree limbs from crashing down onto your roof or get the sycamore top off your power lines, the quicker your frazzled nerves will begin to settle down.

Into the Trenches

The December 2007 ice storm left my property buried under tons of danger-ously unstable debris. Shocked by the extent and suddenness of the devasta-tion—and rattled by large limbs that continued to crash onto the roof—I left an emergency phone message for my arborist, who was already inundated by similar calls from frantic clients. But because he had manicured our trees just two weeks earlier, the arborist gave our property high priority. He had the dan-gerous debris both on the ground and still in the shattered trees cleared away within a matter of days.

The felling and complete removal of all six of the fatally damaged trees took a couple of months, three different cutting crews, and multiple pickups by a city-contracted debris-hauling company. But those first several days of trans-forming the landscape from a Class 1 disaster zone to the point where it was safe to go outside again was a major step forward, both for our property and our psyches. By early spring, we were emotionally and physically ready to begin replanting.

Sandra Dark

Help Your Neighbors

"Misery loves company" might sound like just another trite saying, but when it comes to natural disaster there is nothing hackneyed about the value of sharing your shock and distress with others in practical ways. Why? For one thing, when an extreme-weather event encompasses an entire community or region, the initial aftermath of nature's worst can leave you feeling particu-larly isolated. That makes it almost impossible for you to put your loss into perspective.

So even if you have plenty of cleanup work to do on your own property, pausing to reach out and help a neighbor remove a tree limb from his driveway or rake up storm debris from her yard can help you to recognize that you are not alone in this. In the process, you might even discover that your personal catastrophe is not the worst in your community.

But reaching out can do more than just help you gain perspective. By extending

Dangerous tangle of debris left by an ice storm. Courtesy of Sandra Dark.

The same site less than a week later. Courtesy of Sandra Dark.

a helping hand to assist others who have suffered landscape destruction, you might obtain important word-of-mouth leads on experts, community programs, and other practical information that can help you deal with your damage. *Note: Word of mouth can be particularly helpful when power outages have limited your access to important sources of information. But beware of false rumors, which can run rampant under such conditions. Confirm and clarify information; for instance, if you hear that storm debris will be picked up at curbside, contact city officials to find out how it should be bundled, and how much volume you are allowed.*

Finally, reaching out provides you with opportunities to warn friends and neighbors against hiring nonexpert tree trimmers. Nonexperts and outright charlatans might top trees or perform other arboreal misdeeds that would add irreparable layers of man-made damage—and stress—to the natural disaster.

Into the Trenches

The December 2007 ice storm broke large limbs from trees in my sister's backyard and split the trunk of a river birch in her front yard. Anxious to get the damage repaired, she was tempted to hire a tree trimmer who had come knocking on doors in her storm-ravaged neighborhood, soliciting business from desperate homeowners for an exorbitant fee. Instead, we were able to steer her to our own arborist, who did quality work at a fair cost.

Sandra Dark

Look Farther down the Road

Extreme-weather events come in an infinite variety of sizes and conformations, from the powerful gust front that splits your Bradford pear tree in half to the deadly ice storm that leaves an enormous footprint of shattered wood across eight states. The worse the destruction, the more difficult it might be for you to see beyond the mess to a time when your property will not resemble the set of the latest disaster movie.

Therefore, the more extensive the damage, the more important it is to take the recovery process in stages, all the while keeping in mind that nature has the capacity to heal as well as to destroy. No matter how overwhelming the destruction in your yard might seem at the moment, taking the long view is one more way to put the disaster into perspective.

Your landscape recovery will include several primary stages.

The Cleanup

This might require just hours to remove the broken Bradford pear tree. Or it could take up to two or three months to clear away extensive debris from a major disaster if you are on a harried arborist's lengthy call list, or must wait for municipal crews to pick up debris at curbside. Establishing this period in your mind enables you to look past it to the next stages in your recovery period.

Repairing Specimens

This can—and in the case of plant-threatening damage, should—take place alongside the cleanup process. Once emergency repairs have been made, plants can begin their own healing process, which enables them *and you* to start moving forward together out of the disaster.

Restoration

Once the debris has been removed and emergency repairs are made, you can install replacement plants immediately, season and weather permitting, or begin the lengthier process of nursing damaged specimens back to health, which can require a period of several seasons. Because different plants in your landscape might have received varying degrees of damage from the same weather event, you might well have the satisfaction of seeing some specimens restored to a robust condition while others continue to convalesce.

In even the worst landscape disaster, appearances can change dramatically in a remarkably short period of time. Assuming that you are taking actions to bring about that change—beginning the cleanup process and calling in experts when needed—you should be able to look forward to some sense of order returning to your property within as little as a day or so. Even in extreme cases where it might take months for all the debris to be hauled away, just gathering the mess into piles can enable you to move on to the restoration stage.

Within a year or so after planting, your replacement trees and shrubs should be fairly well established. And while your new landscape specimens might take a decade or more to reach maturity, they will be growing steadily during that time, progressively refilling the space in your landscape and in your mind.

Into the Trenches

One year after my big mulberry tree was destroyed by an ice storm, a young oak was already established and thriving in its place. Though it will be many years before the replacement casts the broad circle of cooling shade that its somewhat ramshackle predecessor once did, the more storm-tolerant oak holds the promise of greater resistance to future extreme-weather events. And as if in anticipation of bigger things to come, mockingbirds sing from its twiggy branches.

Sandra Dark

Get Involved In Community Tree Planting

Nothing helps to ease the pain of losing a prized specimen quite like planting a new generation. However hard you work to control and manipulate your landscape, nothing changes the fact that your trees and shrubs are a part of the natural environment, subject to nature's inevitable cycles and at times chaotic whims.

Each tree in your landscape or community is a part of the urban or rural forest, with its own role to play in the environment. So planting new trees and shrubs can help to keep you in touch with the big picture, as well as your own role in the tumultuous, ever-evolving majesty of our planet.

Keith G. Tidball, associate director of the Initiative for Civic Ecology at Cornell University, studies the role of people's relationship to nature in their ability to recover from disaster, especially regarding how community-level greening efforts following conflicts or disasters contribute to their social and ecological resilience: "My research suggests that after sudden events like disasters, some people turn to greening, and that those greening efforts not only help individuals and families cope with disaster, but they also may play a role in helping social and natural systems bounce back more quickly and more completely.

"When individuals and neighborhoods feel like their community is recovering and becoming green again, they have more hope and optimism to further their investment in recovery, resulting perhaps in more greening efforts."

There are times, such as in New Orleans following the wholesale deforestation caused by Hurricane Katrina, when replanting lost trees is imperative for environmental and aesthetic reasons, as well as to restore a city's sense of identity. In a post-Katrina tree-planting campaign, Elysian Fields Avenue received 224 magnolias, live oaks, and willow oaks, all of them 12 to 16 feet tall. And so far, more than 6,000 new trees have been planted in adjoining neighborhoods.

But the regreening campaign involved more than just municipal crews. Recognizing the need for public involvement even in a city that was still traumatized, Parkway Partners of New Orleans recruited and trained 90 volunteers known as Tree Troopers who could offer tree advice and planting assistance in their own neighborhoods.

"After the storm I thought I was a bit brazen asking people to take part in such training when they were not back in their own homes," Executive Director Jean Fahr admitted several years after making her first overtures to flood victims. "But people came and have been wonderful volunteers ever since. It gave them a *purposeful* effort in the recovery."

A Case in Point

When teacher Peggy Rosefeldt moved to the Gentilly district of New Orleans in 1974, among the things that attracted her to her neighborhood were the big 50-year-old trees. Just two blocks from the University of New Orleans campus, the green canopy provided privacy and cast welcome shade in the city's torrid summers. It also helped to purify the air, an important added benefit because of Peggy's breathing problems.

Then the levees broke, leaving her with no house, no job, and no trees. Peggy was living in a cramped FEMA trailer waiting for her house to be rebuilt when she was given the opportunity to become a Tree Trooper for Parkway Partners. After twelve hours of training with some of the best tree experts in the city, she found her calling in helping to reforest her neighborhood. She has personally planted some three dozen trees, and participated in group plantings of hundreds more.

Peggy Rosefeldt speaks for many who joined the Parkway Partners program while they were still in the process of trying to put their lives back together: "It was a way to keep my sanity. It's been a very positive experience for me. It really [provides] a sense of putting down roots again." And helping others put down fresh roots with new trees has had yet another added value: "We may not have known all our neighbors before, but we do now!"

The regreening of New Orleans has lifted the spirits of more than just the foresters, Tree Troopers, and other official participants. From the man in a business suit who stopped on his way to work to help a team of Tree Troopers plant a tree, to passersby who honked horns and cheered on the tree planters along

Elysian Fields Avenue, the slow, incremental restoration of the urban forest has exemplified the city's hope for its future.

Make It a Learning Experience for Kids

If major natural disasters are traumatic for adults, they can be even more so for children. Youngsters tend to be extremely sensitive to the anxieties of their elders, so you can best help them get over the stressful situation by working to overcome your own emotional distress. In the process, you can turn your landscape disaster into a positive learning experience by actively engaging your child in the recovery process. Along the way, you might discover for yourself the simple magic of positive thinking and constructive action.

Normal routines are reassuring to children. So the sooner you can return your household to its old schedules and patterns, the faster youngsters can regain their emotional equilibrium.

Take the time to explain what has happened ("The wind broke the old hickory tree"); what that entails ("We will have to get an expert to fix it" or "We will have to cut it down"); and the endgame ("Then we will all go out and find a new tree to replace it"). Once you break the situation down into such basics, you might find that it is easier for you to come to terms with the disaster as well!

Unless youngsters volunteer, using them as unpaid labor during the cleanup stage is unlikely to create a positive experience. But you might get them interested by putting a positive spin on the work, such as turning the cleanup into a contest to see who can pile up the most debris (and perhaps throwing in the promise of a pizza at the end of the day).

If your children are old enough, get them involved in the restoration process. Take them along to the nursery to help choose a replacement tree. Better yet, allow them to pick out their own tree or shrub to plant and grow, with assistance if necessary.

Before heading to the nursery, encourage your budding foresters to read up on trees and shrubs so they will choose suitable weather-resistant species. Or provide them with a list of weather-resistant candidates from which they can choose (see appendix I). With access to the Internet, computer-savvy kids can be tenacious researchers. In the end, they might be able to teach you a thing or two!

As a family, take part in constructive Arbor Day or community tree-planting activities. This can help both you and your children better grasp the importance of trees to your community and to the environment. Along the way, you will learn to better appreciate the part your own landscape plays in the greater urban or rural forest.

Do not forget the importance of schools and youth organizations in the wake of a natural disaster.

A Case in Point

Following Hurricane Katrina, Parkway Partners planted large live oak trees on the grounds of the Martin Luther King School for Math and Science as part of the ReLeaf New Orleans program. In the process, Parkway Partners also handed out maple saplings to students who were part of an environmental science class at the school. The excited children took these saplings home to plant in their own yards in the city's devastated Ninth Ward.

"Many of those yards are—or were at the time—missing the house that was once there," points out Keith Tidball, noting that schools are important anchors to the community. "A large percentage of students commute to the school so that they and their parents can remain rooted to the neighborhood. Some of the children live as far away as Kenner and St. Charles Parish."

For those youngsters, small maple saplings can grow into enduring symbols connecting their pasts to their futures.

In the spirit of regreening New Orleans after Hurricane Katrina. Courtesy of Keith Tidball/ Parkway Partners.

Living Memorials

In response to the profound emotional trauma caused by the tragic events of September 11th, the USDA Forest Service created its Living Memorials Project at the behest of Congress. There is now a national registry for special green spaces that have been built as places of solace where people can walk or sit and find peace. (For more on this, go online to www.livingmemorialsproject.net.)

But a tree or long-lived shrub also can serve as a lasting living celebration of almost any landmark occasion, from the birth of a child, to the dedication of a new home, to the return to near normalcy following a catastrophic extreme-weather event. The Forestry Commission of St. Louis, Missouri, encourages citizens to plant trees in public parks through its Tree-Membrance Program as a tribute to a special person or occasion, or simply to say, "I love you." Such living gifts can continue to celebrate your sentiment for generations to come. For both memorial and celebration trees, check out the Arbor Day Foundation site at www.arborday.org.

Welcoming Change

The bottom line is that your personal, community, or regional landscape has taken decades and sometimes centuries to evoke everlasting memories. Though traumatic, an extreme-weather event can open an opportunity to create new memories and to reflect on our place in this great complex world of ours.

So relax, take another deep breath, and remember: as much as we would like to think that we are in control, we are not and Mother Nature has a plan all on her own.

Also, take your blessings in small doses. While the devastation may seem overwhelming, think small. A simple planting of colorful annuals in an otherwise gray, devastated landscape can go a long way in providing hope for the future.

Dean Hill

Prepare to Cope

Most scientists looking into the future think that ongoing climate change will continue to intensify extreme-weather events. The increased volatility is likely to put greater and more frequent pressure on your landscape throughout your lifetime.

Taking measures to prevent as much damage to your valuable trees and shrubs as possible, and then taking swift and appropriate action when catastrophes do occur, are the best ways for you to maintain the worth of your real estate—and your peace of mind.

Acknowledgments

Books such as *Weatherproofing Your Landscape* are not created in isolation. Besides the many experts and landscape owners who appear within these pages, the authors also would like to thank Loretta Worters, vice president of the Insurance Information Institute, for her patience and care in responding to our many questions; J. David Hucker, registered consulting arborist, for taking the time to explain the complex process of valuating landscapes; Tracey Payton, horticulture extension agent, for setting the gold standard for Cooperative Extension agents across the country; and Wayne McEndree, CPA, for invaluable help with tax matters. In addition, we want to express our heartfelt appreciation to Gina Panettieri, for being everything an agent should be and more, acquiring editor John Byram, for sharing our vision of a book that could help besieged landscape owners everywhere come to terms with this age of increasingly volatile weather extremes, and copy editor Ainslie Gilligan, for going the mile and then keeping right on going.

Appendix I

Trees and Shrubs for Extreme Weather

The natural tolerance of tree and shrub species to extreme weather can vary from region to region, and be influenced by additional factors ranging from hardiness zones to microclimates and soil conditions. So a particular species might be tolerant of a form of extreme weather in one locale, but less so in another. For instance, some experts consider eastern arborvitae (*Thuja occidentalis*) to be tolerant of ice and snow, while others class the shrub as highly susceptible to frozen stuff. Likewise, eastern redbud (*Cercis canadensis*) has a reputation for being flood tolerant in some regions and intolerant in others.

Also, a species that is tolerant of one or more type of extreme-weather event might be highly intolerant of other forms of extreme weather.

Therefore, the following lists should be used as only rough guidelines. Trees and shrubs are long lived, so it is important to make *the* best possible and best-informed *choices* when selecting your landscape's big-ticket plants. Before making your final choices, check with local nurseries or your Cooperative Extension office to make sure the species you have in mind are suitable for your specific landscape and growing conditions.

Note: For the most part, plants native to your area are more tolerant of the extreme conditions common to your locale. Hardiness zones can vary somewhat depending upon local conditions. And fire resistance can vary depending on the dryness of the plant material and on whether the fire is slow or fast moving.

Key:

(D) Drought tolerant
(F) Flood tolerant
(W) Wind tolerant
(IS) Ice and Snow tolerant
(Fi) Fire resistant

The Twelve Hardiness Zones (in degrees Fahrenheit):

12: 50° to 60°
11: 40° to 50°
10: 30° to 40°
9: 20° to 30°
8: 10° to 20°
7: 0° to 10°
6: -10° to 0°
5: -20° to -10°
4: -30° to -20°
3: -40° to -30°
2: -50° to -40°
1: -60° to -50°

Acacia [*Acacia* species] (D, F, W) Zones 9–11
Alder, black [*Alnus glutinosa*] (F, W, IS, Fi) Zones 3–7
Arborvitae, eastern [*Thuja occidentalis*] (F, W, IS) Zones 2–7
Ash, black [*Fraxinus nigra*] (F, W) Zones 2–5
Ash, green [*Fraxinus pennsylvanica*] (D, F) Zones 2–9
Ash, white [*Fraxinus americana*] (F, W, Fi) Zones 4–9
Aspen, quaking [*Populus tremuloides*] (F, Fi) Zones 1–7
Bald cypress [*Taxodium distichum*] (D, F, W, IS) Zones 4–10
Barberry, Japanese [*Berberis thunbergii*] (D, F, W, IS) Zones 4–7
Beech, American [*Fagus grandifolia*] (D, W, IS, Fi) Zones 4–9
Birch, paper [*Betula papyrifera*] (F, W, Fi) Zones 2–7
Birch, gray [*Betula populifolia*] (D, W) Zones 3–8
Birch, river [*Betula nigra*] (D, F, W, Fi) Zones 4–9
Bird of paradise, Mexican [*Caesalpinia gilliesii*] (D, W) Zones 8–11
Box elder [*Acer negundo*] (D, F) Zones 3–8
Buckeye, Ohio [*Aesculus glabra*] (D, F) Zones 4–7
Buttonbush [*Cephalanthus occidentalis*] (F) Zones 5–9

Buttonwood [*Conocarpus erectus*] (W) Zones 10–11
Catalpa [*Catalpa* species] (D, F, W, IS) Zones 4–8
Cedar, eastern red [*Juniperus virginiana*] (D, F, W, IS) Zones 2–9
Cherry, black [*Prunus serotina*] (D, W) Zones 4–8
Cherry, cornelian [*Cornus mas*] (F) Zones 4–7
Chinese pistache [*Pistacia chinensis*] (D) Zones 6–9
Chokecherry [*Prunus virginiana*] (D, Fi) Zones 2–10
Coffeeberry [*Rhamnus californica*] (D, Fi) Zones 7–9
Cottonwood, eastern [*Populus deltoides*] (F) Zones 3–8
Crabapple [*Malus* species] (D, W, IS) Zones 4–8
Crabapple, Dolgo [*Malus pumila "Dolgo"*] (F, Fi) Zones 3–9
Cranberry, American [*Vaccinium macrocarpon*] (F) Zones 2–6
Crape myrtle [*Lagerstroemia indica*] (D, F, W) Zones 7–9
Dogwood, flowering [*Cornus florida*] (W) Zones 5–9
Elderberry, American [*Sambucus canadensis*] (D, F) Zones 3–9
Elm, American [*Ulmus americana*] (D, F, W) Zones 2–9
Elm, lacebark [*Ulmus parvifolia*] (D, F, W) Zones 5–9
Elm, Siberian [*Ulmus pumila*] (D, W) Zones 5–9
Elm, winged [*Ulmus alata*] (F, W) Zones 6–9
Fir, white [*Abies concolor*] (D) Zones 4–7
Ginkgo [*Ginkgo biloba*] (D, W, IS) Zones 3–8
Golden rain tree [*Koelreuteria paniculata*] (D) Zones 5–9
Hackberry, common [*Celtis occidentalis*] (D, F, W, Fi) Zones 3–9
Hawthorn [*Crataegus* species] (D, F, Fi) Zones 4–8
Hawthorn, downy [*Crataegus mollis*] (F) Zones 3–6
Hickory, shagbark [*Carya ovata*] (D, F, W, IS) Zones 5–8
Hickory, mockernut [*Carya tomentosa*] (D, W, IS) Zones 4–9
Hickory, water [*Carya aquatica*] (F) Zones 8–11
Holly, American [*Ilex opaca*] (D, F, W, IS) Zones 5–9
Holly, deciduous [*Ilex decidua*] (D, F, W, IS) Zones 5–8
Holly, yaupon [*Ilex vomitoria*] (D, F, W) Zones 7–9
Hornbeam, American [*Carpinus caroliniana*] (D, F, W, IS) Zones 3–9
Indigo, false [*Amorpha fruticosa*] (F) Zones 3–9
Inkberry [*Ilex glabra*] (D, F, W) Zones 5–10
Ironwood, black [*Krugiodendron ferreum*] (W, IS) Zones 9–11
Juniper [*Juniperus* species] (D, F, W) Zones 3–9
Kentucky coffee tree [*Gymnocladus dioica*] (D, W, IS) Zones 3–8
Larch, eastern [*Larix laricina*] (F) Zones 2–8
Laurel, Texas mountain [*Sophora secundiflora*] (D) Zones 7–10

Leatherwood [*Dirca palustris*] (F) Zones 4–9

Linden, American [*Tilia americana*] (D, W) Zones 3–8

Linden, littleleaf [*Tilia cordata*] (D, F, W, IS) Zones 3–7

Locust, black [*Robinia pseudoacacia*] (D, W) Zones 4–8

Locust, honey [*Gleditsia triachanthos*] (D, F, Fi, W) Zones 3–9

Magnolia, southern [*Magnolia grandiflora*] (D, F, W) Zones 6–10

Mahogany, alderleaf mountain [*Cercocarpus montanus*] (D, Fi) Zones 6–9

Manzanita [*Arctostaphylos* species] (D, W, Fi) Zones 7–10

Maple, Amur [*Acer ginnala*] (D, IS, Fi) Zones 3–9

Maple, Japanese [*Acer palmatum*] (W) Zones 5–8

Maple, Norway [*Acer platanoides*] (D, W, IS) Zones 3–7

Maple, red [*Acer rubrum*] (D, F, W) Zones 3–9

Maple, silver [*Acer saccharinum*] (D, F) Zones 3–9

Maple, Florida sugar [*Acer saccharum* subspecies *floridanum*] (D, W, IS)
    Zones 7–9

Monkey flower, sticky [*Diplacus aurantiacus*] (D, Fi) Zones 8–9

Mulberry, white [*Morus alba*] (F) Zones 4–8

Myrtle, southern wax [*Myrica cerifera*] (D) Zones 7–11

Oak, black [*Quercus velutina*] (D, W) Zones 3–9

Oak, burr [*Quercus macrocarpa*] (D, F, W, IS) Zones 3–8

Oak, Englemann [*Quercus englemannii*] (D) Zones 8–11

Oak, Gambel [*Quercus gambelii*] (D) Zones 4–7

Oak, live [*Quercus virginiana*] (D, F, W, IS) Zones 7–10

Oak, myrtle [*Quercus myrtifolia*] (W) Zones 8–10

Oak, Nuttall [*Quercus nuttallii*] (D, F, W, IS) Zones 4–9

Oak, overcup [*Quercus lyrata*] (F) Zones 5–9

Oak, pin [*Quercus palustris*] (D, F, W, Fi) Zones 4–8

Oak, post [*Quercus stellata*] (W) Zones 5–9

Oak, red [*Quercus rubra*] (D, W, IS, Fi) Zones 3–8

Oak, shingle [*Quercus imbricaria*] (F) Zones 4–8

Oak, Shumard [*Quercus shumardii*] (D, W) Zones 5–9

Oak, swamp white [*Quercus bicolor*] (F, IS) Zones 5–8

Oak, water [*Quercus nigra*] (F) Zones 6–9

Oak, white [*Quercus alba*] (D, W, IS) Zones 3–9

Olive, Russian [*Elaeagnus angustifolia*] (D, W, IS) Zones 3–8

Palm, cabbage [*Sabal palmetto*] (W, F) Zones 8–11

Palm, date [*Phoenix dactylifera*] (W) Zones 8–11

Palm, windmill [*Trachycarpus fortunei*] (D, F, W, IS) Zones 7–10

Palo verde, blue [*Cercidium floridum*] (D, W) Zones 9–10

Pecan [*Carya illinoinensis*] (D, F, IS) Zones 6–9
Persimmon [*Diospyros virginiana*] (D, F, W, IS) Zones 4–9
Pine, Austrian [*Pinus nigra*] (D, F) Zones 4–7
Pine, limber [*Pinus flexilis*] (D) Zones 4–7
Pine, ponderosa [*Pinus ponderosa*] (D, Fi) Zones 3–7
Pinyon, Mexican [*Pinus cembroides*] (D) Zones 5–8
Plum, American [*Prunus americana*] (D) Zones 3–8
Plum, Chickasaw [*Prunus angustifolia*] (W) Zones 6–9
Privet, Regel [*Ligustrum obtusifolium* variety *regelianum*] (F) Zones 4–7
Privet, swamp [*Forestiera acuminata*] (F) Zone 6
Redbud, eastern [*Cercis canadensis*] (D, F, W) Zones 4–9
Rose [*Rosa* species] (D, W) Zones 1–11
Serviceberry, shadblow [*Amelanchier canadensis*] (D, F, W) Zones 4–7
Snowberry [*Symphoricarpos albus*] (F) Zones 3–8
Spirea [*Spirea* species] (D, W) Zones 4–9
Spruce, black [*Picea mariana*] (F) Zones 2–5
Spruce, Colorado blue [*Picea pungens*] (D) Zones 2–8
Spruce, Norway [*Picea abies*] (D, W, IS) Zones 3–7
Spruce, white [*Picea glauca*] (F, IS) Zones 2–6
Sweetgum, American [*Liquidambar styraciflua*] (D, F, W, IS) Zones 5–9
Sycamore [*Platanus occidentalis*] (D, F) Zones 4–9
Tulip tree [*Liriodendron tulipifera*] (F) Zones 4–9
Tupelo, black [*Nyssa sylvatica*] (D, W, IS) Zones 4–9
Tupelo, water [*Nyssa aquatica*] (F, W) Zones 6–9
Viburnum [*Viburnum* species] (D, F, W, IS) Zones 2–9
Walnut, black [*Juglans nigra*] (D, F, W, IS, Fi) Zones 4–9
Water elm [*Planera aquatica*] (F) Zones 6–9
Willow, black [*Salix nigra*] (F) Zones 2–8
Willow, pussy [*Salix discolor*] (D, F) Zones 4–8
Winterberry, common [*Ilex verticillata*] (F) Zones 3–9
Witch hazel, common [*Hamamelis virginiana*] (F) Zones 3–8

Salt-Tolerant Species

Buttonwood [Conocarpus erectus] Zones 1–11
Cedar, bay [*Suriana maritima*] Zones 10–11
Golden rain tree [*Koelreuteria paniculata*] Zones 5–9
Holly, yaupon [*Ilex vomitoria*] Zones 7–9
Oak, live [*Quercus virginiana*] Zones 7–10

Oleander [*Nerium oleander*] Zones 8–11

Palm, cabbage [*Sabal palmetto*] Zones 8–11

Palm, hurricane [*Dictyosperma album*] Zones 8–11

Palmetto, saw [*Serenoa repens*] Zones 8–11

Privet, Regel [*Ligustrum obtusifolium* variety *regelanium*] Zones 4–7

Serviceberry, shadblow [*Amelanchier canadensis*] Zones 4–7

Wax myrtle, southern [*Myrica cerifera*] Zones 7–11

Appendix II

Species Ratings

The species rating (or species value) for a tree or shrub is just one element of an intricate set of factors used by an appraiser to estimate the monetary value of a landscape specimen. Arriving at the species rating itself involves a complex analysis of how well a particular species thrives in your geographic location.

This "desirability quotient" includes how well a species is adapted to an area's climate and soil, and even its pests. As climate or other conditions change, so can the rating of an individual species. For instance, ash trees carried a high species rating in Indiana landscapes until the infamous emerald ash borer arrived on the scene in 2004, causing the death or weakening of tens of millions of trees. As a result of the devastating, ongoing infestation, ash tree species are no longer recommended for the area, and are expected to experience a precipitous drop in future ratings lists.

The desirability of different tree and shrub species are rated by percentages, ranging from 0 to 100. The higher the percentage a species has in your geographical area, the more desirable that species is considered to be for your locale. And the more desirable the species (along with other factors), the higher its monetary value and replacement-cost valuation are likely to be.

The rating earned by any given species can vary from region to region. For instance, a palm tree that garners an 80 percent rating along the Gulf Coast would receive no rating at all in the Great Lakes region, far outside its hardiness zone. Ratings also can vary from state to state. So while an eastern white pine

(*Pinus strobus*) might receive a 90 percent rating in Nebraska, it might average only 57 percent in Georgia.

Ratings can even differ from one area of a state to the next if there is a significant difference in growing conditions. So the species rating of a Japanese maple grown in northern Indiana can be 20 to 40 percent lower than one grown in southern Indiana. Likewise, a salt-tolerant species with a modest rating when grown in an inland landscape might rank higher along the coast, where storm surges or salt spray can be a problem. Or a species acclimated to the Rocky Mountain heights of western Colorado might not thrive at all in the lower altitude of eastern Colorado's high plains.

To give you a better idea of how ratings lists can vary, here are species samples from two areas of the country having widely different growing conditions: New England and Southern California. As you can see, most of the highly rated species on the New England list are not even on the Southern California list—and when a species does make both lists, its rating differs.

New England

(Courtesy of the New England Chapter of the International Society of Arborists.)
Aspen, quaking (*Populus tremuloides*) 20–30
Beech, American (*Fagus grandifolia*) 90–100
Birch, paper (*Betula papyrifera*) 70–80
Box elder (*Acer negundo*) 30–40
Fir, Douglas (*Pseudotsuga menziesii*) 80–90
Fir, white (*Abies concolor*) 80–90
Ginkgo (male) (*Ginkgo biloba*) 90–100
Hackberry, common (*Celtis occidentalis*) 70–80
Hickory, shellbark (*Carya laciniosa*) 80–90
Hornbeam, European (*Carpinus betulus*) 80–90
Kentucky coffee tree (*Gymnocladus dioica*) 80–90
Larch, European (*Larix decidua*) 80–90
Maple, Japanese (*Acer palmatum*) 90–100
Maple, three-flower (*Acer triflorum*) 80–90
Pine, eastern white (*Pinus strobus*) 80–90
Serviceberry, shadblow (*Amelanchier canandensis*) 70–80
Shadblow (*Amelanchier arborea*) 70–80
Spruce, Norway (*Picea abies*) 80–90
Tamarack (*Larix laricina*) 80–90
Tupelo (*Nyssa sylvatica*) 90–100

Southern California: Coast Influence

(Courtesy of the Western Chapter of the International Society of Arboriculture. *Note: The WCISA plant-appraisal guide lists ratings in given numbers rather than ranges.*)

Acacia, Bailey (*Acacia baileyana*) 70
Avocado (*Persea americana*) 90
Bald cypress (*Taxodium distichum*) 90
Bird of paradise, Mexican (*Caesalpinia gilliesii*) 90
Box elder (*Acer negundo*) 10
Cedar, Atlas (*Cedrus atlantica*) 90
Chaste tree (*Vitex lucens*) 90
Crape myrtle hybrids (*Lagerstroemia*) 90
Eucalyptus, rainbow (*Eucalyptus deglupta*) 90
Fig, rustyleaf (*Ficus rubiginosa*) 90
Ginkgo (male) (*Ginkgo biloba*) 90
Hackberry, common (*Celtis occidentalis*) 50
Jacaranda, yellow (*Schizolobium excelsum*) 90
Macadamia, smoothshell (*Macadamia integrifolia*) 90
Magnolia, southern (*Magnolia grandiflora*) 90
Maple, Japanese (*Acer palmatum*) 50
Oak, California live (*Quercus agrifolia*) 90
Palm, pindo (*Butia capitata*) 90
Pine, Norfolk Island (*Araucaria excelsa*) 90
Redwood, dawn (*Metasequoia glyptostroboides*) 90
Sycamore, Mexican (*Platanus Mexicana*) 90

While the species rating of a specimen is an important factor in determining its monetary value, how does a high or low rating affect you if you need to replace a plant?

If you lose a large, mature specimen to an extreme-weather event, disease, or infestation, you obviously cannot replace it with another tree or shrub of the same size. So replacement costs are based on the standard planting stock that is available at your nearby nurseries, and the species rating of a tree can be a good reflection of those local prices. For example, a four-inch-caliper tree of a species having a 20 percent rating in your locale might cost $60 to replace, while the same size tree of a species having a 100 percent rating might cost $850.

Regional species-ratings lists are available through the International Society of Arboriculture (see appendix III for contact information). And in some cases, you can find them through your Cooperative Extension office, or online.

Also, if you have your landscape specimens valued by a certified arborist or registered consulting arborist, that expert can inform you as to the desirability—or lack thereof—of each of your tree and shrub species. This information, along with other factors such as a plant's location, importance to the landscape, and utilitarian value, can help you make informed decisions as to what kind of effort, if any, you should put into trying to save a tree or shrub that has been injured by fire or an extreme-weather event.

Appendix III

Resources

Professional Associations

International Society of Arboriculture (ISA): P.O. Box 3129, Urbana, IL 61826; phone: 217-355-9411; e-mail: isa@isa-arbor.com; Web site: www.isa-arbor.com.

American Society of Consulting Arborists (ASCA): 9707 Key West Avenue, Suite 100, Rockville, MD 20850; phone: 301-947-0483; e-mail: asca@mgmtsol. com; Web site: www.asca-consultants.org.

Tree Care Industry Association (TCIA) (formerly National Arborist Association): 136 Harvey Road, Suite 101, Londonderry, NH 03053; toll-free phone: 800-733-2622; Web site: www.treecareindustry.org.

American Society of Landscape Architects (ASLA): 636 Eye Street NW, Washington, DC 20001-3736; toll-free phone: 888-999-ASLA (2752); Web site: www. asla.org.

Lightning Protection

Lightning Protection Institute: P.O. Box 99, Maryville, MO 64468; toll-free phone: 800-488-6864; e-mail via Web site: www.lightning.org. *Information on lightning-protection systems for trees is also available from Tree Care Industry Association.*

Rain-Guttering

National Rain Gutter Contractor Association (NRGCA): 3125 28 Street SW, Suite 7, Grandville, MI 49418; toll-free phone: 866-446-1515; e-mail via Web site: www.nrgca.org.

Water-Collection Systems

American Rainwater Catchment Systems Association (ARCSA): 919 Congress Avenue, Suite 460, Austin, TX 78701; Web site: www.arcsa.org.

Landscape Rain Gardens

Rain Garden Network: phone: 773-773-5333; e-mail: info@raingardennetwork. com; Web site: www.raingardennetwork.com.

Plants

American Forests Historic Tree Program: P.O. Box 2000, Washington, DC 20013; toll-free phone: 800-368-5748; e-mail: historictrees@amfor.org; Web site: www.historictrees.org.

For lists of trees and shrubs that are native to your area, contact your local Cooperative Extension office, and go online to find state and local native-plant societies.

Mycorrhizae

Hort Enterprises: P.O. Box 2448, Pompano Beach, FL 33061; phone: 954-046-3580; toll-free phone: 800-966-4678; Web site: www.hort-enterprises.com. *Web site includes a list of trees and shrubs and the types of mycorrhizae they use.*

Mycorrhizal Applications, Inc.: toll-free phone: 866-476-7800; e-mail: Info@ Mycorrhizae.com; Web site: www.mycorrhizae.com.

Government

National Flood Insurance Program: toll-free phone: 888-379-9531; Web site: www.floodsmart.gov.

811 (Web site for locating utility lines): www.call811.org.

Recommended Reading

Brickell, Christopher, and David Joyce. *American Horticultural Society: Pruning & Training*. DKAdult, 1996; hardcover; 336 pages.

Hill, Lewis. *Pruning Made Easy: A Gardener's Visual Guide to When and How to Prune Everything, from Flowers to Trees*. Storey Publishing, LLC, 1998; paperback; 224 pages.

Larsen, F. E., and W. E. Guse. *Propagating Deciduous and Evergreen Shrubs, Trees, and Vines with Stem Cuttings*. Pacific Northwest Cooperative Extension Publications; 12 pages. Available through Washington State University, P.O. Box 645912, Pullman WA 99164-5912 or by toll-free phone at 800-723-1763 or online at http://cru84.cahe.wsu.edu/cgi-bin/pubs/PNW0152.html.

Mizejewski, David. *National Wildlife Federation: Attracting Birds, Butterflies & Backyard Wildlife*. Creative Homeowner; paperback; 128 pages. Available online at http://www.nwf.org.

USDA Forest Service. "How to Prune Trees." (Extensive illustrated guidelines.) Available online at: http://bit.ly/34BFl8.

Index

American Forests Historic Tree Program, 167, 224

American Society of Consulting Arborists (ASCA), 223

American Society of Landscape Architects, (ASLA), 223

Arboriculture, International Society of (ISA), 223

Arborist, certified or registered consulting: cost of, 105; for custom designed rehabilitation program, 133; for damage assessment, 116; and French drains, 108; hiring a, 104–5, 133, 223. *See also* Experts, hiring

Architect, landscape, 105–6, 223; cost of, 106; and damage control, 116; and French drains, 108

Armillaria root disease, 144

Bark damage, 92, 96–97; by hail, 6; by lightning, 99; repairing, 96, 99; by string trimmers, ix, 143

Borers, stem, 147–48

Bracing. *See under* Tree supports

Branch collar, 55

Cabling. *See under* Tree supports

Canker diseases, 145

Climate change, vii, 2

Cobra system. *See under* Tree supports

Collateral damage: causes and consequences of, 149; damage control for, 149–50; prevention of, 126

Competition: from crowding, 43–44; and drought, 76; from turf grass, 42–43, 76

Construction damage: by grade changes, 60; prevention of, 60–62; by soil compaction, 60; by trenching, 60–61

Crane, hiring, 124–25

Cross-border damage, 97–98. *See also under* Property liability

Crown loss, 89–90

Crushed plants, 90–91; by snow, 9

Damage, assessing

—Class 1 damage, 84; insurance coverage, 88; limbs, dangling, 87–88; limbs in power lines, 86; limbs threatening structures, 88; severe structural damage, 87; uprooted utility lines, 87

—Class 2 damage, 84–85; bark damage, severe, 92; crown loss, major, 89–90; crushed trees or shrubs, 90–91; emergency grafting, 92; flooding, 92–94; foliage wilt, discoloration, 94–95; limb failure, major, 88–89; split trunk, 90; uprooted plants, 91–92

—Class 3 damage, 85; bark damage, moderate, 96–97; leader loss, 95–96; limb failure, moderate, 95

Damage, hidden, 19, 84

Debris removal: reducing costs of, 126–27. *See also under* Removing plants

Deicing chemicals, 73–74

Design, importance of, 172–76

Disease, 19, 45; armillaria root disease, 144; canker diseases, 145; diagnosing, 143; pythium and phytophthora root diseases, 145–46

Do it yourself: designing for, 114; emergency care, 101–4; safety rules for, 102–3; utility line dangers, 103–4, 129; when to, 102. *See also under* French drains; Guttering; Pruning; Rainwater collection system; Transplanting

Drainage, 44–45, 157

Drought, 9–14; at-risk regions, 13–14; contributing conditions, 13; damage by, 12–13; and lawn reduction, 76–78; mulch during, 78; plant response to, 10–12; water, recycled, 79; watering during, 75, 78–79; water needs, prioritizing, 74–75; water rationing, 75, 180–81. *See also* Watering

—adapting plants to, 75–76; competition, reducing, 76; crown reduction for, 76–77; and fertilizer, 76, 78

—damage severity factors, 12–13; competition, 13; duration, 12; location, 12; new plantings, 12–13; plant health, 13; root problems, 12; soil conditions, 12; species, 13; temperature, 13; watering technique, 13

Dry zones, 45

Emergency care: checklist, 121; delaying decisions, 120–21; do-it-yourself, 102–4

Emotional recovery: community involvement, 204–6; helping neighbors, 200–202; involving kids, 206–7; living memorials, 208; looking ahead, 202–4; post-Katrina New Orleans, 197–98, 204–6; taking action, 199–200. *See also* Post Traumatic Stress Disorder

Epicormic growth, 139–41; and flood stress, 15

Evergreens: and snow damage, 8, 73; and winter mulch, 134–35

Experts, hiring: choosing a reliable, 108–9; cost effectiveness of, 108; danger signals when, 109–11; in an emergency, 112; saving money when, 113–14; getting a second opinion, 119–20; necessity of signed agreement, 109; value of, 101; where to find, 111–12. *See also under* Arborist, certified or registered consulting; Architect, landscape; French drains; Guttering; Rainwater collection system

Fertilizing: after soil test, 136–37; and collateral growth, 135; damaged plants, 122, 135–37; during drought, 76, 78; how and when to, 136–37; and infestations, 135; lawn fertilizers, 136; over-fertilizing, hazards of, 137; and pest and disease resistance, 135

Flood, 14–17, 79–81; at-risk regions, 17; cause of damage, 15–17; common symptoms, 15; contributing conditions, 17; guttering, emergency, 80; guying, emergency, 80; mulch, removing, 81; tolerance to, 92–93; tree standing in water, 81

—damage severity factors: age and size, 17; depth and duration of flood, 16; flowing or stagnant water, 16; season, 16; soil conditions, 16; species, 16

Flood insurance. *See* National Flood Insurance Program

Foliage wilt, 15; and flooding, 94

French drains: contactor, hiring a, 107–8; cost of, 107; do-it-yourself, 108; and root systems, 45

Frozen stuff, 6–9, 69–70; at-risk regions, 9; contributing conditions, 9; cause of damage, 7–9; emergency bracing, 70. *See also* Ice; Snow

—damage severity factors: age and size, 8; burial, 8; melt-off, 8; shape, 8; species, 7–8

Goldhamer, David A., 76

Grade changes, 60

Grafting, emergency, 92

Grey water (recycled water), 79

Guttering: contractor, hiring a, 106; cost of, 106; do-it-yourself, 106; for drought conditions, 79; emergency, 80. *See also* National Rain Gutter Contractor Association

Guying. *See under* Tree supports

Hail, 6; bark repair, 96

Hedge, crushed, 181. *See also* Pruning; Replacing loss

Heirloom plants, 154–69; annual inspection, 157–58; propagating (*see* Propagating plants); protecting, 155–58; replacement alternatives, 167, 224; the Survivor Tree, 158; usage alternatives, 167–68

Herms, Dan, 135

Holistic landscape, 172

Ice, 6–9; deicing chemicals, 73–74; emergency support, 69–70, 73; removal of, 70–72; and the

Survivor Tree, 71; weight of, 6. *See also* Frozen stuff; Snow

Infestation. *See* Pests

Inspection, annual, 157–58

Insurance, landscape: endorsements (riders), 191–93; homeowners policy coverage, 189–91; insuring single specimen, 192–93; and taxes, 193 (*see also* Tax deductions); valuating specimens (*see* Plants, assessing value of)

Integrated Pest Management (IPM), 148–49

Invasive plants, 183–84

Katrina, Hurricane, 150; emotional recovery from, 197–98, 204–6, 207; New Orleans tree loss, 14, 197–98; restoration, 177, 204–6, 207. *See also* New Orleans restoration

Landscape appraisal: cost of, 37–38; as defensive weapon, 39; report contents, 39

Landscape appraiser: when to hire, 36–37; finding reputable, 39

Landscape durability, 20–23

Landscape restoration. *See under* Replacing loss

Landscape value: importance of knowing plant values, 20–21; real estate value of, vii–viii

Lawn, reducing, 76–78

Leader loss, 95–96

Liability, property. *See under* Property liability

Lightning: assessing damage from, 18, 98–99, 152; likelihood of strike, 18; and pines, 98, 117; protection systems, 66–67, 223–24; when to remove tree, 17, 98

Lightning Protection Institute, 223–24

Limb, dangling, 87–88

Low areas, 44, 81

Memorials, living, 208

Microclimates, 24

Mulch: during drought, 78; during wet conditions, 81

Mycorrhizae, 137–38, 224

National Arborists Association. *See under* Tree Care Industry Association

National Flood Insurance Program, 191, 225

National Rain Gutter Contractor Association (NRGCA), 224

Native species: converting to, 77–78

New Orleans restoration: Parkway Partners, 198, 205, 207; Tree Troopers, 205–6. *See also* Katrina, Hurricane

Palms, stem damage to, ix

Pests, 19, 146–48; and fertilizer, 135; identifying, 147; and insect-friendly landscape, 149; Integrated Pest Management, 148–49; nematodes, 94–95; stem borers, 147–48

Phytophthora root disease, 145–46

Pines: and flooding, 92; and lightning, 117; and nematodes, 94–95

Plant durability: and adaptation, 22; age and size, 22; foliage, 23; and plant habit, 22–23; and pruning, 22; and soil conditions, 21; and species suitability, 22, 40–45; and sun and shade, 21; and weather tolerance, 21–23, 40–41

Plants, assessing value of: age and size, 25, 33–34, 119; do-it-yourself assessing, 32–36; health factors, 25; importance of knowing value of, 20–21, 31; improving value of plants, 29–30; for insurance purposes, 192; intangible value, 37; location factors, 26; plants that devalue property, 26–29; single tree, 38–39; species, 25; species ratings, 219–22; when to hire appraiser, 36–37. *See also* Landscape appraisal; Landscape appraiser

Plants, undesirable, 26–29, 41–42

Plants, vulnerable, 41–42

Plant selection: for extreme weather, 21–23, 40–41, 213–18; mistakes in, 184–85; transplants, choosing healthy, 178

Post Traumatic Stress Disorder, 177, 197. *See also* Emotional recovery

Power lines. *See under* Utility lines

Preventive health: and disease, 45; and drainage, 44–45; and dry zones, 45; evaluation, importance of, 45–46; and infestation, 45; and low areas, 44; and overcrowding, 43–44; root zones, protecting, 43; and soil, 42–43; and turf grass competition, 42–43

Propagating plants: from cuttings, 159–61, 165; disseminating offspring, 166–67; expert, hiring an, 159; guidelines for, 225; nursery for, 163–64, 166–67; from seeds, 161–65; the Survivor Tree, 158, 166; transplanting seedlings, 164–65; from volunteers, 166

Property liability: assessing ownership, 97; cross-border damage, 97–98; insurance coverage, 190–91

Property line maintenance: preventive, 62–63; who pays for, 63. *See also* Property liability

Pruning: basic guidelines for, 48–51, 53, 225; and branch collar, 53, 55; to build strong structure, 48–51; curbside trees, 51–52; do-it-yourself, 53–56, 138–39; and double trunks, 48; for drought, 76; epicormic growth, 139–41; expert, when you need an, 138–39; preventive, 47–56; pythium root disease, 145–46; to reduce buildup of frozen stuff, 48; to reduce hazards, 51; restoration, 121–22, 138–41; six rules of, 53–54; structural flaws, 51; and tree ridge, 55; tree topping, 27, 54, 141, 185; when to prune, 48, 54, 141; wound paint, 54, 138

Rain garden, 44, 180, 224

Rain Garden Network, 224

Rainwater Catchment Systems Association, American (ARCSA), 224

Rainwater collection system, 79; contractor, hiring a, 106–7, 224; cost of, 107; do-it-yourself, 107; systems available, 106–7

Real estate values: and damaged plants, 116–17; improving marketability, 175–76; and landscape, vii–viii, 1, 101–2; and long-term care, 133; and trees, 1–2

Rehabilitation: delaying decisions, 120–21; expert advice, 116, 133; when property is on market, 116–17; rehabilitation program, 121–23, 133; restoration pruning, 121–22; restoring vigor, 133–34

Removing plants: collateral damage, avoiding, 126; conditions for, 62, 117–18, 152–53; cost of, 125; costs, reducing, 126–27; crane, hiring a, 125; dangers of, 123; debris removal, 126–27; delaying decisions, 120–21; doing it yourself, 123; expert, hiring an, 123–25; getting a second opinion, 119; liability, 123; preventive removal, 62; transplanting, 118

Replacing loss: adding color, 182; adding food production, 182; avoiding cookie-cutter plants, 176; avoiding impulse shopping, 176; consulting experts, 173, 178, 180; correcting landscape shortcomings, 179–83, 186–87; design, importance of, 172–75; energy costs, reducing, 182; extreme-weather tolerance, improving, 176–78; eye-appeal and balance, 173–74; hedge, damaged, 181; holistic landscape, 172; long-term vs. short-term choices, 178–79; lower maintenance, 175; New Orleans, post-Hurricane Katrina, 177; noise and unsightly view,

181; phantom tree, 178–79; planned evolution, 174; plant selection mistakes, 184–85, 187; problem solving, 81, 173; real estate value or marketability, improving, 175–76; size, 185, 187; spacing, 185; staged installation, 175; transplant size, 176; updating landscape, 171–72; wildlife enhancement, 182–183

Root system: depth of, 4, 11; and drought, 11; and French drains, 45; and mycorrhizae, 137–38; and old specimens, 156; protecting, 43, 156; space, 41; understanding, 133–34

Salt: and New Orleans flooding, 150; and species selection, 150–51, 217–18; treatment for, 150

Scott, Jud, 138

Snow: at-risk regions, 9; burial by, 8–9; cabling, emergency, 73; cause of damage from, 7–9; contributing conditions, 9; evergreens, bent, 73; removal, 72; salt-saturated, 150; soil, compaction of, 60; storing snow, 73; testing, 46–47; tree damage from, 6–9; and tree removal, 126; understanding, 42–43

Species: for extreme-weather tolerance, 21–23, 40–41, 213–17; native, 66; ratings, 219–22; salt-tolerant, 150–51, 217–18; selection of, 40–41; wildfire resistant, 66

Specimens, old, 119

Specimens, valuating. *See under* Plants, assessing value of

Staking. *See under* Tree supports

Structural damage, hidden, 19

Stump removal: cost of, 128–29; do-it-yourself, 125, 129–30; natural, 130–31; professional, 125, 128–29

Survivor Tree, 37; and ice storm, 68, 71; new growth, 100, 120; offspring, disseminating, 166; propagation of, 158; as symbol, 154

Tax deductions, 193–96; declaring, 194; documentation for, 194–95; filing limits, 195; proof of damage, 193–95; self-insurance, 196

Tidball, Keith, 204

Topping. *See under* Pruning

Transplanting: for design, 30; do-it-yourself, 118; emergency, 118

Tree, fallen, 15, 81; cross-border, 97–98; damage caused by, 2; old trees, 5; and saturated soil, 15; and shallow soil, 4. *See also* Property liability; Uprooting

Tree Care Industry Association (TCIA) (formerly National Arborist Association), 223

Tree habits, 23–24, 42

Tree removal. *See under* Removing plants

Tree ridge, 55

Trees, curbside, 51–52

Tree shapes. *See under* Tree habits

Tree spacing, 33, 185

Tree supports: bracing and cabling, 59–60, 141–43; Cobra system, 143; costs of, 143; do-it-yourself, 143; expert, hiring an, 142–43; and flooding, 80; guying and staking, 58–59; what to look for, 141–43

Trenching and root damage, 60–61. *See also* French drains

Trunk, double, 48, 90

Trunk, split, 90

Uprooting, 91–92

Utility lines: buried, 103–4; fallen, 86; limbs on, 86; marking, 103–4, 129, 225; uprooted buried, 84, 87

Valuating plants. *See under* Plants, assessing value of

Water, recycled, 79

Watering: during drought, 75; lawn vs. trees and shrubs, 56; location of, proper, 56; methods for, 13, 74–75, 78–79; and microconditons, 57; and precipitation, 134–35; preventive, 56–57; quantity and frequency of, 56–57, 75; timing of, 56; to winterize, 57, 134; winter mulch, 135

Water rationing, 180–81

Water sprouts. *See under* Epicormic growth

Water uptake, tree, 10

Wet areas, 180

Wildfire: damage, assessing, 98; emergency measures, 82, 151–52; and native plants, 66, 151–52; reducing threat of, 63–66; resistant species, 66

Wildlife, planting for, 225

Wind: at-risk regions, 6; contributing conditions for, 6; damage by, 2, 3–4; supports for, emergency, 69; and tipped trees, 2, 4–5

—damage severity factors: age and health, 4–5; plant exposure, 3; property topography, 3; root anchoring, 4; sail area, 4; species, 4; wind velocity, 3

Wound paint, 54, 97

Journalist Sandra Dark's work has appeared in a wide range of publications, including *Gardening How-To*, *Organic Gardening*, *The Family Food Garden*, and *Mother Earth News*. Dark is a member of the Garden Writers Association and the American Society of Journalists and Authors.

Dean Hill, member of the American Society of Landscape Architects, is cohost and landscape designer for the DIY Network's *Grounds for Improvement* television program and the author of *Grounds for Improvement: 25 Great Landscaping & Gardening Projects*.